YOU AND OTHERS

YOU AND OTHERS

REFLECTIVE PRACTICE FOR GROUP EFFECTIVENESS IN HUMAN SERVICES

LINDA McKINLAY
OKANAGAN COLLEGE

HEATHER ROSS
OKANAGAN COLLEGE

Toronto

Library and Archives Canada Cataloguing in Publication

McKinlay, Linda, 1948–
You and others : reflective practice for group effectiveness in human services / Linda McKinlay, Heather Ross.—1st ed.

Includes bibliographical references and index.
ISBN-13: 978-0-205-46514-9
ISBN-10: 0-205-46514-5

1. Social group work—Textbooks. I. Ross, Heather, 1961– II. Title.

HV45.M42 2008 361.4 C2006-903425-7

ISBN-10: 0-205-46514-5
ISBN-13: 978-0-205-46514-9

Editor-in-Chief, Vice-President of Sales: Kelly Shaw
Executive Acquisitions Editor: Ky Pruesse
Signing Representative: Katie McWhirter
Executive Marketing Manager: Judith Allen
Supervising Developmental Editor: Suzanne Schaan
Production Editor: Amanda Wesson
Copy Editor: Dana Kahan
Proofreader: Judy Hernandez
Production Coordinator: Sharlene Ross
Composition: Laserwords
Art Director: Julia Hall
Cover Design: Anthony Leung
Cover Image: Photodisc
Chapter Illustrations: Sam McKinlay

20 21 22 CP 15 14 13

Printed and bound in Canada.

To the groups that inspire us . . .

Linda and Heather

Contents

Preface ix

Chapter 1: Reflecting on You 1

Group Process in the Helping Professions 1
Using This Text 3
Reflection in the Helping Professions 7
The Reflection Tool 11
Sample Reflection 1 16
Sample Reflection 2 18
Blank Reflection Tool 22

Chapter 2: Group Dimensions 24

Studying the Dimensions of Groups 24
Common Elements of Groups 26
A Reflection Tool Example 39
Sample Reflection 3 39
Blank Reflection Tool 45

Chapter 3: Group Development 47

Examining Group Development 47
Effective Group Function 48
Historical Theories of Group Development 56
Group Development and Effective Group Function 61
Final Comment 71
Blank Reflection Tool 79

Chapter 4: Leadership and Group Roles 81

Group Roles 81
Shared Leadership 85
Leadership Issues in Groups 100
Formal Leadership Roles 106
Blank Reflection Tool 115

Chapter 5: Power in Groups 117

Power in Groups 117
The Concept of Power 119
Forms of Power 121
Empowerment 125

Developing Power Through the Lifespan 127
Communication Skills and Power 130
Power and Leadership Roles 135
Final Comment 141
Blank Reflection Tool 148

Chapter 6: Decision Making from a Shared Understanding 150

A Context of Shared Understanding 150
Methods of Decision Making 151
Factors That Affect Decision Making 159
Conflict Defined 164
Conflict Behaviour 166
A Model for Resolving Conflict 172
Blank Reflection Tool 181

Chapter 7: You and Others 183

Integrating the Learning 183
Concluding the Base Group Experience 184
Reflective Practice and Ongoing Assessment 186
Group Contexts in the Helping Profession 187
Self-Assessment Framework 188
Sample Self-Assessment Framework 191
Professional Considerations 196
Blank Self-Assessment Framework 198

Glossary 201
References 209
Index 211

Preface

We have created this text as an introduction to group skill development in the helping professions. We chose to use the process of reflection to deepen student learning and to focus on the relevance of group process theory to each student as an individual.

All the professions that encompass work in human service require effective group participation and leadership. Graduates of training programs in human service find themselves daily in group situations, whether they work with families, in teams, on committees or in any of the countless group structures inherent to the profession. As well, students in their role as learners must function in a group when they spend time in the classroom and other institutional training contexts. The important years spent as students offer the opportunity to lay the foundation for ongoing group skill development. Chapter 7 of this text provides students with a self-assessment framework that will help them take their group process learning into their practice and support the ongoing refinement of their interactions with others in group contexts.

For over 15 years, we have been teaching students the skills of interpersonal relationship building and effective group participation in early childhood education. In that time, we have found that there are a number of resources available to support our teaching of interpersonal skills, yet very few of those resources link the professions of human service to effective group participation. This text is designed to help learners link group theory to group practice through the use of real-life examples in human service. This process of linking theory to practice provides students with the opportunity to see how the theory finds application in professional contexts linked to their training and supports them in evaluating their own effectiveness in group contexts.

Our approach is based on our teaching philosophy that students need interactive exercises and real-world case study examples in order to best assimilate and accommodate their thinking about the vital role they play in all groups. As well, the focus on reflection as a conduit for growing self-awareness helps support students as they try out their individual styles of group participation. In the work of human service, reflective practice is the foundation for ongoing professional judgment and must be taught, supported and practised.

The first chapter of this text is a foundation, preparing students for the exercises, reflection suggestions and case studies in the chapters that follow. Chapters 2 through 6 provide exercises and reflection suggestions to help reinforce theoretical principles, while at the same time focusing attention on the student's immediate experience of significant issues raised. Chapter 7 is a closure chapter designed to summarize the content of the text and to provide a structure for ongoing evaluation of group skill development.

Instructor's Manual

We have written an instructor's manual, available for downloading from the Pearson Education Canada online catalogue http://vig.pearsoned.ca for use alongside the text. The most important components of this resource are the extended rationales and general commentaries related to facilitating each exercise and the suggested answers to the case studies.

The exercises in the text are designed to be facilitated by instructors. The information in the instructor's manual offers suggestions and background information based on our experience with each exercise. The exercise can be adapted, condensed or expanded, and inspire questions that further enhance student learning. You will find it helpful to review the online instructor's manual prior to exploring each individual chapter and implementing exercises in class. The exercises are reflective in nature and are meant to be discussed and debriefed upon completion. We have successfully implemented all of the exercises included in this text in the classroom and have found that students benefit from their relevance.

Suggested case study answers are offered to help you better understand our intentions when we created each case study with the chapter content in mind. In our experience, students often come up with ideas and suggestions that even we had not considered. We have had great success using case studies as assignments.

Throughout the text a reflection icon highlights suggestions for individual student reflection opportunities based on chapter content. These questions help point out areas that might be significant to the students' personal experiences. The reflection tool explained in Chapter 1 helps students work through this process. We suggest that students be asked to complete reflection tools as an additional assignment and to reflect either on the questions posed throughout the text or on other class content of particular significance to them as they progress through their course of studies. We have provided completed reflection tool samples in Chapters 1 and 2 and have included four additional samples for the rest of the text in the instructor's manual.

Acknowledgments

The inspiration for this work comes from our friend and colleague Diana MacDonald, whose teaching and mentorship introduced us to the importance of paying attention to group process and provided the foundation for our own ongoing self-awareness and growth.

The following people provided helpful feedback on the manuscript at various stages:

Robert Basso, Wilfrid Laurier University
Geraldine Boates, Mohawk College
Carole E. Harlow, University College of the Fraser Valley
Susan Leslie-Berkis, Humber Institute of Technology and Advanced Learning
Lynne Peters, Confederation College
Laura E. Taylor, University of Windsor

We would also like to thank those people in our lives who, as always, continue to support us in the work we do. This includes our parents, our children, our friends and our colleagues. Special thanks to Sam McKinlay for his creative talents, understanding and ability to capture whatever we asked of him in artistic form.

A special thank you to Rachel Stuckey, our developmental editor, for her incredible capacity to succinctly, yet fully, respond to our writing with articulate feedback and suggestions.

Chapter 1

Reflecting on You

Objectives

In this chapter, students will acquire the knowledge, skills and attitudes to:

1. Link the study of group process to self-reflection.
2. Value the impact of group participation on the professional practice of human service.
3. Define the process of reflection.
4. Develop an understanding of why reflection is important to working in groups.
5. Appreciate the value of ongoing reflection in professional practice.
6. Understand the rationale and overall organization of this text's approach to developing the ability to work successfully in groups.
7. Understand how to use the reflection tool.
8. Prepare for ongoing use of the reflection tool to deepen their level of self-awareness throughout the rest of the text.

Group Process in the Helping Professions

The practice of working with people involves understanding groups and all of the factors that make those groups function effectively. This is a foundation skill in all human service professions. The learning has already begun as you take on the role of a student within the classroom context. The classroom offers many opportunities to explore your role in groups as you participate in discussions, work on student group assignments and relate to your peers. Using the student group experience to risk experimenting with new behaviours and having peers offer feedback on these new behaviours create a most effective forum for learning.

Your choice to enter a helping profession signals an interest in understanding how you can function as a productive team member, as well as how you might support the healthy group involvement of your future clients. We define the practice of human service as including services for young children, youth, adults in care and people with disabilities, and other health and social service professions that provide the consistent support of a trained caregiver. All of these care positions require a depth of understanding about the way we work in groups and our ability to reflect on our own behaviours.

Group contexts might include the staff or team you work with on a daily basis, your clients, the families of the clients in your care, professional groups within the discipline, multidisciplinary groups involved in various aspects of client support and community committee groupings that require your expertise. As the work of human service continues to grow and change, professional involvement in groups of all kinds is vital to the quality of support for the people in your care. This means you have to learn the skills to feel competent and helpful at all levels of group function.

Understanding the ways groups develop helps you make decisions about how much time and effort you are willing to commit as a group member. You may have found yourself in group situations where you wonder how much your participation has contributed to the group and what others might be thinking about your contributions. Learning how such elements as trust, cohesion, productivity and overall group transformation develop in groups over time will help you evaluate your impact and make changes that can improve both the function of the whole group and your own role in its progress. As well, understanding some of the historical research on group development, principles of leadership and the power dynamics that occur in all kinds of group contexts will contribute to your ability to evaluate your role. Only when you create some kind of framework based on well-known principles of effective group function can you feel assured that the changes you make will have a positive impact.

We all have certain natural abilities when participating in groups. Identifying those natural roles creates the foundation for any kind of change. In order to do this we have to move out of our comfort zones and see how we might take on other roles when necessary to improve situations in groups. You can start by stepping back and asking yourself what kind of group member you might be. What kind of history have you had in groups? Have you received feedback about your style of interaction in group settings, either with friends or others you may have worked with in the past? Have you ever felt that you would like to be more effective in certain groups? Are there certain groups you feel comfortable in and others where you feel more isolated? These questions exemplify areas you might pay attention to as you learn about group development and take a closer look at how you can build upon your natural abilities.

In all groups, effective function is dependent on the behaviours of all the individual members. And, even though whatever happens in that group is a consequence of how the behaviours of its members mix, match or challenge each other, once a group forms, it creates a life of its own. It is an example of how a whole becomes larger than the sum of its parts. Once the whole is created, it can flourish, stall or simply fall apart. All of these outcomes are the responsibility of its members. Obviously if all group members are aware of how to contribute to successful group function, there is a high probability that the group will flourish. The skill of self-reflection is central to that process of contributing.

Using This Text

As a new student, the development of skills that contribute to your effectiveness in groups begins the minute you enter your program of study. The learning experience includes group work both in and out of the classroom with content that spans both the theory and practical components of your training program. In classroom situations you may be working in groups during an interactive exercise or during the accomplishment of an assignment. In your practicum or fieldwork you will find yourself working in teams with on-site professionals, having to make real (sometimes rushed) decisions. The ability to understand the ways and means of moving into a group, interacting within the group, and at the same time fulfilling the learning requirements of field practice is a necessary **competency**, or the knowledge, skills and behaviours needed to meet the standards of practice for that individual profession. This competency comprises not only the standards of your field of practice but also the framework for your program of training. Upon graduation, you will apply these skills daily with families, in teams, in supportive mentoring roles, on committees and in any of the countless group functions inherent to the profession.

While the skills of group participation can be taught in the classroom environment, it takes ongoing practice and reflection on your own behaviour to create a personal skill set that becomes a natural part of your interactions on a daily basis. Every situation, every individual and every moment of the day become variables that impact the ways and means of becoming an effective participant within groups. You learn best with opportunities to participate in groups, read about groups in the real world and observe group process in action.

A workbook-type guided approach is based on the teaching premise that students need interactive exercises and real-world examples in order to best assimilate (or accommodate) their thinking about the vital role they play in groups. This is called reflective practice and is the foundation skill that assures that the experiences have meaning for you. As well, *reflection* becomes a natural part of the process of working in all new group contexts as you move into professional work. Ultimately, this constant process of reflection will contribute to your sense of *professional judgment*. **Professional judgment** is another foundation competency in the helping professions. It involves the constant review, consideration, internal dialogue and self-analysis necessary to those who move in and out of others' lives on a regular basis.

Because there is never only one right way of dealing with the many situations inherent in working with others, reflection and professional judgment provide a way of processing each experience, deciding upon the best response and then learning from its consequence. Groups are the forums for learning how to best engage in this process. Reflection is the tool that makes the best of this learning from both a personal and professional perspective.

This text is designed to develop those skills of reflection in ways that make full use of the classroom group context. This will provide a forum to risk being in groups through exercise situations that simulate the work of the helping professions. It is important that you take these opportunities to risk, learn and then debrief experiences in order to practise the process of reflection and professional judgment. You can then link the theoretical work discussed in each chapter to the exercises in ways that can later be explored through the opportunities for guided reflection.

The transition from pure theory within the structure of a classroom setting to the reality of everyday human service practice is a major step. The classroom is a place to risk and learn. Once in the field, and inevitably the profession, the examples change, the variables are not as clearly delineated and individuals are rarely predictable. Developing the skills of ongoing reflection and professional judgment in the classroom context will provide you with the tools necessary to deal with these variables in real practice.

Chapter Structure

The theory components of each chapter include a researched overview of group-process theory in the well-known areas of group definition, group development, leadership and group roles, power and group dynamics and group decision making. This theoretical overview lays the groundwork for later reference, as well-known principles and understandings about group process are looked at from the experiential, and then the reflective, perspectives.

Theoretical components are then explored through the use of classroom exercises. Traditionally, classroom exercises in group process have students working through some rather unrealistic scenarios like problem solving with other survivors of a plane crash on a snowy mountain or making speedy decisions about what to take into their closet bomb-shelters after a nuclear attack. And, even though who you are is who you are regardless of the content of the classroom exercise, it is important to us that you have a chance to take part in exercises that seem more relevant to the student in human service. Hopefully, these exercises are relevant to present-day student experiences, with opportunities to observe and participate in groups and obtain the necessary feedback from others. These experiences provoke the reflective thinking that links your own personal experience to the theory being explored.

Chapters 1 and 2 include examples of personal reflections; Chapters 1 to 6 have a blank copy of the self-reflection template. The template (discussed later) will help support your process of personal, internal dialogue as inspired by components of the theory, the class exercises and the case-study examples. It is designed to ask the basic question, What meaning does this have for me? Each chapter's content is explored within the realm of personal awareness, with the outcome of setting your own direction for successful participation and interaction in groups. The reflection engages a process of professional judgment that will hopefully become a natural component of both your student experience and your professional experience. Suggestions for reflection are included throughout the text, identified by a reflection icon in the margin.

Case studies from the real world of the helping professions will complete each chapter of this text. These real-world examples will provide the narratives that serve to link the theory components to relevant practice. Issues and concerns will be explored through the use of questions that serve to provoke thinking. We believe that these questions will evoke a deeper level of analysis and, in turn, will help you to look more carefully at the *why*, the *how* and the *what-might-have-happened-if* of a particular situation. This way the theoretical principles are used for analysis, which in turn reinforces learning. For some, this may resemble a critical reflection approach to a particular scenario, and for others, it will simply be a process of questioning that helps to link theory to action. The provocation questions are meant for dialogue as well as for internal processing, after you ponder the reflection component of each chapter.

We have created case studies in each of the following contexts:

- Student — to analyze classroom situations that are real and relevant to you in the present
- Team — to exemplify issues that await you in your practical field learning and in the human service professions
- Community — to explore various aspects of community work that will help you understand the impact of individual professional behaviour in a context that includes many disciplines

Each case study contains questions that require written comments from you and eventual group discussion with classmates. Suggested responses to each case study are included in the instructor's resource manual.

Ongoing Small-Group Feedback

In order to best process the classroom theory, exercises, case studies and reflection opportunities, we suggest that at this point members of your group-process class create small groupings of individuals who meet on a regular basis to share experiences and impressions. This becomes what is sometimes referred to as a **Base Group**, a small grouping of students who meet on a regular basis in a confidential communication forum. We believe it is helpful to bear witness to others' learning and to give and receive feedback in some kind of consistent context. Feedback can then be used to enrich reflection. As well, Base Group members can observe each other for specific skill development, supporting learning and offering input into strategies each member might find useful to his or her own effectiveness in groups. Base Groups meet during class time (see Exercise 1.1 to Exercise 1.3), and are planned in conjunction with your instructor.

EXERCISE 1.1 CREATE A BASE GROUP

Objectives:

1. To create a context for communication and support for the duration of this course
2. To experience relationship building with a diversity of individuals
3. To share perspectives and engage in the process of giving and receiving feedback while learning about group process

PROCESS:

Create a grouping of four to six students. This grouping will stay together for the entire course and will be called a Base Group. Think carefully about your choice of Base Group colleagues. It is important that you feel comfortable with the people you will be communicating with on a regular basis. However, it is also important that you step out of your comfort zone and experience different perspectives when giving and receiving feedback.

Different member choices might include:

- Someone you trust
- Someone you feel comfortable with, yet do not really know that well

- Someone you think is quite different from you, although there seem to be some similarities of opinion (based on your early observations)
- Someone you really do not know well at all, outside of your comfort zone

This Base Group will meet either at the beginning of class, just before class ends, or both at the beginning and end of a class session. If the meeting is at the beginning of class, it will offer a short time (five minutes) to share areas of growth each member is working on and will include a possible determination of what each member might want others in the Base Group to observe that day.

A meeting just before the end of class offers the opportunity to debrief the class session and to give each other feedback that was contracted before the class started. Because the text suggests a number of student exercises and case-study discussion questions, there should be many bits and pieces to discuss.

EXERCISE 1.2 BASE GROUP DISCUSSION SUGGESTION

Objectives:

1. To begin the process of small-group inclusion through shared experiences
2. To share perceptions of an ongoing small-group discussion forum

In your Base Group, share with each other the kinds of small groups you have been a part of.

Work through each of these questions with each other:

- What positive and negative memories do you have from those experiences?
- What perceived status did you have in those groups?
- What role did you play in those groups?
- What challenges and opportunities* do you foresee in a Base Group arrangement?

* You may want to share these challenges and opportunities in an instructor-facilitated discussion with the whole class.

EXERCISE 1.3 CREATE A NAME

Objectives:

1. To continue the process of small-group inclusion through shared experiences
2. To represent the unique personalities of the Base Group

In your Base Group, create a name that somehow represents all individuals in the group. Share aspects of yourselves that help others know who you are. The Base Group name should symbolize the essence of your Base Group in some way.

Once you have decided on a name, discuss how you came to that decision. Make some notes about how the decision was made, paying attention to how the discussion was structured (for example, whose ideas were used, how long it took to decide, who talked the most and who was quiet). These notes will be referred to later in the book.

It is important to recognize that this kind of interactive small group is different from the groups that focus on exploring deeply personal feelings and the reasoning behind certain individual behaviour patterns. These kinds of groups, often called encounter groups, training groups or therapeutic growth groups, involve a deeper level of disclosure and risk. We want you to view Base Groups as an opportunity to explore the concepts covered throughout this text with the help of observations and feedback from others. Both Base Groups and therapeutic groups share the characteristics of risk taking, personal growth and changes in behaviour. They differ in the level of disclosure of intimate personal detail.

Reflection in the Helping Professions

We all find ourselves in groups of some kind at some time in all aspects of our lives. We all participate in these groups, see them start and end, and in whatever way we choose, reflect on how, why and what we may have said or done during these group times. Whether or not you actually identify this process of internal debriefing as *reflection* is a very individual matter. And depending on the essence, makeup, task, goal or simply the purpose of your being in a group context, your behaviour makes a difference. Internally debriefing your part in that group is simply a human thing to do. And this process of internal dialogue serves a very important purpose for those who have chosen to become professionals in the service of other human beings. It guides your practice while being modeled for, or taught to, clients in your care.

Unfortunately reflection does not come easily to many. Those who believe they are reflective may be simply scratching the surface that defines true critical reflection. Hopefully this text will assist in helping you dig beyond that well-scratched surface and move you into a critical reflection process that helps you identify real elements of learning about yourself. This will then assist in making your performance in group work of all kinds more effective.

The Process of Reflection

What exactly does the process of reflection look like? How do we know we are in a time or place of reflection? Is it intuitive or does it involve some kind of behavioural action, like discussion or actual behaviour change? How do we know we are actually reflecting deeply enough to change? All of these questions are legitimate and, again, are contingent upon the context, motivation and individual/personal level of awareness you find yourself in.

When we reflect, we sort things out after the event. **Reflection** involves processing our thoughts. It is either an internal narrative (thinking about what has occurred) or external narrative (talking to someone about what has occurred) that re-tells the story of the events of the recent (or sometimes not-so-recent) past. Reflection usually effects change. For most of us this means taking what happened in a situation, looking at it in terms of what we already know or have experienced and then moving forward.

Some would call reflection "**constructive process**". By this we mean that reflection provides an opportunity to ponder new information in terms of what is familiar to us by assessing this information with reference to our existing beliefs and values.

After much pondering, we eliminate what no longer seems to be working and make changes in our behaviour that may work better in the future. As you reflect, you take the time to step back and actually look at the story of *you*. By doing this you reinforce the meanings of new facts, ideas and questions within your personal context. This is truly a healthy human process because it sorts things out in meaningful ways.

Usually we judge ourselves in some way with personal reflection, mentally assessing our behaviour and comparing it to our existing beliefs or values. For example, if you received feedback that others in the group are intimidated by your tone of voice, you might think about how accurate the feedback was and then consider your values and beliefs about how people should treat each other respectfully in groups. You might decide to change your tone of voice and try out new behaviours in the group. Or, after considering the feedback, you might come to the conclusion that before making any changes you need more information from other sources. What you are doing here is reflecting more deeply on the meaning the feedback has for you and comparing it to existing values about how you think people should be treated. The process of reflection helps you take the time to consistently build on your growing self-awareness about how effectively you work with others.

Many of us take the time to work at self-reflection. Some of us mull over events deliberately and take mental note of what perceptions seem different or the same. Others of us write about the *doing* and then, afterwards, step back and read about ourselves in a place of self-assessment. And still others of us have witnesses in our lives. These are the close confidantes who have the ability to truly listen and to mark changes or similarities in our interpretation of events as we tell our stories. And, there are those of us who simply *are* in this world, who feel little need to pay much attention to our behaviour. Unfortunately, in the practice of working with others, not paying attention to our behaviour is not an option. Our behaviour has a major impact on those we work with. The need to reflect, adapt and evoke change is necessary to our practice.

Theories of Reflection

Donald Schon (1983) describes two types of reflection, *reflection-on-action* and *reflection-in-action.* Reflection-on-action occurs after an incident has occurred. The example above, when you reflected upon feedback you received, is an example of reflection-on-action. It occurred after you received the feedback and took the time to re-assess your behaviour in the situation.

Reflection-in-action takes place while a particular event is actually occurring. For most of us, reflection-in-action is an extremely difficult process. This is because taking the time to think about our responses or about the variables affecting the way we are interacting with others while we are actually in the situation can be very confusing. However, with time and experience, you can develop the ability to be consciously aware of what is going on around you and make modifications and adaptations based on what you think might be helpful at any given moment. For some, this becomes an intuitive process. The following example exemplifies the differentiation between reflection-on-action and reflection-in-action.

> You are a member of a group of students who have been in the same program together for about eight months. During that time, you have been doing a number of group assignments and have had the opportunity to

> pick and choose the groups you work in. You have noticed students in the class who take a similar approach to you to assignment work. Their ideas are similar to yours, they have similar values and their work ethic approximates the way you like to approach a task. As a result, you have invited a number of these people to join you in a current class assignment. The decision making about whom you have chosen has been based on your own observations, your past group experiences with these people and your impression of the similarities you have. This would be an example of Schon's reflection-on-action. (In other words, you have thought back on your past experience to gain insight about what you think is going to be a successful group experience.)
>
> Once you are in this group together, you continue to observe the others working alongside you on the assignment, noting the skills and abilities each member brings to the task. As well, you see that there are decisions that have to be made that will contribute to the success of the group task, and you offer suggestions for dividing the remaining tasks. This would be an example of reflection-in-action. (You are contributing to the effectiveness of the group *during* the accomplishment of the task.)

This link between reflection and practice is further explored in Cranton's (2002) discussions about **transformative learning** theory. According to Cranton, critical reflection helps us re-examine our point of view once we have experienced the consequence of some significant event. This re-examination may change our beliefs and values in some way, while helping us discard any of the more distorted aspects of that experience. The way we remember a particular experience is not always accurate. Often, what we remember is clouded with assumptions and subjective interpretations we automatically make about the people involved and the events that took place. The change in beliefs and values and discarding of assumptions is considered a transformative experience because we have changed our thought processes (and ultimately our behaviour) in some way.

It is healthy to test out our first reaction to others, particularly during those times when we sense discomfort or receive feedback. Linking possible assumptions to our own beliefs and values allows us to do the sorting out that clears the issues and helps us decide whether we need to change our behaviour. Looking carefully at assumptions that might cloud your perceptions of a situation is the basic premise of the reflection tool we provide in this text to support your reflection. All of this process is learning in action and, whether or not we are aware of it, learning reconstructs our thinking, feeling and behaving in order to move us forward in healthy ways. Otherwise we become trapped in misinterpretation, judgment and our own "right way".

Unearthing our beliefs and values about any given situation is not a simple process. It requires taking the time to look at the assumptions we often make, pinpointing their origin and investigating how they might be affecting our behaviour with others. A step-by-step guide can make this a bit easier, yet still requires insight and the openness to challenging these assumptions. Although challenging our assumptions (and ultimately our beliefs and values) is not a comfortable process, it can open up our own personal awareness about who we are and why we behave the way we do.

Whether this practice of reflection leads to a transformative change in our behaviour depends on whether we are happy with our patterns of behaviour and whether we are comfortable with their impact on others around us. We may choose to make changes, or we may decide we like the way we are. Regardless, moving into a place of objectivity through reflection and looking at often unconditionally-accepted beliefs and values open the door to enhanced self-awareness and increased interpersonal effectiveness.

Reflection and Group Process

As practitioners in services that affect others, it is vital for us to engage in consistent, meaningful, and introspective reflection. This must happen both during and after our participation in the group contexts in which we work. Because we are in the business of working with people we must find some way to self-monitor in order to dig away at personal, often hidden, agendas in a process that examines our own behaviour in groups. The term **hidden agendas** will be more thoroughly explored later in the text and is defined as those personal goals we do not openly express in the group because they are different from the goals the group is working toward. The process of self-monitoring brings our hidden agendas to the surface and helps us more openly examine the beliefs and values that affect our behaviour. This is important to our effectiveness with others, either as group facilitators or as group members. Only through our ability to engage in this process of self-discovery can we effectively work in groups and model the process for those we work with.

In the previous section we discussed how enhanced self-awareness leads to greater interpersonal effectiveness. As we constantly examine beliefs and values in the context of the varying groups we find ourselves a part of, our behaviour becomes more consistent and more congruent with our beliefs and values. As both student learners and human service professionals, this process must become a part of our practice. Consistency and congruency are the hallmarks of exemplary competence in the helping professions. We are always in a place of learning about ourselves and about others. Many believe that the ultimate goal of critical thinking and learning requires us to move beyond simply accumulating content or information. Reflection allows us to take the content to a deeper level, to organize it and move into what some call a lifelong learning approach. That way we avoid becoming simply passive receptors of knowledge and experience. In the work of the helping professions the *process* of building relationships and supporting others drives exemplary practice.

Mezirow (1997) discusses **habits of mind**, which he defines as the habitual, routine ways we think, feel and act, based on our early experiences and cultural heritage. According to Mezirow, the process of critical reflection is vital to breaking down those habits of mind that we often resort to in group situations and that impair our judgment and keep us trapped within our own frame of reference. Again, this process questions assumptions, beliefs and values and occurs in a social context. In today's ever-changing world, this is now the necessary competency for those who must work in any kind of group environment. For Mezirow, self-reflection moves us out of our comfort zone and into a place of what he terms "autonomous thinking:"

> The common presumption . . . is that the essential learning required to prepare a productive and responsible worker for the twenty-first century must empower the individual to think as an autonomous agent in a collaborative context rather than to uncritically act on the received ideas and judgements of others. (p. 8)

Again, we see the value of reflection in a group context, not only within the sphere of human service but within all aspects of an individual's life as a member of society. The focus here is on collaborative process and the willingness to consistently examine what may be assumptions or judgments that create barriers to healthy, open and productive social relationships.

As we come to the end of this theoretical discussion of reflection, some important points can be made about its value to our own growing sense of self-awareness and the development of group skills in the professional practice of supporting others:

The Importance of Reflection

1. It helps us to examine the past events of our lives, mix them with new learning and then make changes that will enhance our effectiveness in social situations.
2. It helps us to unearth the "story of us" in narrative form, reinforcing our interpretation of new facts and clarifying the meaning of experiences for us.
3. It helps us to examine our beliefs, values and assumptions as we look more carefully at why we behave the way we do in new situations.
4. It sorts out the information we have just learned and makes sense of it.
5. It digs for hidden agendas.
6. It improves our professional practice through constant self-review.
7. It "tabs" or catches thinking and feeling at a moment in time.
8. It gives us a chance to step back from an event and take a closer look at our role in it.
9. It contributes to interpersonal effectiveness.
10. It promotes change, which, in today's world, keeps us vital and effective in our work.
11. It is the opportunity that allows those special moments of insight (those "light-bulb moments") to occur that allow us to transform into a new way of being in the world.

The Reflection Tool

Reflection and Transformative Learning

We have designed a template, or **reflection tool**, to guide you in the process of what we earlier discussed as transformative learning. Transformative learning differs from basic reflection on content in that it involves consideration of and deliberation on the assumptions upon which we base our interpretations and points of view. As we grow and mature, we create frames of reference that relate to all aspects of our lives. These frames of reference are formed from our experiences (cultural expectations and the expectations in society and experiences in our family of origin) and create the foundation for the way in which we make decisions, form judgments, and decide how we will behave in any given situation. As you look at the reflection tool sample on page 16, you will see that Question 3 seeks to uncover the beliefs and values that form frames of reference.

Staying rooted in a particular frame of reference may limit your openness to new possibilities and personal growth. On the one hand, it is comfortable to stay with what is familiar. On the other hand, remaining in your comfort zone may get in the way of new information and insights that could lead to a more inclusive, well-rounded way of being in the world. The way to assess your "rootedness" is through questioning and exploration of the beliefs, values and assumptions you hold. This can be a very risky thing to do. The reflection tool is a guide to help you with this questioning.

The reflection tool follows the format of "What?", "So What?", "Now What?" to help you focus your thoughts on the meaning an incident had for you and the significance any insights might have for your future practice or behaviour.

Sections of the Reflection Tool

(Please refer to the blank reflection tool at the end of this chapter.)

What?

This section asks you to briefly describe the event, awareness/insight, or information (chapter reading) that stands out for you in the moment. It is simply a description of what you want to reflect on more deeply.

So What?

Questions 1 to 4 ask you to derive meaning from the situation you described. Question 1 asks you to identify the emotions that arise when you think of the situation. An emotional response is often our first clue that something is going on within us that might merit a closer look and be a potential growth spot. Often when we experience emotions, particularly uncomfortable emotions, we blame the person or the situation for our feelings and don't spend time exploring to find out what it is about us that might be contributing to our emotional response. Do not be surprised if different emotions arise that may contrast with or contradict each other, depending on the point of view you take when thinking about the situation or concept. Differing emotions exemplify the term *mixed emotions* and indicate an ability to step back and reflect from different perspectives.

Taking an objective look at the origin of these emotions opens the door for us to move deeper into the real meaning a situation has for us, our role in co-creating the situation and the potential for change either in our point of view or our behaviour (or both).

Question 2 asks you to explore your emotions further to help you better understand your reactions. It helps to focus on the emotion that seems most significant to you in the moment. Think about the feeling that seems most relevant and try to determine what contributes to that emotion. Most likely it will come from your past, your family history or other impactful experiences.

Question 3 addresses your assumptions and beliefs and values (frame of reference) and asks you to question their impact and validity. This is a difficult process and involves the ability to step outside your personal perspective and look objectively at the ideas and feelings you have with respect to the situation described.

Assumptions are immediate thoughts and ideas that arise when we first react to a person, a situation or a concept we have never considered before. Assumptions may or may not be accurate and affect our perception and experience of any situation. They also contribute to our emotional response to that situation. We must avoid believing in these immediate assumptions. If they are not investigated we may find ourselves responding in unhelpful ways based on an inaccurate initial perception.

For example, if you were in a group situation where someone kept cutting you off you might assume that:

- The person is inconsiderate.
- The person doesn't realize she was cutting you off.
- What you have to say isn't important or interesting.
- The person knows a lot more about the topic than you do.
- It is acceptable to interrupt or cut people off in this group, and other group members are not concerned about being interrupted.

As you can see, the assumptions range from what you think might be true about the individual, to what you think about yourself, to what you think might be true for other members of the group. When you are considering what assumptions might be contributing to your reactions, it is important to step back from your emotional responses and consider assumptions you might be making about other less personal aspects of the situation. In this example, you are looking not only at your own irritation, but also considering assumptions you are making about what the group or person might be experiencing. All these thoughts contribute to your emotional response, yet so far you don't know for sure that any of them are true. What is important here is to take the time to brainstorm about what the range of assumptions might be.

Beliefs and **values** are more ingrained patterns of thoughts and feelings. They arise from family rules and expectations as well as from the expectations of the society in which you grew up. Beliefs and values reflect what is deeply important to us in relation to the issue we are reflecting on. Beliefs are what we think is true, while values are what we hold to be important. With respect to the above example, your beliefs and values might be:

- It is disrespectful and impolite to cut people off.
- Individuals have a right to be heard on an equal basis.
- When you are working with others, everyone's contribution is valuable.

As you can see in Exercise 1.4 on page 14, it is not always easy to discriminate between assumptions and beliefs/values. Unearthing assumptions, beliefs and values helps us to reconsider ways that we might be jumping to conclusions about situations. Distinguishing between immediate assumptions and ingrained beliefs and values contributes to our ability to differentiate between what drives us as human beings (beliefs and values) and the judgments we make (assumptions). We often act based on these assumptions when they might be inaccurate because we do not take the time to verify them.

Question 4 helps you to make connections about how your assumptions and values relate to the current circumstance. This question is intended to deepen your understanding of how your frame of reference contributes to your interpretation of the situation.

EXERCISE 1.4 ASSUMPTIONS, BELIEFS/VALUES

Objectives:

1. **To discriminate between assumptions and beliefs/values**
2. **To become familiar with the process of identifying assumptions and beliefs/values**

The following statements represent either an assumption or a belief/value. With reference to the descriptions above, work with a partner to label each statement.

1. A true friend is supportive, no matter what. __________
2. Men should not marry each other. __________
3. Other people think I'm weird. __________
4. All Canadians have the right to a good education. __________
5. Having lots of money ensures happiness. __________
6. Someone who is overweight eats only junk food. __________
7. Teenagers who take drugs have had poor parenting. __________
8. Global warming is having a detrimental effect on the environment. __________
9. He has lots to say so he must know a lot. __________
10. They are not working as hard as me on this project so they must not care about getting a good grade. __________

Discuss with the class any surprises or challenges you may have had with this exercise.

Answers:

1. Belief/Value 2. Belief/Value 3. Assumption 4. Belief/Value
5. Assumption 6. Assumption 7. Assumption 8. Belief/Value
9. Assumption 10. Assumption

Sometimes beliefs and values keep us stuck in one place. We become so attached to a specific outlook on life that we are unable to entertain new or different possibilities. If personal growth is the desired outcome, critical reflection on our patterns of thought is the path to achieving that goal.

Question 5 directs your attention toward the potential for a change in your behaviour. Changing your behaviour is not always the desired outcome. This question asks you to consider why a change might be valuable. There are always consequences to our actions. Here you are looking at why or why not a change in your behaviour might be an effective or useful choice.

Now What?

This section asks you to put the insights gained through the previous process into your present context. How will you apply this learning to your life? Question 6 asks you to identify specific behaviours to experiment with (as linked to the chapter) while Question 7 asks you to consider how you might sabotage change. Sometimes we allow our fear of what might happen to prevent us from exploring new possibilities.

Objectives

Once you have identified potential changes, you will set specific goals for yourself. These goals will be most effective if they are specific behavioural changes that you can make within a short time frame.

What Questions Remain?

This section offers you an opportunity to frame your learning as a question for the class. You might find yourself confused about something that you would like more input on, or you might reach an insight that could challenge others in the class to go deeper into their own learning. We have included two examples that focus on unique group-process issues that might arise in classroom experiences. These are meant to help you see how to use the reflection tool throughout the rest of the text. As well, we close Chapters one to six with a blank version of the tool for your own use. The two examples will help you add meaning to what has just been described as components of the reflection tool (see pages 16 and 18).

Using the Reflection Tool

The example on page 16, Sample Reflection 1, outlines how a learner might use the reflection tool after receiving feedback that she takes over the group by asking many questions and suggesting next steps.

Notice that:

- In Questions 1 and 2 the learner recognizes her emotional response and, rather than reacting from it, looks to see where it might be coming from. She realizes that this is new feedback for her, that her perception of her behaviour is different from that of the group (I thought I was being helpful . . .), and that perhaps the group is being unfair. In other words, by asking "why" she takes the time to analyze that first emotion, adding depth to the reflection.
- In Question 3 the assumptions (her immediate thoughts that occurred upon receiving the feedback) contain two elements: her immediate leap to believe that everyone agrees with the feedback and the assumption that she is being powerful in an undesirable manner.
- For beliefs and values (frames of reference that have formed throughout her lifetime), she focused on the use of power identified in the "Assumptions" section. In this example, it is the link with power that caught the learner's attention rather than an in-depth exploration of asking questions and making decisions, which is what the original feedback was about. This "going with the flow" of the reflection is not only acceptable but encouraged.
- At the end of Question 4 the learner is questioning what is behind the feedback from the group's perspective. Rather than immediately assuming the feedback requires her to change her behaviour, she is considering the possibility that only a small portion of the group interpreted her behaviour in the way that resulted in the feedback she was given.
- In Question 6 the learner is looking at ways to meet her own needs as well as the needs of the group. Considering a change in behaviour does not necessarily mean abandoning everything you hold dear.
- A potential revelation was identified in Question 7 and explored further in the "What Questions Remain?" section when the learner frames questions for the class about power and questions herself about her own judgments and need for control. Both sets of questions might be explored in class.

Sample Reflection 1

What?

What stood out for you in this chapter? Describe a reading, exercise, incident, person's behaviour, etc.

Class gave me feedback that I dominate the group process. I ask a lot of questions, and I make decisions about what we should do next without checking them out.

So What?

1. Emotional impact?

- Surprised
- Defensive
- Angry

2. Why do you think you had this emotional response?

- Never had this feedback before
- Don't want to think of myself as interfering with others
- Don't like it when others do this and now I'm being told I'm like that
- I thought I was being helpful in offering ideas for next steps
- I don't think it's fair to be so critical when I was just trying to help

3. What assumptions might you be making in this situation? What beliefs and values were touched off by this situation?

Assumptions:

- Everybody agrees with this feedback.
- It's accurate — they're right in their assessment that I behave this way.
- It's not OK to be this way — bad use of power.

Beliefs and values:

About the feedback:

- Power is bad.
- People in power take advantage of others.
- People don't like people in power so they don't like me.

About my response/feelings:

- Decisions need to be made in order to move on.
- It's a waste of time to keep talking about how people feel.

4. Write about the meaning this has for you. Some helpful questions might be: Do you think your values might be clouding your interpretation of the situation? If so, how?

Possibly. I'm jumping to a negative assessment of myself by believing that power is bad and that everyone in the group sees my behaviour as unhelpful.

Have you been affected by similar situations in the same way? How have you responded?

Yes. I was in a group where one person kept trying to get the group to do things the way she wanted. I felt intimidated and didn't say much — I shut down. I don't want to be responsible for shutting people down.

5. Is it important for you to change your behaviour? Why?

Maybe. I'm not sure how many people in the group see me as dominating, and I'm not sure whether those who do would tell me they don't like it.

If the group is telling me my style is hindering group process, then it would be a good idea for me to figure out how to incorporate my desire to get the task accomplished with a way that helps others feel included and respected.

Now What?

6. Based on the learning from this chapter, what other behaviours might you consider?

- Going with the flow
- Checking in more to see if the group is ready to consider next steps
- Asking first for ideas from others before expressing my own ideas

7. What might stop you from engaging in these new behaviours?

- My need to get on with things
- Frustration at taking a long time to do something that could be accomplished faster
- Sounding awkward and timid rather than confident and in control

Objectives

- Check with the group to see if they see me as being powerful in a negative or unhelpful way
- Share my thoughts about different behaviour I could engage in from Question 7, and see if they think this would be helpful
- If yes, practise
- If no, ask for input about what they think would be helpful or clarify the purpose of their original feedback

What Questions Remain?

- Is being powerful bad?
- What does good power look like in group process?
- How does a group get to decisions without someone pushing to get there?
- What judgments do I make about people who sound timid and awkward?
- What is it about me that I need to be in control of, and how might that hinder my work with others?

On page 18, Sample Reflection 2 uses a learner's observations of other people in her group and the impact their behaviour is having on her as a way of getting clear about what she might do next.

Notice that:

- In Questions 1 and 2, even though the learner is frustrated with the behaviour of group members, her focus is on what is contributing to her own reaction. In other words, she is not blaming others for her feelings or looking to make her feelings their fault. She is considering what might happen if the behaviour continues the way it does as a way of clarifying her emotional response.
- In Question 3 her assumptions are concentrated on what she thinks about the immediate situation — that she is the only one experiencing discomfort, judgments that others don't care about their performance as much as she does and that speaking out is dangerous.
- When she explores her beliefs and values she gains increasing clarity about the importance of a strong work ethic and how this affects her interpretation of the other group members' behaviour. She recognizes that harmonious relationships are important to her, hence her hesitancy to speak out. If she had come from a different set of background experiences, she might believe that "the squeaky wheel gets the grease" and that speaking out might be seen in a more positive light. Note that there are no right or wrong answers in filling out the reflection tool. It is geared toward helping you gain some insight into what contributes to your current position in order to more clearly consider other possibilities.
- Question 4 asks the learner to look at what might prevent her from being more open-minded about the situation. In this example, the learner recognizes that she has some ingrained ideas about how groups operate which might prevent her from being open to other possibilities for effective group functioning. Also, she sees that because being successful is so important to her, it is hard for her to relax and have faith that the group might simply be going through a stage and things will get back on track.
- In Question 6, the learner integrates information from the chapter on group effectiveness with her own awareness of the importance of a strong work ethic in order to come up with options that will meet her own needs and the needs of the group. She merges group theory with her own deepening awareness of what she has come to believe she is capable of doing in this situation.
- Question 7 focuses on her fear of how she will be perceived by others. Again, this question helps her to identify what might stop her from risking new behaviour.
- The "Objectives" section outlines the goals she believes are workable for her. This question is meant to nudge the learner toward action rather than simply formulating options without pursuing them.
- In the "What Questions Remain?" section, the questions that the learner forms for class discussion focus primarily on group process. They come out of the learner's assumptions and beliefs about how groups function. She is questioning whether her beliefs are valid and is seeking input from others. She is also questioning how people perceive those who speak up and express concern about people's behaviour.

Sample Reflection 2

What?

What stood out for you in this chapter? Describe a reading, exercise, incident, person's behaviour, etc.

There is a group assignment due in two weeks. The group is spinning its wheels — nothing is getting accomplished. Everyone is arguing, going off task, joking around — they don't appear to be taking things seriously.

So What?

1. Emotional impact?

- Frustration
- Irritation
- Fear of not getting the work done
- Anxiety
- Confusion

2. Why do you think you had this emotional response?

- I want to do well in school; this is not going to get done; I'm not going to get a good mark; marks are important to me.
- I think we should be able to do this — I don't understand why this is so hard.
- I'm scared that other people in the group are going to let me down.
- I think I'm going to end up doing all the work to make sure we do well.
- I'm not sure what to do; I'm worried that if I say something, people will get mad at me and not like me anymore.

3. What assumptions might you be making in this situation? What beliefs and values were touched off by this situation?

Assumptions:

- I'm the only one frustrated with the way the group is working.
- Other people don't value their marks as much as I do — they don't care.
- Groups are supposed to work well together.
- People won't like me if I say something.

Beliefs and values:

- Working together makes the job go faster — "many hands make light work".
- Good marks mean you've learned more/worked harder.
- Hard work is a reflection of commitment and dedication.
- People have to work hard to reap positive benefits.
- People don't like complainers.
- Harmony is important among group members.

4. Write about the meaning this has for you. Some helpful questions might be: Do you think your values might be clouding your interpretation of the situation? If so, how?

I see groups as functioning in a certain way. The purpose of groups is to get the job done. Is this close-minded?

My need to succeed might be getting in the way of me trusting the process.

Have you been affected by similar situations in the same way? How have you responded?

No. The groups I've been in have always been successful.

5. Is it important for you to change your behaviour? Why?

Yes, I have to do something. This assignment is too important for me not to do well.

Now What?

6. Based on the learning from this chapter, what other behaviours might you consider?

- I could speak up and express my observations and concerns.
- I could check to see if anyone else perceives things the way I do.
- I could do all the work myself.
- The book talks about the importance of maintenance — maybe I could loosen up a bit and join in the joking.

7. What might stop you from engaging in these new behaviours?

- Fear of rejection and isolation
- Self-consciousness — others might think I'm weird or sucking up to the instructor.

Objectives

- Give feedback to the group to help us get back on task — clearly share my observations about arguing, joking and off-task behaviour
- Ask if anyone else is frustrated with the process
- Practise/enhance my assertiveness by risking giving the feedback

What Questions Remain?

- Is it OK for people to joke around and argue?
- What level of task focus is necessary for a group to be effective and highly successful?
- How far can a group go in a state of chaos?
- What kind of impact does a person speaking up have on group functioning?
  - Back on track?
  - Shut it down?

Use of the Reflection Tool

This chapter and Chapter 2 include an example of a reflection that links to the theory content of each chapter. As well, we have included a blank copy of the reflection tool for your own use. There will be suggestions from us throughout the text, where certain issues or personal reactions might merit the opportunity to reflect on the meaning of an exercise, issue, or any new content learned. You may want to use the tool to reflect on those critical issues or you may have an immediate experience in class (or in other group situations) that merits a reflective "dialogue". A guided opportunity to look carefully at sensitive issues should be one of the first processes you engage in as you debrief certain group experiences. At first this process may feel somewhat confusing and awkward. Eventually the questions will come more easily to you. It is our hope that this guided reflection process will eventually become so natural to you in your practice that it will occur without the cumbersome process of capturing the introspection in writing.

Summary

Understanding the ways that groups function most effectively is a foundation skill in the practice of working with people. This understanding develops from studying elements of group structure, the ways groups develop over time, how leadership skills affect group function and the dynamics of power in all group interactions. Only then can those who have chosen to work in helping professions not only participate productively and effectively in groups, but also facilitate the skill development of others with whom they associate in practice.

Linking principles of group theory to actual classroom experiences and case studies from the field and community helps to solidify learning about effective group function. Personal reflection further supports this process. When significant events occur in group contexts, self-reflection helps us analyze how we responded and how we might make changes in our group interactions to become more competent group members.

Through the use of a guided reflection, we can more carefully examine those assumptions and values that might be affecting our impressions of the role we take in groups. We can then make decisions about whether we might change our behaviour. Self-reflection may also contribute to personal growth that extends beyond our work in groups and affects our behaviour in everyday life.

Key Terms

Assumptions *(p. 12)*
Base Group *(p. 5)*
Beliefs *(p. 13)*
Competency *(p. 3)*
Constructive process *(p. 7)*
Habits of mind *(p. 10)*
Hidden agendas *(p. 10)*
Professional judgment *(p. 3)*
Reflection *(p. 7)*
Reflection tool *(p. 11)*
Transformative learning *(p. 9)*
Values *(p. 13)*

Case Studies

The following case studies capture the experiences of some students who have just learned about the expectations of a human service course that teaches skill development while working in groups. With all case-study examples, we encourage you to answer the questions on your own and then share your ideas with others, either in your Base Group or as a whole class. The following two examples may seem strangely familiar to you.

Case Study 1.1 **Issues with the Process of Reflection**

CATEGORY: STUDENT

Padwell is a student in his second semester of a two-year community support-worker diploma program. He has just started a course that focuses on skill development for working effectively in groups. As well, he has become part of a Base Group of five other students in the class. He and a couple of people he has worked with on assignments in his first semester are in this group, along with a couple of people he does not know that well yet feels comfortable with, based on the few times they have met.

One of his assignments involves filling out a guided reflection for various parts of the course based on his emotional reactions to the content. Padwell becomes quite concerned about the process of reflection and comments to students in his Base Group that he questions why so much attention is being paid to this. He is not sure of its value when other skill areas are more concrete and understandable. As well, he is not used to discussing his emotional reactions to things that bother him because it is not something he has been encouraged to do in his family. Some of the other Base Group members seem a bit confused about the reflection process as well, yet do not seem to have the same emotional reaction as Padwell.

QUESTIONS:

1. Can you relate to Padwell's concerns? If not, why? If so, what other issues might you have with the process of reflection?
2. How might Padwell make use of his Base Group to feel more comfortable with the process of written reflection, using the tool provided?
3. Should Padwell be exempt from filling out and submitting reflections based on his reactions to content throughout the course? If so, why? If not, why?

Case Study 1.2 **Base Group Members**

CATEGORY: STUDENT

Twenty-six students in a human service certificate program are given the opportunity to divide into Base Groups of five or six. Over a period of about half an hour, students move around the room, choosing members based on the instructor's suggestions (someone they trust; someone they are comfortable with, but do not know that well; someone new and different, yet similar in some ways; and someone outside their comfort zone). There is a bit of confusion in the classroom, and eventually groups of five and six are formed. Alexis, Gemma, Ewan and Sachan are left without a group.

Alexis and Ewan have been in classes together and worked successfully on a small group project in the first semester. They have been in classes with Sachan or Gemma, but do not know them well. The instructor suggests that all four make up a Base Group. After a few moments of discomfort and a bit of embarrassment about feeling like "left-overs", they say hello to each other and then class time is over.

Alexis and Ewan have lunch together and share their concerns about the fact that Sachan and Gemma might not make the best Base Group colleagues. They share their few experiences with both classmates, noting that Sachan seems like a punk rocker, with her many body piercings and gothic style of dress and really weird-looking friends at the college. Gemma is the mother of two grown children and seems to be from a different generation, based on some of the input she has offered in class discussions. They end their conversation totally disgusted with the idea of Base Groups altogether and feel forced into a situation that may be a total waste of time.

QUESTIONS:

1. What challenges do you think await this Base Group, based on the impressions Alexis and Ewan are sharing with each other?
2. What opportunities await this Base Group, based on its membership?
3. How do you think Alexis and Ewan might deal with their concerns?

Reflection Tool

<table>
<tr><td colspan="2">What?
What stood out for you in this chapter? Describe a reading, exercise, incident, person's behaviour, etc.</td></tr>
<tr><td>So What?
1. Emotional impact?</td><td>2. Why do you think you had this emotional response?</td></tr>
<tr><td>3. What assumptions might you be making in this situation? What beliefs and values were touched off by this situation?

Assumptions:

Beliefs, values:</td><td>4. Write about the meaning this has for you. Some helpful questions might be:
Do you think your values might be clouding your interpretation of the situation? If so, how?

Have you been affected by similar situations in the same way? How have you responded?</td></tr>
<tr><td colspan="2">5. Is it important for you to change your behaviour? Why?</td></tr>
</table>

Now What?

6. Based on the learning from this chapter, what other behaviours might you consider?

7. What might stop you from engaging in these new behaviours?

Objectives

What Questions Remain?

Chapter 2

Group Dimensions

Objectives

In this chapter, students will acquire the knowledge, skills and attitudes to:

1. Identify the dimensions that define groups.
2. Understand what elements of group contexts contribute to optimal group performance.
3. Analyze real-life scenarios and consider ways to improve group effectiveness using the dimensions discussed in the chapter.
4. Understand how modifications to group elements can affect productivity.
5. Begin the process of personal reflection through exercises, case studies and Base Group interaction.

Studying the Dimensions of Groups

Just how do we define *groups,* and why is it important to do so? Johnson and Johnson (2006) suggest a number of ways of defining groups. **Groups** exist when members influence each other and set common goals, when there is a sense of interdependence within the membership and group participation feels rewarding to individuals, when relationships function within a framework of mutual norms and expectations, and when individuals interact directly with others on a regular basis.

We are also in a group if we simply believe we are part of a group. This definition is important in the world of human service because it clearly defines the kinds of professional groupings we connect to in less concrete settings like advocacy work. We perceive that we are part of a group of advocates who support the best care for our clients, yet we may never know exactly who all of the members are, and we may not connect directly with others who support our professional values. Nonetheless, we most certainly consider this to be a grouping vital to our profession, and we make it our responsibility to find the best ways to connect to other group members — online, through annual conferences or through monthly newsletters (see Exercise 2.1).

EXERCISE 2.1 DEFINING GROUPS

Objectives:

1. To tap your perceptions of what defines a group
2. To explore the many ways you might experience groups
3. To reach some common definition of groups based on your experience
4. To begin to familiarize yourself with group terminology
5. To explore your idea of what and who may or may not be classified as a group

Using all members of the class for this exercise, choose about four or five of the simulations from this listing:

- Three people standing in line at a blood-bank clinic after September 11, 2001
- Five people on a committee representing a number of child and youth care agencies in an urban context
- Four students forced to do an assignment together for marks
- Four people stuck in an elevator
- Six friends organizing a Halloween party
- Six people from different departments in a health unit with offices along a short hallway
- Five employees in a group home on different shifts
- Ten people in a chat room

Each group prepares a short skit for the whole class, with members engaged in a discussion about the context in which they find themselves. For example, four people stuck in an elevator would obviously discuss why they are not moving and just when and how they might get moving again.

As each simulation is played out, student observers will discuss:

1. How are the members interacting with each other?
2. Is interpersonal communication style important here?
3. Are there any expectations or rules that may direct the way these members function?
4. Is there some kind of structure to the way the members exist together in this context?
5. How does each member influence one another?
6. Do any of these members have a goal in mind?
7. Are individuals that comprise this group using it to achieve any personal goals?
8. Based on your answers to Questions 1 through 7, would you say this was a group? Why or why not?

After completing the skits, return to your small simulation groups and with consideration of the many defining attributes of the term *group*, brainstorm what you think might be a general definition.

Share these definitions with the whole class and note common and divergent points of view. Post them in the room for future reference and spontaneous alterations as you move through the rest of this chapter's material.

We see value in taking a closer look at the elements and factors that comprise groups. These elements and factors are often referred to as the dimensions of the group. Understanding the unique contexts of every group you find yourself a part of helps you make decisions about how you contribute to its function. In many ways this contribution is a personal investment on your part — an investment that is dependent on the context and the reason the group exists.

We make decisions about our level of commitment to each group situation on both a conscious and an unconscious level. Your role may look quite different in a discussion group of five students during a quick 15-minute in-class task compared to a project group that has to complete an assignment outside of the classroom over a period of one month. The amount of time spent together, physical space, size and membership of the group and overall reasons for the group's existence all interrelate as variables that affect the way each group functions.

By looking at the common elements inherent in a definition of groups, we can link them to some of the group types you are part of as both a student and a practitioner. Taking the opportunity to discriminate among some of the significant elements that can affect group function helps educate us as we move into group situations. We can then ask ourselves the following questions:

1. What do I have to take into consideration when forming the best group for a particular task or activity?
2. What do I have to do to make the best of an assigned group situation?
3. What is going to affect my performance in a particular group?
4. What is going to affect the group's performance?

Common Elements of Groups

By examining general categories that help define how groups exist we can better understand the elements of those groups and predict some of the dynamics that might affect their function. As a new group member, this helps you give careful consideration to ways of adapting your behaviour prior to taking part in any kind of group function. This is not to say that we are encouraging you to form some kind of judgment or preconceived notion about how any new group situation will play out for you. What it does mean is that you can better understand the challenges and opportunities implicit in the groups you are a part of and use that knowledge in ways that make those dynamics enhance productivity and enjoyment of the overall experience.

The characteristics that merit consideration when examining defining factors in groups are both directly observable and indirectly observable. Cragan and Wright (1995) suggest that directly observable characteristics include communication styles, space, time and size of the group. Indirectly observable characteristics include interdependence, norms, structural patterns, goals and perceptions.

We have considered Cragan and Wright's suggestions in developing an adapted list that will identify some of the common elements, or dimensions, of groups. In addition to considering Cragan and Wright's categories we have included communication patterns, personality factors and the nature of the task as variables that affect group dynamics, based on the work of Patton, Giffin and Patton (1989).

The eleven elements are as follows:

1. Size of the group
2. Time you will be together
3. Context (where you are together and who is in the room)
4. Norms (both assumed beforehand and decided on with the group)
5. Preconceived notions about purpose and your role
6. Group goals
7. Assumptions about members and roles
8. Communication patterns
9. Personality factors
10. Nature of the task
11. Interdependence (the ability to work together toward a common goal)

All of these elements interrelate and affect each other. Because they interrelate, the whole function is clearly more than the sum of the individual elements. As well, the miniscule shift of one element will create a change in the dimension of the group's function and will affect all the other elements. Something as simple as shifting the time a group meets to accomplish a task will in some way affect group goals, membership, necessary norms, communication patterns, the impact of the context and the level of interdependence members have with each other.

We must take time to unravel these elements in terms of your work in the helping professions in order to avoid possible pitfalls that could be prevented through an advanced awareness of these common factors.

Defining the Elements of Groups

1. Size of the Group

Social scientists have debated whether two people can be defined as a group. Can two people working in partnership actually be called a grouping? That may have to be left up to you to decide. Perhaps it is more helpful to ask ourselves whether a group of two people is seen as productive, effective and ideal in the accomplishment of a task. Is a group of two an ideal minimum group size? When two people have different points of view about an issue, decision making has the potential for an impasse because of an inadequate level of the interpersonal expertise necessary to reach a shared understanding or because the decision making becomes automatic and possibly narrow-minded. A third party (or more) changes the dynamic and may alter one of the other party's perspectives or may add yet another dimension to the discussion altogether. That makes for a richer process of decision making or direction setting because of the addition of a perspective that either adds weight to an idea or moves discussion into a whole new realm (Brilhart & Galanes, 1992; Johnson & Johnson, 2006). Therefore, an effective minimum group size might be three.

But what about maximum size? It is difficult for large groups to work together on a common task or decision. For example, if you could imagine your entire class of students trying to come together to make a decision about something, group size could become unwieldy. Individuals would not get enough air time, some students might lose interest and begin side conversations or opt out of participation due to sheer aggravation, group leadership might become a big question and it might be very difficult to balance the needs of both the introverts and extroverts in the room.

With all of these questions in mind, it is obvious that if the goal is to reach a decision in which the members feel valued for their input and committed to the final outcome, then this group size is likely to be ineffective and counterproductive. It is difficult for a group of this magnitude to meet in its entirety to formulate decisions together. Typically groups of this size break down into sub-groups or committees in order to manage some of the issues discussed above.

Researchers seem to agree that when looking at a group's ability to complete tasks and make mutually satisfactory decisions, smaller groups of five to seven members are the most successful (Brilhart & Galanes, 1992; Johnson & Johnson, 2006; Slater 1958).

2. Time Together

Obviously, the time a group is actually together has an impact on its function, its productivity and its overall effectiveness. Time taken for individual meetings, the time between meetings and the time the group works together over a series of meetings in the completion of a task all affect the group's development and function. It is also a dimension of groups that can significantly affect our commitment to a particular group. In a classroom situation, for example, students will commit much less energy to an in-class small-group discussion than they will to a graded assignment that spans a longer period of time over a semester. Similarly, in the professional context, the ways groups function may change depending on the length of time the group has worked together or the expectation of commitment to a common task.

The history of our role in a group of employees significantly affects our role, our level of risk taking and the perceptions others have of us in the work setting. The longer a group is together, the greater the likelihood of smoother decision making based on members' increased understanding of each other's strengths and weaknesses and contributions to group functioning. Time also may enhance group member accommodations for certain idiosyncrasies as individuals grow to understand or appreciate each other's behaviours.

3. Context

Environment/Where you are together: Physical environment is such a significant factor! It sets the tone for any group function in obvious and not-so-obvious ways. There should be a match between the purpose of the grouping and the physical context where it takes place. Too often this factor is ignored when preparing a setting for groups to function. As educators, we are constantly aware of the effects of classroom environment on student learning. Room temperature, square footage, table placement, chair comfort, visual appeal, lighting — the list of environmental factors is endless.

There is likely no need for a staff of three to hold their weekly staff meeting in the company boardroom. However, consider this recent experience of a community committee of representatives deciding on a job description for the position of supervisor of a parenting education project in a small town in northern British Columbia. This group of dedicated and very busy childcare stakeholders was called together to advise the regional Ministry for Children and Family Development on the job description and was asked to meet at the local Ministry office. The group of six professionals met in the hallway of the regional office and was told that the regional manager had been called out of town suddenly and had suggested they meet anyway. After ten minutes of waiting in the hallway and three phone calls checking out meeting locations in the building, the meeting was held in a training lab found empty by a helpful secretary. A key member (human element) was missing and the meeting place had three different kinds of chairs and a very small octagonal table. The meeting began late and had to be hurried because the room would not be available for more than 60 minutes.

This example helps us visualize the importance of consistency between the physical environment and the importance of the task. The roles each of the members of this group played during the decision-making process were affected by their waiting in the hallway, the seating arrangements, the meeting room itself and the inconvenience of all the moving around. In this type of situation, some group members will find discomfort hard to move beyond, and others will simply take it in stride. Either way, productivity will be affected. And, less obviously, the meeting context pays little respect to the commitment of this kind of community working-group. There is a certain inconsistency here.

The bottom line is that group members are affected by the message they receive in whatever environmental context they find themselves working in. Surroundings affect how you feel and inevitably how you function.

Human element/Who is in the room: Imagine the following scenarios:

1. There is a group-home staff meeting (six staff) to decide on a work plan for an adult with disabilities new to the home. One of the staff has his eight-year-old daughter sitting off to the side entertaining herself until the meeting is over and dad is ready to take her home for the day.
2. You have been meeting with a childcare committee (12 members) every two months for over a year, and now there are three new representative community members.
3. You are in a class of early childhood education students, and there are two men and twenty-four women.
4. You are in a full-day workshop on working with difficult people. One of the people in the workshop is someone who has been irritating you over the past two months. This person has just been promoted to case manager and constantly hovers over you, intimating that you could be doing a better job.

How might the **human element** (the people physically present in the group) affect how people relate to each other? In the first scenario, the fact that one group member has a child nearby will affect his contribution simply because he has someone he knows and loves within his visual frame. Others may try to accommodate the child, which could interrupt the flow of decision making and undermine the overall creativity of the planning. In the second scenario, the three new members will literally change the face of the committee and completely adjust communication patterns. In the third scenario, the gender imbalance will be a dimension that might affect the subject matter and depth of personal sharing

EXERCISE 2.2 HUMAN ELEMENT

Objectives:

1. To analyze the potential impact of the human element on group function
2. To reflect on how you might adjust your personal style in certain human contexts

In groups of six, consider the scenarios suggested in the text on page 29, and discuss how group members might be affected by either the human circumstances or individuals in the environment. Ask yourselves the following questions:

1. What potential accommodations might you or other members in each of these groups make in these situations?
2. How might these accommodations challenge group effectiveness? How might they enhance group effectiveness?

Note your suggestions on chart paper and be prepared to share them with the whole class.

during class discussions while creating an opportunity for hearing diverse perspectives. Finally, in the fourth scenario, having the person you find irritating in a workshop about working with difficult people might be just too much to bear (see Exercise 2.2 for further analysis of how the human element can affect groups).

During your discussion, note similar situations you may have found yourself a part of, and share your experience of how these groups were affected by individuals in the environment. This might be an excellent opportunity to use the reflection tool to explore more deeply memories of any experiences you have had and the impact the experiences had on you.

4. Norms

Every group has a set of **norms**, a system of rules and expectations that develops to guide the behaviour of group members. These rules may be openly discussed and obvious to all group members or may develop subconsciously as a result of the behaviour of the people present.

When people form groups, both *preconceived* and *mutually decided* norms exist. By **preconceived norms**, we mean that individuals have expectations resulting from their backgrounds, their socialization and their general experiences that they bring to group situations. For example, if you were heading into a meeting with your college instructors, you would anticipate that there would be certain expectations about the language used, the start and end times and the acceptability of topics for discussion. If, however, you are meeting a group of friends that you see on a regular basis, the categories of preconceived norms will not change (that is, you will still have expectations about language, time together and topics of discussion) but the content of those categories will be very different. In other words, you enter these situations with these notions before the group has even established itself. Preconceived norms may or may not become a reality as the group progresses (see Exercise 2.3).

Mutually decided norms are often a result of some kind of discussion about how a group will operate when it is underway. Examples include how members ask questions, who talks when, whether there is an assigned group leader, how an assigned group leader is addressed, whether first names are used, how much time the meeting will take and whether an agenda is necessary. It is impossible to list all of the potential norms a group may create in order to operationalize its existence. The important thing to remember is that these kinds of norms are generally understood, and the expectation is that all group members will adhere to them (Cragan & Wright, 1995; Johnson & Johnson, 2006). See Exercise 2.4.

In reality, many mutually decided norms fall by the wayside in deference to the way that patterns of behaviour actually grow and become the accepted norms of the group. These are the real norms that remain relatively constant within the group over time.

EXERCISE 2.3 DEFINING NORMS

Objectives:

1. To understand the impact of norms on group behaviour
2. To develop a list of expected classroom norms that most members of the group can agree to

On your own, think of three groups you belong to (e.g., your class, a sport or hobby group, a group of close friends, etc.) In each of these groups, identify:

1. Some preconceived ideas about the norms that existed in the group before you became a part of it.
2. The initial norms that were decided consciously.
3. The norms that have remained over time.

Check back with each of these groups, and see if the other members of the groups agree with you. Were there any surprises for you?

EXERCISE 2.4 CONTEXT-SPECIFIC NORMS

Objectives:

1. To compare norms that evolve in different contexts
2. To analyze contexts and discuss how and why norms evolve in different environments

In a group of three, discuss two different classes you have had over the past year. In discussion of these classes, share:

1. Some preconceived ideas about the norms that existed in each of the classes (even if the ideas are based on rumours you have heard) before you became a part of them.
2. Any initial norms that were decided consciously by the class.
3. Any operational norms communicated by the instructor.
4. The norms that have remained over time.

In your group, note agreements and disagreements and prepare to discuss these with the whole class.

In the same group, list norms you would like to see established for the whole class.

As a whole class, share these norms and list them on chart paper. Discuss when they should be re-visited.

In your reflection for this exercise, you may want to note how you experienced this process and whether you are willing to conform to these norms.

5. Preconceived Notions about Purpose and Your Role

In contrast to preconceived norms, there is the *preconceived notion* you may have about your role in a particular group with respect to its purpose.

Before we take part in any kind of group activity, from a simple discussion group in class to something as complicated as a large community forum, we usually have some kind of **preconceived notion** or idea of how the grouping will look and what the task will be. We are not always conscious of this expectation, yet it colours our experience even before we set foot in the context. For example, an instructor may break up a large class into discussion groups for a particular task. Your preconceived notion is that the small group will discuss the topic assigned. When you meet with the small group, one member takes this opportunity to talk about a recent family crisis. You may experience a brief period of awkwardness, given that the discussion has taken a much different direction than you had expected. Your behaviour may be affected in a variety of different ways, depending on the importance of the task and your values and beliefs about doing what you are told. Again, this affects your personal contribution to group function and is a dimension that merits consideration.

You may also have preconceived notions about your participation or your role in a group. For example, you may see yourself as an ordinary, run-of-the-mill participant in groups. You comment on topics of discussion when you have input, you support others as they creatively problem solve and you ask questions when something is unclear. You do not see yourself as ever taking centre stage in a discussion. Consequently, it may come as a surprise to you if other participants actually view you as a group leader. They listen to your comments and often change decisions based on your input. A potential conflict may arise if group members try to put you into a position you do not identify with. This may even become more problematic if they try to formalize your role by appointing you spokesperson or leader.

As another example, you may have the perception that you are ill-equipped to productively contribute to a committee you have been assigned to because you do not think you have the knowledge or experience to offer anything of relevance. As a result you remain silent during group meetings. Your role in this group is that of a silent member, which in turn affects group function. Other committee members may overcompensate for your lack of input, ask for your opinion and generally become irritated with your behaviour. Prior to becoming a part of this committee group, you will have already created a dimension that will affect its function.

Let us return to the earlier scenario in which six well-regarded stakeholders were pulled together to create a job description in advance of a selection committee for the supervisor of a new parenting education program. Each member of this short-lived group represented a community service that would refer families to the parenting centre. Most likely members of this group worked with each other in some capacity on various committees in their community. However, they were now all together for the first time and were waiting in the hallway.

As this scenario played out in terms of group process, that first 60-minute meeting would have been affected by the preconceived expectations each stakeholder had regarding the expertise and the role they would need to play in the interchange. The time spent together may or may not have been productive. Much would have depended on the adaptability of each group member, as the members had to create a process that included understanding each other's role in the committee, respecting the input of each stakeholder and actually creating a job description such that the work was meaningful. In the human service sector, this is not as difficult as it might seem. That is, committees come together, complete a task in representative roles and then move on. The question we must ask ourselves is: how do we learn how to cope in these kinds of situations in such a way that we are able to quickly assume our role, and even more importantly, understand, respect and work with others who must play their role? And, we must cope in this way without letting preconceived notions get in the way of group process and effectiveness.

6. Group Goals

Group goals can be a defining factor for the existence of a group. If the goals of the individual members of a group can be achieved by those members independently, then why bother with the work of group decision making? As with other elements or dimensions of groups, goals exist at different levels, both for the individuals within the group and for the group as a whole. Group goals are a determining, integrated factor that affects all of the other dimensions we have discussed. They affect the size of a group, the amount of time it must spend together, its level of interdependence and even the context in which the group finds itself.

We believe that when group process gets stuck, often it is a result of the whole group's lack of clarity about goals. As well, it is important to note that some group members might bring individual goals to the group that may or may not be explicitly communicated to all members. These unstated individual goals are often defined as hidden agendas. Again, hidden agendas have an effect on all of the other elements that comprise group dimensions.

To determine the goals of any group, it is helpful to ask yourself the following questions:

1. What is the purpose of your group? Why are you together? What is your reason for being a group?
2. What is it you need to accomplish?
3. How will you know you have done what you need to do as a group?

Effective goal setting must be a cooperative effort. **Goals** must clarify for every group member in a meaningful, realistic, relevant and attainable way what it is the group is going to do. By coordinating both individual and overall group goals and making these goals as specific as possible, conflict can be lessened so that everyone accepts the process. If the goal setting is agreed on from the beginning, then even minor alterations to the direction of a group can be dealt with without too much frustration on the part of group members. Effective goal setting should also include some kind of time element for the more specific task-related goals. That is, there should be an agreed-on length of time when these specific goals will be met (see Exercise 2.5 on page 34).

EXERCISE 2.5 GOAL SETTING

Objectives:

1. **To practise goal setting for a variety of tasks**
2. **To work together in a simulated situation to identify practical, attainable goals**

The following task scenarios require some concrete goal setting. Break into five groups with each group taking one scenario. List goals that will assure effective and cooperative task completion. If there is some kind of time limit on any of the goals, make sure to abide by it.

1. It is May and you have been asked to plan an all-day Saturday presentation/conference in November. The theme of the conference is the importance of healthy early childhood development to healthy communities. Two speakers have to be invited and a luncheon served.
2. It is February, and your group is going to plan the June post-convocation celebration.
3. You are working on a group assignment. The project is a design for an inclusive playground to be built in downtown Toronto, beside a low-income apartment complex. Accommodations must be made for children with disabilities, from three to twelve years of age.
4. You are part of a brand-new team of childcare and youth care diploma-trained individuals asked to come together to work on a program for young teens in a centre that is already fully operational.
5. You are part of a small group of students asked to give feedback to the college cafeteria on the poor quality of the food being served lately.

After each group has completed the determination of goals, prepare to share them with the whole class.

7. Assumptions about Members and Roles

Individuals make assumptions about other group members and have expectations about their level of participation and interest in the group. It requires a heightened level of self-awareness to identify these assumptions and link them to your decision making about your participation in the group. A simple example is a class of students planning a graduation party. Assumptions might be that everyone is interested in having a graduation party, that all class members want to participate in a lively discussion of party plans and that everyone is willing to come to consensus on decisions that are made.

Before you were a student in your current program, what thoughts did you have about how other students would behave in your class? What thoughts did you have about how you would behave in this class? As you look back on the first few days of class, how have your experiences either matched or not matched your expectations? You may want to use your reflection tool to deepen your thinking on this question.

Cragan and Wright (1991) discuss how some of our stereotypical judgments of group members based on common factors such as age, gender, race, education, income and occupation affect our own behaviour in the early stages of group development. These authors acknowledge how very difficult it is to isolate the impact of these variables on group behaviour. The reflection tool is useful for identifying possible first impressions you might have of particular group members, for analyzing how those impressions might influence your expectations of those group members and for anticipating how both your first impressions and your expectations might affect your behaviour. The impact of first impressions differs with every group we are part of, and it is important to enhance our level of self-awareness about just how and when they might get in our way. A deeper understanding of individual group members as the people they really are will minimize the possible detrimental effect of our initial perceptions of them. How do we do this? We communicate in ways that allow us to share real information about each other.

8. Communication Patterns

In later chapters we will closely examine the impact of communication style on leadership and power issues that affect group dynamics. However, when considering common elements of group dynamics, one relevant factor that affects how a group might define itself is the observable way in which its group members interact with each other. By **communication patterns** we mean the frequency and quality of the actual ways each group member connects with other group members. These more obvious verbal and non-verbal interaction patterns can affect the overall defining nature of any group in process. Often these patterns are the result of attempts to lead the group or expressions of power. The origin of each group member's contribution to group process will be explored later in the text. Whatever the motivation, it is important to recognize the impact of such defining factors as level of participation, shifts in exactly which group members are communicating with each other and any interaction-pattern changes in group function.

Exercise 2.6 (see page 36) will help to illustrate these kinds of observable patterns and their effect on others' assumptions about the dynamics of particular groups.

9. Personality Factors

Group-member personality traits obviously affect the function and dynamics of any group. Motivation and general disposition are two particularly relevant considerations. Patton, Giffin and Patton (1989) discuss factors like sociability, activity level and seriousness as personality characteristics that affect the interpersonal environment of any group decision-making context. The social dispositions of any mix of individuals will surely affect the way in which group members interact with each other and function effectively as a working unit. As well, the motivation to succeed as a member of a team and the ability to see the importance of people working together toward a common goal are traits that affect group dynamics. If you find yourself part of a group where one or more members feel forced to be there or prefer working independently on tasks, the dynamic will feel different from the dynamic of a group in which all members are excited to be there and are anxious to work together.

Personality factors that have the potential to affect group function seem almost endless, and, as explained later in this text, express themselves in a variety of ways. They can either be seen as functional, providing leadership to the group, and sharing power and influence to move the group forward, or they can block healthy group progress when expressed through dysfunctional patterns of behaviour. Either way they are factors that define the group and affect the dynamics of interaction.

EXERCISE 2.6 COMMUNICATION PATTERNS

Objectives:

1. **To observe natural communication patterns that occur in a large group**
2. **To practise identifying those assumptions you might make about group dynamics when observing the interaction among members**
3. **To learn about your own interaction patterns**

Five members of the class volunteer to observe the rest of the class in discussion. The class members sit in a circle, and the five observers make note of every person's seating position each on his or her own large piece of chart paper.

Observers each work (in sequence) for a five-minute shift, drawing arrows to represent who talks to whom during the discussion. Each observer works only on his or her own schematic, with a fresh drawing being used for each observed portion of the discussion. Observers should also make note of the time period of the discussion during which they noted interactions.

Once the observers are ready, the rest of the class members, in their noted seating locations, discuss the following issue regarding an approach to scheduling classes and come up with a list of the advantages and disadvantages of the approach:

Your program of studies is looking at the value of moving to a four-day-a-week teaching schedule (with Fridays off). Consequences include a longer school day and shortened lunch hour in order to accommodate the training hours required of your program. There are other advantages and disadvantages of moving to this schedule. What might they be from your perspective? You have about 25 minutes to discuss this.

Once the discussion is complete, observers share their observation templates, indicating the interaction patterns represented by arrows.

The class then discusses the following:

1. What impressions in general are you left with when hearing about the interaction patterns observed during this discussion?
2. If you were a group member, did you feel left out of the discussion? If so, what impact did this have on the quality of the outcome?
3. If you were a group member, did you feel that you were quite vocal? If so, what impact did this have on the overall discussion?
4. Were there some people who talked more often to certain people than to other people? If so, who were they?
5. Over time, was there a shift in the interaction patterns and the overall productivity of the group (that is, its ability to come up with a number of advantages and disadvantages to the new scheduling idea)?

Once the whole class has discussed these questions, Base Groups come together to talk about individual reactions to this experience and the impact on personal learning.

*An alternative to this assignment would be to videotape the entire group discussing this question and then have everyone in the class observe communication patterns.

10. Nature of the Task

The nature of the task that a group is seeking to accomplish together affects not only the goals of the group, but also the dynamic interaction of its members. Therefore, it can be seen as one of the common elements of group function and a defining factor in the very existence of the group.

Steiner (1972) describes four common kinds of work accomplished in groups. *Additive tasks* are those tasks where each group member completes a portion, all portions are added together and then the work is complete. An example of this kind of task might be an assignment for which each student member of a group completes a component of the work, it gets stapled together and submitted to the instructor and is then done. If each component is marked separately, then there are very few decisions to be made, and it is truly an additive task. If, however, a mark is given to the whole group, then the task is deemed *conjunctive.* The product of a conjunctive task is more mutually dependent for group members, even though group members still contribute separate components to the work. In the group-assignment example, all student group members must do a good job for the mark to be high for all.

Disjunctive tasks are tasks that are completed by the most expert member of the group. This person takes responsibility for the quality of the product, and the rest of the group depends on his or her expertise for the success of the work. Using a student-assignment example, a disjunctive task might be one in which a group of students is creating a floor plan for a care facility, and one member of the group has a mother who is an architect and has assured the group that he can get the help he needs to complete that portion of the assignment. In this example, the other members of the group are counting on the expertise of one group member, but are not themselves contributing to that portion of the task.

Finally, *discretionary tasks*, according to Steiner, have a more balanced dynamic, with group members needing to make joint decisions about how they use their member strengths to produce a high-quality product. If students are working on a project, this would involve careful consideration of each group member's contribution and a consistent process of checking in with each other to ensure that the way in which they have decided to do the work is meeting the standards that they have defined for themselves.

Each of the four kinds of work described here has an impact on the way the group members structure their work, set their goals and use their resources. Ultimately, the importance of the decisions to be made and the overall significance and magnitude of the task affect any group's dynamics.

11. Interdependence

We will discuss the element of *interdependence* more thoroughly later in the text when we explore the ways groups develop. It is important to recognize that the level of interdependence plays a key role in member satisfaction during group process and is significantly linked to the level of trust members have in each other, interpersonal style and particular stages in group development.

We see **interdependence** as the level at which members of a group work together toward a common goal.

Examples might include:

- The way in which group members divide up tasks, allowing all members to contribute to the final outcome
- Times when members ask each other for support or when group members are supportive of each other when the process of decision making or task accomplishment gets blocked
- Times when members take responsibility for checking in with each other, yet are autonomous in their own contributions

EXERCISE 2.7 LEVELS OF INTERDEPENDENCE

Objectives:

1. To examine alternative levels of interdependence in the completion of tasks
2. To predict how levels of interdependence might affect the quality of task completion

In this exercise we return to the five scenarios explored in Exercise 2.5. Return to the group that you were in for this exercise and retrieve the goals listed for your scenario.

With reference to the concept of interdependence explained above, envision a way of working together that exemplifies a low level of interdependence. Simulate a scenario for the whole class that demonstrates some of the behaviours that highlight a low level of interdependence.

Now, go through the same process and produce a simulation for that same group that exemplifies a high level of interdependence.

As you play out both of these scenarios, discuss with your group the ways that varying levels of interdependence might affect the quality of the task.

As you prepare to move into any group situation, your commitment to the task or to the goals of the group affects its level of interdependence. There is a continuum of interdependence that is not only affected by every individual's commitment to the task but also by the importance and immediacy of the task at hand. Going back to our classroom-project scenario, there is a big difference between the interdependence experienced by a small group of students doing an impromptu class exercise and that experienced by that same group of students working together on a short-term project for marks. In the first example, the stakes are low and the level of commitment is as diverse as the people you find yourself joining in discussion. The level of interdependence you might feel with others in the group depends on things like how many people are in the discussion, whether the task is helpful to your own understanding of the classroom material and whether you are taking responsibility to record or report on any discussion or decision making that is taking place. You are not particularly concerned if everyone in the group seems totally committed to the task at hand. In the latter example, where there is a group project to be accomplished requiring a high-quality product, you would want to be in a group of committed members willing to function together and create something of value. The stakes are high, and there is a mark involved (see Exercise 2.7).

Summary

Identifying the elements that define groups helps us better understand the factors that might have an impact on a group's effectiveness. As well, our role in any group situation will be affected by the dynamic interaction of these elements.

There are both directly observable and indirectly observable characteristics that merit consideration when examining the variables that affect the ways groups function. Directly observable characteristics include the size of the group; the amount of time it will be together; where the group is together, the human element in that context; and the interactive communication patterns of group members.

Indirectly observable characteristics include the norms or rules group members follow when working together (either assumed beforehand or decided while the group develops), preconceived ideas group members all have about the purpose of the group and their roles as members, group goals, assumptions group members make about everyone's membership in the group, different personality styles of group members, the kind of work the group is assigned to do and the ability of group members to work interdependently toward a common goal.

By examining these elements more closely we can learn to identify potential issues in all of our group contexts and make the necessary adaptations to improve productivity and overall enjoyment of the group experience.

A Reflection Tool Example

Sample Reflection 3 on page 40 is an example of a completed reflection tool linked to the theory covered in this chapter. In this situation, the student has been experiencing discomfort about the behaviour of one of the members in her Base Group. The example relates to the elements discussed in the "Human Element" section of this chapter on page 29.

Sample Reflection 3

What?

What stood out for you in this chapter? Describe a reading, exercise, incident, person's behaviour, etc.

I'm in a Base Group with a person who brings up personal experiences in class that I find offensive. Others in the class and I laugh when she does this.

So What?

1. Emotional Impact?

I feel offended, uncomfortable, intimidated, uneasy, anxious, apprehensive and a little bit resentful.

2. Why do you think you had this emotional response?

The situations she describes are far removed from how I live my life and what I value. I'm not sure how to respond to her. I don't know what's coming next.

3. What assumptions might you be making in this situation? What beliefs and values were touched off by this situation?

Assumptions:

- She wants me to buy into her way of life.
- There is an expectation that I support her—that I agree with her and enjoy her comments/stories.
- Her stories are true.
- She believes her approach to life is the way to be in this world.
- She is trying to impress me (the class?).
- People are laughing because they enjoy what she is saying.

Beliefs, values:

- I believe she is wrong.
- The topics she brings up are inappropriate for class discussion.
- Professionals don't talk like this.
- People in the human service field should be more sensitive to what others are comfortable hearing.

4. Write about the meaning this has for you. Some helpful questions might be:
Do you think your values might be clouding your interpretation of the situation? If so, how?

- This question addresses Element 7: Assumptions about everyone's membership.
- I'm worried that my values are preventing me from connecting with this person; that she won't have anything of value to offer this Base Group.
- I'm afraid that I'm so caught up in my judgments that I cut myself off from her, preventing myself from hearing anything she has to say in order to protect myself.

Have you been affected by similar situations in the same way? How have you responded?

- I have a few friends that get raunchy and I ignore it; it seems different in a social situation. Still, I'm cutting myself off.
- This is a new program for me, and I didn't think I'd be hearing this kind of language and these kinds of topics in this realm.

5. Is it important for you to change your behaviour? Why?

Yes. I'm in a Base Group that is supposed to be helpful to my learning and my practice. Shutting down will not be helpful and will contribute to others' perceptions about me. I might end up isolating myself and look like a prude.

Now What?

6. Based on the learning from this chapter, what other behaviours might you consider?

- Now that I've identified some of my assumptions, I'm hoping that I can be more open to interacting with this person regardless of our differences.
- I'm going to try to catch myself if I find myself tuning out or disengaging when she contributes to the group.
- I'll try not to laugh when she tells her stories.
- I may have to express my discomfort.

7. What might stop you from engaging in these new behaviours?

- Fear of sounding like a prude
- Fear of sounding judgmental
- Not being one of the gang
- Not having enough self-awareness in the moment when something shocking is said
- The shock of the story may make it hard not to laugh as laughter is an almost automatic defensive response.

Objectives

1. Be more proactive in engaging her in conversation
2. Be more conscious and aware of my responses to her storytelling — work on not laughing
3. Be open in learning to appreciate her role in this Base Group — look for the positive impact she may have on our group
4. Share my discomfort if the behaviour continues

What Questions Remain?

1. How does a person confront inappropriate sharing in a productive manner?
2. What are the expectations of a professional about types of conversations in a learning forum?

Key Terms

Communication patterns *(p. 35)*
Goals *(p. 33)*
Groups *(p. 24)*
Human element *(p. 29)*
Interdependence *(p. 37)*
Mutually decided norms *(p. 30)*
Norms *(p. 30)*
Preconceived norms *(p. 30)*
Preconceived notions *(p. 32)*

Case Studies

In this chapter, the case studies will question your understanding of significant group elements that may or may not affect the function of particular groups. In turn, they will offer you a chance to anticipate ways the elements might shift to enhance group effectiveness and maximize group potential. This analysis is significant for your professional learning because it creates the framework within which you can make decisions about your level of commitment in group situations. Whenever we are in a group, there are some elements that are beyond our control. They still affect us in some way, and might still have the potential for minor adaptations that would improve group function. There are other elements we definitely have some control over.

As we described in Chapter 1, the case studies in this text will explore issues in the classroom (Student), in the work of your discipline (Team) and in the multidisciplinary community (Community). These categories will help you to apply the ideas within your present contexts and prepare you for the contexts you will experience in your professional life.

Each case study contains questions that require written comments from you and eventual group discussion with classmates. Suggested responses to each case-study question are included in the instructor's resource manual.

For each one of the following five case studies, the learning objectives remain the same and focus on the elements discussed in this chapter:

- Size of the group
- Time together
- Context: where you are together; who is in the room
- Norms: assumed and decided
- Preconceived notions about purpose and your role
- Group goals: reason for the group's existence
- Assumptions about members and roles
- Communication patterns
- Personality factors
- Nature of the task
- Interdependence (the ability to work together toward a common goal)

Case Study 2.1 **First Week of Class**

CATEGORY: STUDENT

You are just beginning a diploma program in child and youth care that will take two years to complete. There are 26 students in the group — 7 men and 19 women. In this program you will be spending six hours a day in the same classroom. Two three-hour classes are held per day from 8:30 to 11:30 a.m. and 12:30 to 3:30 p.m., with coffee breaks at 10:00 a.m. and 2:00 p.m. The classroom adequately holds 26 people, has two fairly small windows and about 15 octagonal tables (for one or two people) that form a large table if you move them together in a puzzle-like way. There are bulletin boards on the wall, and after one week of class, these are starting to fill up with chart paper from group work.

Of the 19 women, four are over the age of 35, and one student is 50. The rest of the women are in their 20s. Of the seven men, one is 35 years of age, and the remaining six are in their 20s. All of the men are single. Of the women over 35, one is divorced, one is single and the other two are married with children. Of the women in their 20s, four have young families, three are at various stages of commitment and the rest are single.

It is the last day of your first week of class. You have now met all three instructors in the program and are well aware of all of the courses you will take in this semester (along with assignment expectations). You have discovered that all the instructors prefer an experiential teaching style, where you are often in small-group discussions with a variety of people, reporting back to the whole group and having the opportunity to interact with everyone throughout each class. In one of your classes (interpersonal skills) you have been told to expect hands-on learning that will encourage you to "be real, in the moment". Risk taking and personal sharing will be encouraged and will be your avenue of interpersonal skill development.

You have noticed that most people in the class put up their hands to ask questions and there is usually a significant silence when the instructor poses a question to the group. Friendships are beginning to develop in the group and side talking amongst certain people is just starting to occur when the instructors are talking. This seems to happen in all of your classes.

QUESTIONS:

1. Which group elements are significant, and what effect might they have on the group experience to date?
2. How might you modify some of these elements to improve the atmosphere and experience of this class?

Which of these elements might affect your commitment and comfort level in this case study and why?

Case Study 2.2 **Project Work Group**

CATEGORY: STUDENT

You are in a human service worker one-year certificate program at a college in northern Ontario. It is the third month of the program (closing in on the end of the first semester). You have a major group assignment worth 35 percent of the total grade. The instructor has blocked off three classes for group-work time in class. Because the groupings were not evenly distributed, you are in a group of three and everyone else is in a group of four (groups are picked out of a hat). After hearing the criteria of the assignment, you realize that there is a lot of work to do for three people. The instructor has assured you that there is enough time to get this work done in class, plus about two or three hours out of class, if all goes smoothly. The project involves some independent research and then some quality time together integrating all of the pieces. There is an oral component to this assignment, along with a written piece.

Your other two group members are people you have never worked with before. You have noticed that one of the people in your group is generally very quiet in class, and the other (a friend of yours) makes strong contributions to class discussion and gets good grades. You and your friend both work at Tim Horton's on different shifts, two evenings a week and on weekends.

Your first meeting was during class time. It seemed to be a bit chaotic and non-productive. As well, the rest of the groups were meeting in the same classroom, and it was noisy. The product of the first meeting was a discussion of the assignment and distribution of research responsibilities. You are still concerned about the amount of work to be done and whether your group will be able to create a quality assignment.

QUESTIONS:

1. Which group elements are significant, and what effect might they have on the group experience to date?
2. How might you modify some of these elements to improve the atmosphere and experience of this class?

Case Study 2.3 **Budget Meeting**

CATEGORY: TEAM

Greenway Childcare Centre and Treetops Childcare Centre are two daycares housed in one building and overseen by a director. Each centre has its own supervisor and two assistants (about 25 children in each centre). The director is responsible for overall staffing, budget allocations and overall administration.

In the Greenway Centre, the supervisor is relatively new (three months), with one assistant who has been on staff for 10 years and the other who has just graduated from the diploma program at the local college. In the Treetops Centre, the supervisor has been there for about 10 years (is a good friend of one of the assistants at the Greenway Centre) and the assistants have been there one year and three years.

Each centre has its own staff meetings every two weeks and the supervisors meet with the director about once a month. The Greenway supervisor and the new assistant have some fresh new programming ideas that they would like to implement, which will require some ongoing funding for the first year.

The budget is set yearly, and the director sends a directive to each centre asking them to think about any capital or operating budget wants, needs and changes. It is now time for the annual budget meeting, and the director has decided to hold this meeting with both supervisors at noon in the staff room during their one-hour lunch break. She has brought in sandwiches.

QUESTIONS:

1. Which group elements are significant, and what effect might they have on the upcoming budget meeting?
2. How might you modify some of these elements to improve the atmosphere and experience of this budget meeting?

Case Study 2.4 **Certified Education Assistant (Teacher's Aide)**

CATEGORY: TEAM

You are a diploma graduate from a human service program and have been employed as a teacher's aide at Berryland Middle School in Oakville, Ontario. You are working with Charlie, a 13-year-old boy with autism. He is very verbal, is able to focus on tasks and has only a slightly modified education plan. However, he tires easily and becomes distracted by noise or movement. He is used to working in a classroom with only a few children, with lots of visual supports and you nearby to prompt him if necessary. He becomes very agitated (verbally abusive and physically aggressive) when he sees he is not able to complete his work. He has three different teachers in three different classrooms, all with different teaching styles and expectations for the behaviour of children in the class.

It appears that the social studies teacher is able to adapt to Charlie's outbursts and is teaching content that is holding his interest. Charlie loves to draw, yet it appears that the art teacher is very structured and authoritarian. She does not tolerate noise in the room and insists on very specific ways of approaching the material. Finally, the English teacher simply ignores what Charlie is doing and makes little effort to include him in the class.

You have been working with this child since he was nine years of age and have transitioned with him from elementary school to grade 7 in middle school in the fall. It is now November.

Charlie is having great difficulty coping with the different expectations from each of the teachers, and you are concerned for both his emotional well-being and his academic success. The teachers have come to you, wanting to meet in hopes of better meeting the needs of this child. You have been waiting for this opportunity and offer to set up a meeting after the school day is over.

QUESTIONS:

1. What elements will you be paying attention to in preparation for this meeting and why?
2. How might your preconceived notions about the teachers who work with Charlie affect the dynamics of this particular meeting?
3. Identify the goals for this meeting (not goals for Charlie).

Case Study 2.5 **Program Advisory Committee**

CATEGORY: COMMUNITY

You are a second-year diploma student in a two-year rehabilitation assistant program in a community college located in Calgary, Alberta. There are about 30 students in your second-year class and 28 in the first-year class. You have been asked by the community program advisory committee chairperson to represent both the first- and second-year classes on a sub-committee of the advisory group charged with the task of completing the regular five-year evaluation of the program. This person was given your name by the chair of your program department after checking with you. You are not too sure why you have been asked, but feel quite proud of this representative position.

The subcommittee consists of seven members, from faculty- and community-stakeholder groups (e.g., the local hospital rehabilitation clinic, the human service worker program chair, the supervisor of a local physiotherapy clinic, etc.). You have had your first meeting and the group will continue to meet once every month for the next six months. Meetings will be held on Wednesday from 6:30 to 8:30 at night.

QUESTIONS:

1. If you were a student on this committee, what would make your time and participation in this group comfortable and effective, with reference to the elements discussed in this chapter?
2. How do you think you might gather important input from the two groups of students you are representing on this committee? Briefly explain the pros and cons of each idea.

Reflection Tool

What?

What stood out for you in this chapter? Describe a reading, exercise, incident, person's behaviour, etc.

So What?

1. Emotional impact?
2. Why do you think you had this emotional response?
3. What assumptions might you be making in this situation? What beliefs and values were touched off by this situation?

Assumptions:

Beliefs, values:

4. Write about the meaning this has for you. Some helpful questions might be: Do you think your values might be clouding your interpretation of the situation? If so, how?

Have you been affected by similar situations in the same way? How have you responded?

5. Is it important for you to change your behaviour? Why?

Now What?

6. Based on the learning from this chapter, what other behaviours might you consider?

7. What might stop you from engaging in these new behaviours?

Objectives

What Questions Remain?

Chapter 3

Group Development

Objectives

In this chapter, students will acquire the knowledge, skills and attitudes to:

1. Identify the stages of group growth and development.
2. Understand their own behaviour and the behaviour of others in groups during each of the stages of group growth.
3. Examine the criteria of effective group development.
4. Explore the relationship between stages of group development and effective group process.
5. Reflect on the effects of personal communication style on group effectiveness.

Examining Group Development

In this chapter, we will take a close look at the ways groups develop over time. Common behaviours of group members as they work through the time they spend together have been of interest to well-known theorists who have unearthed fairly consistent stages of group development. Later in this chapter, we will take a closer look at these stages of group development and explore the relationship between these stages and the behaviours that affect group effectiveness. This is important to the work of students and field practitioners in human service because it offers necessary insight into our own and other's effectiveness in groups over time. In our field of practice we must use this insight consistently because our work is rarely done alone. As well, our role will often be to model, mentor and facilitate the progress of groups we work with on a daily basis. Your awareness of how you and others progress as a group in your classroom setting will have a direct influence on ways you reflect on the function and effectiveness of groups in the profession.

By first examining the criteria that we and others might recognize as an effective group in action, we can then take a closer look at some well-known theories of group development, with the objective of exploring ways we might better understand our own part in that process. With that understanding comes awareness and reflection on bettering group function in our student, professional and community contexts.

Effective Group Function

Observable Characteristics of Effective Groups

In Chapter 2, the dimensions of groups were explored in the important consideration of which elements have the potential to affect group function. The next questions to explore might be, What might a group that is functioning effectively look like? How might we recognize a healthy functional group of people working together on a particular task? As observers, what will we actually see the participants doing?

Conference-Planning Example

Imagine you are watching a meeting in progress. It is a committee planning a conference, and the event is going to take place about a month after the meeting. There are 10 people on the planning committee, and they are meeting around a large table in the boardroom of a health unit. Based on our discussion in Chapter 2, the group is a relatively workable size, and the environment for the meeting suits the group membership (the members are all from the same early childhood development professional organization, and the conference is on the nutritional needs of infants and toddlers). This group has met for about a year, approximately once a month. For the past two months the meetings have been every two weeks because the date for the event is close. A timeline has been created and the group is generally on track, based on long- and short-term goal completion. Now you are able to observe them at work. What would you see happening in this group of hard-working conference planners to offer evidence of effective process?

More than likely there will be a clear meeting structure. The structure is probably a product of ongoing goal clarification throughout the period of time this group has been meeting. How will this show itself in the behaviour of the group? Generally through the confidence you see in all committee members as they begin to discuss the conference-planning tasks for this particular meeting. If there is any confusion about the current tasks at hand, members will take immediate responsibility for clearing up that confusion, and the member responsible will respond in a non-defensive way.

Because planning-committee members take responsibility for getting their own needs met, there is a relatively easygoing and expedient process of clarifying the work to be done. Group members will discuss their feelings about not only the decision making at hand, but also about the way the process of working through those decisions might be going. Being aware of both thoughts and feelings will be seen as legitimate and important. Because this planning committee is closing in on the date of the event, the feelings of anxiety will not be seen as interfering with the event, but rather as a shared group experience that is acknowledged, talked about and then superseded by the work to be done.

All of the members' contributions in this meeting will be seen as important and will be listened to seriously. Members will check with each other during the give and take of conversation, making sure that they are clear about contributions before they either agree or disagree. Each member will speak from his or her own perspective, yet it will become very obvious that each diverse point of view (in this case from each stakeholder in fields linked to early childhood development) will be welcomed and probably sought out. As each committee member represents his or her own community group, this will look like a sharing process with each person contributing something valued to the whole planning team.

Innovative ideas do not detract from the process because there is some kind of structure in place that allows for input and decides its relevance. When a new idea comes to the table, the group will either celebrate its usefulness to the planning of the conference, alter it to fit the task at hand or shelve it for another time. Decision making may take different forms depending on whether more information is required or a simple show of hands can move the process along. Either way, the committee sees itself as an entity in which all members are valued and all contributions taken seriously. It appears to move together, with individual members committed to a quality product.

The tone of the meeting will appear relaxed, yet focused. The participation in the meeting will be generally high with members functioning in a way that seems natural to them. Most of the time, committee members will check to see what effect particular ideas may have on other members. Because all group members will be painfully aware of the proximity of the conference, most will honour the fact that most of the earlier decision making must remain as is, and only last-minute issues will take precedence.

Each person will look confident in his or her own power, and will not appear afraid to engage in controversy by disagreeing with points raised by other group members. When conflicts or controversies arise, group members will respond with open and active discussion that generates a creative interchange of new ways of looking at the controversial issues. Again, because individuals are clarifying messages they hear and checking out messages they themselves share with others, disagreements or challenges may be common (and welcomed [see Exercise 3.1]).

EXERCISE 3.1 OUTSIDE LOOKING IN

Objectives:

1. To identify behaviours that contribute to group effectiveness
2. To link identified behaviours with the elements of groups discussed in Chapter 2

In your Base Groups, take a close look at the conference-planning description and discuss examples of interactions or behaviours that appear to contribute to this group's effectiveness.

For each example discussed above, illustrate how these points might actually look. For example: "All members' contributions in this meeting will be seen as important and listened to seriously." To illustrate this in real life, group members would look at the person talking, paraphrase the speaker, have open body language and acknowledge the points the person is making.

Discuss the ways in which the behaviours you identified link to the elements of groups discussed in Chapter 2.

Share your observations with the whole class.

Participating in an Effective Group

In order to take an even closer look at what comprises effective group process, it helps to alter our perspective somewhat and look at what might actually feel like a functional, successful group experience. Only then can we work through what has been theorized as the stages of group development and enhance our own sense of what feels right or not right and our sense of how we might contribute to more effective group function. We have looked at the more observable indicators of effectiveness; now let's examine the less observable factors that tell us the group we are a part of is functional and worth our time and commitment.

Think back on a time when you worked with a group of people in the accomplishment of some kind of project, task or sporting event. This could be in a club or volunteer organization, or even more recently on a student assignment. You could also use a personal example where you have planned a family reunion, a celebration with friends or a major event like a wedding. Try to capture either the positive or negative feelings you had during the entirety of the planning and implementation process. We do this by looking at the less observable factors of *personal effectiveness*, *trust*, *cohesion*, *productivity*, and level of *transformational change* when examining group effectiveness.

Personal Effectiveness

We all like to feel useful in any group situation. We want to know that we effected change in some way. This is as much about what others think of our participation as it is about what we think about how much we have contributed to the group's task or function. A sense of **personal effectiveness** overlaps somewhat with feelings of cohesion, yet merits special consideration because the degree to which we feel effective contributes to our sense of self-worth. Lack of personal effectiveness results in feelings of inadequacy, low self-efficacy, lack of power and sheer frustration. Frustration will block effective group process.

The antithesis of a healthy and productive group is one in which there is little opportunity to be heard, due to imposed, authoritarian structures, unequal power, the avoidance of conflict and one-way communication among group members (Johnson & Johnson, 2006). When you are a part of such a group you feel powerless and unable to figure out what you could possibly do to improve the situation. In our experience, communication is the first step toward improved group function and enhanced personal effectiveness.

Communication skill development is obviously the prerequisite to effective group process. It is also the backbone of the practice of working in the realm of human service and relationship building. You can access any number of suggestions about ways to communicate your thoughts and feelings to others in the immense body of research available. You can train yourself in all of the well-known techniques to help send and receive messages effectively. And no matter how well you learn and practise ways and means of communication, you will more than likely still find yourself in situations where the process has broken down and lack of communication was clearly at fault.

Often students will go to their instructors with issues related to difficulties in group work. Class projects might be at risk and students might feel totally blocked and ineffective when attempting to work through issues of communication that prevent the work from moving forward. With a **mediated discussion**, groups can identify issues that perhaps have been brewing amongst group members. The process of facilitating discussion may seem magical to the students involved; however, the process is simply a matter of clarifying how messages are sent and ensuring that the listeners are hearing what is being said. The key to mediated discussions is to slow down the communication and ensure that the much-needed skills of sending and receiving messages are being practised in the interchange.

The development of communication skills is a lesson in lifelong learning mixed with the ability to assess our own style of interaction on an ongoing basis. The reflection tool we offer in this text provides the opportunity to look at the effect your communication style might have when working in groups. Suffice it to say, when it comes to a discussion of group effectiveness, communication style is a very significant factor.

Exercise 3.2 on page 52 is designed to help you review well-known and well-practised skills in communicating effectively with others.

Trust

When you feel trusting and trusted in a group of individuals, then most likely you will believe that almost anything can be accomplished that will meet the needs of all members. Groups with high levels of trust feel safe enough to communicate honestly and to share thoughts and ideas openly. This builds on the link between effective communication and effective group function.

How do we define trust and how do we develop it in our groups? **Trust** is an overworked term that many of us take for granted without truly understanding its relevance or components, or even being aware of whether we experience trust in a particular relationship. The development of trust begins with group members taking risks by being open and making contributions that come from the heart. When we share something from the heart, whether it is something about ourselves, an idea about an issue or simply an opinion about something important to the group, we "put it out there". And, when we do this, we usually hope someone actually accepts what we have contributed and responds honestly and openly back to us.

This openness can be called **disclosure**, and is key to understanding trust building. Think about a time when you met someone new and began to see that person socially. As you hung out together, you began to share the details of your life, offering tidbits of information about yourself. Your new friend did the same. The information was revealing and newsy — things you like to do, stories about who is in your family and what you did on the weekend. As the relationship continued, you began to risk sharing less newsy and more opinionated or dramatic and important things about yourself. As soon as you did that, you were risking sharing information that not everyone you meet will get to know about you.

One of two things might have occurred as you opened up to your newfound friend. He or she may have responded with something equally risky and openly accepted your disclosure in ways that felt supportive. Or he or she may simply have listened and responded in ways that continued to be newsy and less risky. If the first occurred, then you will have felt closer in some way to that person. If the second response occurred, then you will have felt vulnerable and concerned that you shared in an unsafe situation. You may even be concerned that the information would be held against you. This is a very uncomfortable place to be, and more than likely you would be more careful and less natural during the development of this relationship. If some kind of mutual disclosure does not

EXERCISE 3.2 COMMUNICATING WITH OTHERS

Objectives:

1. To review interpersonal communication skill techniques
2. To appreciate the impact of group size on your communication style
3. To practise communicating with others

Part I

In pairs, discuss the following: When there is a group assignment for marks, should the instructor assign group members, or should students choose their own group? Explain the rationale for your opinion.

After a five-minute discussion, assess yourself by writing brief answers to the following questions:

When speaking:

1. What was your body language and tone of voice? Consider your posture, eye contact, physical closeness, facial expression, volume and expressiveness.
2. Did you express your feelings openly, without judgment?
3. Did you speak from the "I" position and take responsibility for your own feelings and opinions?
4. How clearly and concisely do you think you expressed your opinions?
5. How did you express disagreement? Consider your level of openness and any changes to body language or tone of voice. Also, did you disagree in a way that acknowledged the other person's thoughts and feelings before you expressed your own?

When listening:

1. What was your body language? Was it appropriate to the message of the speaker with respect to cultural sensitivity and the content of the message itself?
2. Did you paraphrase to let the speaker know you understood what was being said?
3. What body language shifts occurred at times of disagreement?
4. If there was a change in the emotional climate of the speaker's message, how did you respond? Think about how you responded to the change in emotional tone?

Part II

After writing the brief self-assessment above, have the same discussion with four other people.

Use the same criteria to assess your speaking and listening skills in this group. Note the differences for you in this second context.

Part III

After writing the brief self-assessment for Part II, have the same discussion with nine other people.

Use the self-assessment criteria once more and assess your speaking and listening skills in a large group.

After the three parts of this exercise are completed, discuss the exercise with the class as a whole and identify similarities experienced by all members of the class. Note the effect that group size had on your inner experience. Consider your ability to communicate effectively (listening and speaking clearly) and the overall *feeling* you experienced in each group scenario.

eventually occur you may even close off the relationship or choose to spend less time with that person. In social relationships, mutual disclosure feels open, natural and supportive, which in turn fosters a closeness that usually builds over time. Of course, as relationships develop, levels of trust can diminish. We have all had the experience of broken trust in social relationships and have learned that we should never be totally vulnerable and always trusting. Friendships that stand the test of time are built on a high level of trust and openness.

For less personal and more cooperative task-oriented groups to develop in healthy productive ways, the work of trust building is also important. It, too, is a product of openness and a kind of mutual disclosure. Johnson and Johnson (2006) discuss the factors of openness, sharing, support and acceptance as integral to successful, **cooperative group development**. By this we mean that when we are open in a group context, we share our thoughts and ideas easily, putting them out there for all to respond to. If others do the same, we accept those contributions and consider them in a supportive manner while building on the suggested ideas. Levels of trust and **mutuality** (working cooperatively and interdependently toward a common goal) increase through acceptance and support, based on respect for the contributions of others. This respect comes from believing that what we and others offer the group will be accepted as legitimate. This takes work and requires fairly refined levels of communication.

In the practice of human service, trust building is a much needed competency skill at all levels, with clients, with other professionals and with community. Later in this chapter we will look more closely at how our behaviour and the behaviour of others affect the openness and support necessary to group function. Exercises 3.3 and 3.4 explore trust building in groups.

EXERCISE 3.3 WHO'S GOT A LOONIE?

Objectives:

1. To experiment with the concept of trust in a large group
2. To consider your own personal level of risk taking and trust

A volunteer stands up and asks the class, "Who's got a loonie?" and then waits patiently. Eventually someone reaches into his or her pocket or purse and comes out with a loonie. The volunteer walks over, asks for the money and asks the giver, "What are your hopes and aspirations for this group? In other words, what kind of group would you like this to become?" When the giver has answered the question, the volunteer takes the loonie, walks over to another person and hands him or her the dollar, asking the recipient the same question and listening to his or her answer.

Next, the volunteer asks the group, "Who's got a ten-dollar bill?" There is likely some fidgeting and hopefully up pops a ten-dollar bill. The same question is asked of the giver, and then of the recipient of the ten-dollar bill. Now, the volunteer asks, "Who's got a twenty-dollar bill?" Again the question is asked and the transfer of money takes place.

The volunteer asks each person to silently reflect on their thoughts and feelings about risk taking and trusting that the money will be returned. Did you volunteer your money, that is, take a risk? How did you feel? What about when the ante was upped to ten dollars? Twenty? Did you think the volunteers who gave money were foolish?

Do a one-word check around the room regarding how people feel in this moment.

Note: Please see the instructor's manual for the resolution of this exercise.
(This exercise is adapted from an exercise on the High Performance Teams website: http://highperformanceteams.org/home. htm)

Use the reflection tool to delve more deeply into how you link trust and risk taking.

EXERCISE 3.4 PERSONAL TRUST

Objectives:

1. To use personal experience to identify trust-building behaviour
2. To translate personal trust building to the work environment

Think of a relationship you have with someone in which trust is high. Consider the following questions:

1. At what point in the relationship did you begin to feel some sense of trust?
2. What did each person do to encourage trust to develop?

In your Base Group, share your insights and note similarities.

As a whole class, discuss the common elements of trust building that you experienced. Post these elements for the class to see.

Back in your Base Group, with reference to the common elements posted in the class, discuss the following questions:

1. How might trust building look different in a group situation?
2. How do these elements translate to the work environment?
3. Is it always necessary to build trust to have an effective group? Why or why not?

Share your discussion with the whole class.

Cohesion

Cohesive groups are committed to creating a structure that can utilize the strengths of each group member in ways that enhance productivity. The experience of **cohesion** is unique to each group experience. When you feel part of a cohesive group, you are aware that the time you devote to the rest of the members is well-spent and much appreciated by all. In the last chapter we discussed the effect of preconceived notions about our role in groups and the way this might affect our own position in any group structure. When we feel cohesion in a group situation, we feel comfortable in the role we play in connection with others and about the roles we all take on.

Johnson and Johnson (2006) discuss cohesive process as one in which group members maximize their own level of productivity and also the productivity of others with whom they share a group task. Each group member sees a reward not only for his or her own contribution, but also for the place it holds in the task as a whole. When we see the part we play rewarded in itself and in its place in the grand scheme of things, we feel valued.

One of the possible pitfalls of a cohesive group is the potential for a phenomenon known as *groupthink*. Groups can become so closely knit that individual group members avoid expressing disagreement about particular issues or concerns because they value group togetherness and do not want to disrupt consensus. The term **groupthink** was coined by Irving Janis (1972) to describe the experience in which a group's desire for solidarity and unanimity overrides its inclination to critically evaluate alternative solutions or possibilities. When group members operate from a groupthink perspective, they are seeking agreement at the expense of full exploration and assessment of optional courses of action. Members avoid disagreeing or voicing concerns that may lead to flawed or unproductive decisions. According to Johnson and Johnson (2006):

> . . . groupthink is promoted when the group is highly cohesive, when it is insulated from outside criticism, when the leader is directive and dynamic, and when the group does not search for and critically evaluate alternatives. Group members rely on shared illusions and rationalizations to bolster whatever option is preferred by the volunteer. (p. 296)

Brilhart and Galanes (1992) suggest that groups should create fail-safe mechanisms to avoid groupthink patterns of behaviour. By creating structures that ensure that group members consistently analyze and critically review their process of idea sharing and decision making, groups avoid the potential for narrow-minded thinking and decisions based only on the ideas and opinions of the group's members.

Productivity

If we are going to commit time and energy to any group task, we want it to be worthwhile and have some feeling of accomplishment. This is most relevant when we are a part of a working group and there is a task to be done. We experience **productivity** when our work together takes us closer to our goal and generates significant progress. We also want to feel that discussions and decision making are useful and that the group stays on task. It feels good to be able to look at the tangible consequence of our hard work and to eventually reach a common goal. The time is well-spent and we feel we were significant to the success of the project.

Even in those social situations where the goal of the group is to share experiences or offer support to each of its members, there has to be some feeling of accomplishment, or we begin to lose interest in the time we devote to the group. In a way there is still the expectation that the time spent is helpful to you in some way — whether it lightens your mood, supports you at a time of stress or simply offers up a few laughs. Here, productivity is based on how your mood has changed, how much you feel supported or how many times you laughed during the time you spent with your group.

Transformational Change

Sometimes the experience of being part of a group moves beyond productivity, cohesion, feelings of personal effectiveness and trust. In these situations the time spent with a particular group becomes what we like to refer to as a transformational experience. The concept of transformational experience is based on Cranton's (2002) theory of transformative learning discussed in Chapter 1. We introduced the term *transformational* with reference to the process of change that occurs during reflection when new insights lead to a shift in perspective. The reflection tool is designed to help you question your own beliefs and values in ways that help you examine your well-established ways of looking at the world and reconsider their value to your ways of thinking and behaving. Being a part of a highly evolved group of people can actually inspire this process. Through our participation or experience in the group, we begin to sense a shift in our own knowledge of ourselves. We may risk and meet challenges in this group that we never thought were possible before. Or, we may have different insights about others or ourselves as a product of being with others in a group situation. This may have happened because we worked with people from different cultures or walks of life, and that opened us up to experiences we have never tried before. Whatever form this shift takes, we experience a sense of **transformational change**.

Imagine that you have been asked to work on a small committee of students from a variety of programs to nominate students for a representative position in the administration of your college or university. As you work with three other people on this task, you start off feeling a bit confused and not quite sure about your role. All four of you soon discover that even though you come from different programs in the college, you share a mutual goal of achieving power in the institution. This revelation comes around the third time you meet as a planning group, and it ignites much sharing and feelings of mutuality. Through observing others in the group, and their openness to your perspective, you discover that the issue of student representation is more important to you than you thought. You come away from this meeting feeling energized and connected to others in your group. As well, you have a renewed motivation regarding campus politics — something you had thought about before, but were not nearly as excited about until you were a part of this group. This experience has been truly transformational and a direct product of the group process.

Historical Theories of Group Development

Two well-known theories have contributed to our understanding of how groups develop over time. Bruce Tuckman and William Schutz developed their theories in the middle of the twentieth century, and they are still relevant to any discussion of group development today. Each of these researchers has created sequential-stage frameworks that describe the developmental progress of a variety of groups. Even though the stages in both of these frameworks are sequential, groups may cycle between them depending on the situations they encounter. That is, each stage is defined by the way people respond to the task and each other and may be revisited as the people change and the tasks differ over the time the group members are together.

Forming, Storming, Norming, Performing, Adjourning

Tuckman's work in the 1960s was based on a thorough research review of a number of different types of group situations. He extracted commonalities from the literature of that time with a focus on how members of groups interact at different stages of their existence. From this he created a model of group development that describes how a group comes together and then matures over time. The model itself is known as *forming, storming, norming* and *performing*. He reviewed his work 10 years after its origin and, in conjunction with Mary Ann Jensen (Tuckman & Jensen, 1977), added a fifth stage known as *adjourning*. Tuckman's model is a popular conceptual overview of group process and one that logically outlines the interpersonal struggles and celebrations all groups experience as they work together over time.

When groups first come together it is generally a comfortable time. People are nice to each other, and there is a great need to be liked. Tuckman identified this as the

forming stage. There is a focus on trying to figure out why the group is together and what each member of the group is supposed to be doing. Individuals are concerned with the impression others may have about their role in the group, and during this time of determining how members are going to interact with each other, not a lot seems to get accomplished. Nonetheless, it is important to all of the group members that they conceive of themselves as a group with a purpose.

The process of interaction eventually shifts once the group members become clear about why it is they are together and how they will proceed. This shift then moves the group into the stage called **storming**. Now group members begin to question differences in an effort to assert their own individualities. One of the indicators of this storming stage is that group members challenge any perceived leaders that may be emerging from within their ranks. This is a time of conflict and experimentation with power and control. There are big questions: How much influence do I have in this group? Why does that person think they know more than I do? How am I going to be heard in this group? Because of what can only be termed *bids for power*, at this stage the level of task accomplishment continues to be low, and relationships between group members are beleaguered with feelings of dissatisfaction. Some groups never move out of this stage, and the process of interaction becomes almost painful. Other groups take the time to acknowledge and discuss disagreements and continue their work in ways that are less confrontational. They are moving into the next stage of group development.

During the **norming** stage, group members who have worked through the second stage of competitiveness move into a time of greater acceptance and understanding. Group members take the time to listen to each other and work on resolving differences. Groups finally begin to feel some sense of collegiality and what some term as a sense of overall *groupness*. It is a time of consensus and overall well-being. Decision making is accomplished through an accepted structure.

In the **performing** stage, the group continues to experience this sense of collaboration and mutuality and achieves a higher level of trust and interdependence. This happens because the group members begin to share power and appreciate each individual member's strengths as a contribution to the group's task or function. This stage differs somewhat from the norming stage because group members become not only structured in the accomplishment of the task, but also more evolved around the appreciation of each member's ability to contribute in individual ways to the group's function. Relationships become equally as important as the accomplishment of the task. Some believe that not all groups evolve to this point of performing. The task may get accomplished, but the sense of pride in each member's contribution may never be realized.

Tuckman's identification of the stage of **adjourning** brings attention to the importance of group completion and healthy closure. It is a time to recognize a kind of grieving that occurs after the excitement of task completion concludes. If there is recognition of the end of a group process, members can express appreciation for each other and prepare to move on to new endeavours. Without a cleanly recognized closure, the high sense of closeness experienced at the performing stage has nowhere to go. Sometimes group members make promises to get together, but these promises often dissipate as people move on to other things. This leaves a sense of emptiness that could have been avoided with a more formalized opportunity to acknowledge each other. Essentially, in this phase all group members acknowledge together that they are done.

Inclusion, Control, Openness

William C. Schutz developed the Fundamental Interpersonal Relationship Orientation (FIRO) model of group development in the late 1940s and 1950s. This is an interpersonal model of group growth, with a focus on the ways people either express their interpersonal needs or get those needs met while functioning in a group situation. According to Schutz, as we interact in groups we each attempt to fulfill the three basic human needs for inclusion, control and openness (formerly known as affection). The importance of each of these needs to individual group members differs. Schutz looked at both the *desire* each group member has for inclusion, control and openness and the ways each group member *facilitates* these three factors in others. He actually created a scale that measures how a person relates to other group members in terms of his or her own need for inclusion, control and openness, as well as how the individual wants others to express their desires for inclusion, control and openness toward him or her (as cited in Cragan & Wright, 1995).

The way in which we resolve any anxiety we might have about these needs affects the overall dynamic interaction of the groups we are part of, their growth and their effectiveness. It is important for us to take a close look at these three factors of interpersonal function in group situations.

Inclusion

Inclusion is about joining a new group situation and asking ourselves not only whether we feel comfortable in this new context, but also whether we are interested in committing energy to helping others in the group feel comfortable. Schutz's question is, Am I in or am I out? That is, we consciously or unconsciously assess the degree to which we feel a sense of belonging to the group. In this stage group members are checking things out in an effort to build a good impression and to appear to be worthwhile participants. Regardless of whether or not we think this is a group we want to be a part of, Schutz believes that we still have the need to belong and that our greatest fear is that we will be ignored.

Control

Near the end of the inclusion phase, the group reaches a clearer understanding of the reason for its existence and group members begin to feel more comfortable with each other. There is a greater climate of acceptance amongst group members, but this quickly dissipates as the work of the group gets underway and individuals begin to challenge perceived leadership and try to determine their level of influence in the group. Schutz defines the question at this stage as, Am I on top or am I on the bottom? Needs for power and control vary amongst all group members, which makes for an interesting dynamic as individuals jockey for power and position within the group's structure. This is a critical time in a group's development and has the potential for stalling the task at hand.

If you find that you are part of a group situation in which members challenge each other on minor points, argue in ways such that they need to be right and cannot make even small decisions without long and arduous discussion, and the loudest person seems to think he or she has all the power, then you are experiencing the **control** phase of your group. You may even fear that this group may never get it together, but in reality it is experiencing the necessary process of confrontation and influence sharing that helps group members witness each other's growing edges. It is also the time for group members to test out how the group will evolve through the process of decision making. Again, each individual will have a different need for control and a different need for others to exert control over the group.

It is possible that a few groups will not surpass the control issues in this phase and will either stall totally or remain stuck in the bickering phase. Hedley Dimock (1993) suggests that human service professionals "are candidates for arrested development if they are unwilling to go through the trials and tribulations of group building and imagine that they can establish trust and openness . . . ." (p. 15). In the profession of human service we value caring and respectful relationships and may create structures that do not allow trust to be worked through, based on the belief that all people who choose this field are naturally trusting. We may have difficulty accepting the tension that needs to evolve at this stage, and in our zest to make everyone happy, we might have trouble trusting that the difficulties that arise in this control phase are critical and a natural part of any group's development.

Openness

With the structure and power hierarchy established and accepted by all group members comes a time of deeper relationship building. Friendships may form and individuals may be less concerned with their power and influence and more focused on what all group members can contribute to the work at hand. There may even be some sharing of the leadership role to the betterment of a quality product. This is a time of creativity, collegiality and efficiency. For Schutz, the question at this stage is, Am I open or am I closed? Or, Am I close to this group or far away? Again, the need for **openness** will vary for each individual member of the group, even in this more open, intimate phase of group growth.

You will experience this phase of group development when you see people readily sharing their ideas and opinions, when there is an equitable sharing of work to be done and when people's strengths are appreciated and their weaknesses accepted.

We have included a chart (Table 3.1 on page 60) that offers a quick overview of these two theories, outlining some possible questions, issues, feelings and behaviours common to the phases of group development discussed above. We have amalgamated some of the questions you might ask yourself, some of the most evident issues, some of the feelings you may experience and some of the common behaviours observed when groups are in the various stages of development theorized by Schutz and Tuckman. The categories described above are outlined on the left side of the chart, with the indicators described under each developmental stage. This chart helps you to see the similarities between Tuckman's and Schutz's models and helps you to quickly identify the stage your group might be experiencing at any given time in its development.

TABLE 3.1 Individual Experience vs. Phase of Group Development

	Forming, Inclusion	*Storming, Control*	*Norming/Performing, Openness*	*Adjourning, Closure*
Questions We Ask Ourselves	Am I in or am I out? Will people like me? Do I like these people? Why is this group together?	Am I on top or on the bottom? Are people going to listen to me? How much influence do I have?	Am I open or am I closed? How open am I willing to be? What do others have to say?	Are we there yet? How do we end this?
Issues	Belonging Commitment to the group Deserving to be here Dependence	Influence Dominance Power Control Counter-dependence	Task accomplishment, making the most use of each member's resources, interdependence	Putting closure to the group Independence
Feelings	Insecure, anxious, curious, anticipation	Dissatisfied, uncomfortable, lost, worried, powerful	Appreciation, respect, trust, gratitude, pride	Grief, appreciation, emptiness
Typical Group Behaviour	Polite, superficial, getting to know each other, avoidance of conflict or confrontation, continuum of very introverted to very extroverted behaviour	Arguing, confrontation, competition, attempts at leadership, focus on own position rather than the betterment of the group, compliance, submission	Accepting diversity within the group, division of labour, productivity, personal responsibility, acceptance of group structure and leadership, open problem solving	Mutual acknowledgement of the accomplishment of the task, celebrating, disengaging and moving on

Group Development and Effective Group Function

In this section the components of effective group function will be examined within the contexts of each of the phases of group development described in Table 3.1. We have chosen to combine the work of Tuckman and Schutz into four collective phases of group development and taken the liberty of re-titling the stages:

1. Forming, Inclusion
2. Storming, Control
3. Norming/Performing, Openness
4. Adjourning, Closure

As we move through each of the phases of group development, we will attempt to demonstrate how the levels of personal effectiveness, trust, cohesion, productivity and transformational change might play out. Then we will suggest behaviours for your consideration to help the group move through that stage more efficiently.

Forming, Inclusion

Personal Effectiveness

When you head into a new group situation you are armed with all kinds of communication skills. You will have many questions, but your first and most important focus is on you and how you are going to fit into this new place of working with others.

Your style of communication is directly linked to how others will perceive you. It is also significantly related to the communication styles of all the other group members. What you are doing in this stage is discovering how you are going to feel comfortable with all of the other people around you. Those first minutes, hours and, possibly, sessions together will be important to laying the foundation for your own sense of personal effectiveness.

If you are outgoing and talkative, you will be asking others about themselves and probably taking the opportunity to venture into discussion of the task at hand quite quickly. Self-awareness at this stage is important. If there are many introverted, quiet or less forthcoming people in your group, you may come across as overpowering and intimidating.

If you are one of the quieter people in the group waiting to see what the expectations are and letting others carry the discussion, you risk coming across as uninterested. Members might question your commitment and your ability to contribute in a concrete manner.

This does not mean that introverts and extroverts need to make radical shifts in their natural way of entering into new group situations. What is important to personal effectiveness is the ability to use your awareness of your own style of entering into new relationships to better blend with the styles of those around you. This time of group formation is the vehicle that allows that to happen.

Pay attention to how others are responding to you. For example, if you have an extroverted communication style and others in your new group setting appear at ease and interested, and respond to you with open body language in ways that match your way of interacting, then you are probably coming across as non-threatening. If, however, you are met with averted eyes, blank facial expressions, sudden subject changes and conversation directed at just about anyone but you, then you may not be meshing with the people in your new group. Try not to move blindly into new group situations without reflecting on the impact your behaviour has on the other group members. It is possible to adapt to others' communication styles with slight modifications to your own style of interaction. With experience and heightened self-awareness this will become easier.

Cohesion

Cohesion is low at the forming or inclusion stage. Until you reach a level of comfort with your group members, it is hard to move into that place of interdependence described earlier in the section on effective, cohesive groups. One of the interpersonal factors described in Table 3.1 is dependence. Because connections are just starting to be made and are usually superficial, each individual in the group is somewhat dependent on the other members as all members establish their roles and functions within the group. First impressions are important, and members want to be seen as valuable contributors in the eyes of others.

Try not to expect instantaneous mutuality at the inclusion stage. Just remember that cohesion is a natural result of becoming comfortable with each other's styles and abilities.

Trust

Trust is in the infancy stage during the phase of group formation. The initial interactions you have with others form the foundation for the establishment of trust. Because this is usually a time of superficial conversation and cautious sharing of information about ourselves, deeper personal disclosure is not the norm and doesn't feel safe. We often become suspicious of those who disclose personal information too quickly in new group situations, unless the disclosure relates to something that has happened very recently within that person's personal context (e.g., a death in the family).

How can you contribute to a healthy formation of trust at this early stage of group development? You can begin by behaving in a trustworthy manner from the first minute you enter the group situation. Some suggestions for trustworthy inclusion behaviour include sharing information about yourself discreetly, being conscious of the intensity of what you are saying, asking questions that are respectful of boundaries of others, listening to what others are saying without judgment, and showing genuine interest in getting to know the members of the group.

Productivity

In the inclusion stage, expectations of productivity are obviously dependent on the importance of the task at hand. Because the members of the group are getting to know each other and are trying to understand their roles within the group, productivity is usually low while group members are doing the primary work of getting comfortable with the people they are working with. Obviously the more familiar people are with each other, the less time it will take for the group members to move through this stage and get on with the work. However, inclusion still happens in situations where people know each other and have worked together before — it just happens faster.

As well, inclusion is not simply a stage we move through and never revisit as we continue with the work of the group. The group may cycle back to this stage when members leave or new members arrive, or when the task requires any kind of significant change. New factors quickly move the group back into a place of inclusion even if just for an hour while group members re-establish their expectations. Any significant change to a group's work affects its productivity while it quickly or slowly moves back into and out of inclusion.

Think about a time when you were working in some small-group situation on a project and a new member joined your team. You will probably remember feeling curious and a bit anxious about how things were going to play out with the new member. All other established members probably felt the same way. The time spent in a second inclusion stage will depend on how other factors of trust and cohesion were initially established and how long it will take to get back to the work. In the meantime, productivity suffers.

You do not have much control over the level of productivity at this stage. You do have some control over your level of acceptance and understanding that inclusion is a time of getting to know each other and figuring out how all group members will work together.

Transformational Change

Since you are on the cusp of a new group experience, transformational change is something to look forward to and virtually non-existent at the inclusion stage of group formation (see Exercise 3.5).

EXERCISE 3.5 IDENTIFYING INCLUSION BEHAVIOUR

Objectives:

1. **To identify the kinds of inclusion behaviours exhibited in Base Groups with reference to personal effectiveness**
2. **To share with others initial reactions to styles of communication**
3. **To offer feedback to Base Group participants regarding first impressions**

Move into your Base Groups and retrieve your notes from Exercise 1.3 when you first worked together and created a name for your group. Discuss the following:

How did you each communicate during the completion of this first task together? For example, who initiated conversation, who was the quietest member, who asked questions about what you would be doing as a Base Group, etc.?

What level of personal effectiveness did each of you experience after your first meeting together? In other words, were you comfortable with what you contributed, or did you question the value of your participation? How did you feel about the other group members' communication styles?

Offer feedback to each member about his or her style of communication and how it may have helped or hindered your sense of belonging in your Base Group.

Now that you have completed this exercise, reflect on any changes you might have made or appreciated in others that might have helped your inclusion process move more effectively.

Storming, Control

Personal Effectiveness

Once members achieve a sense of belonging (that is, move through forming or inclusion), they begin to feel comfortable enough with each other to challenge the status quo of superficial niceties and begin to promote getting on with the work of the group. Group members have many different ways of attempting to influence the way the group functions at this stage. Ultimately, members begin to push for some structure that allows them to work comfortably together. This may look like hard questioning, argument, disagreement, cliquing and power seeking. Ultimately, each individual is interested in a role that matches his or her own level of personal satisfaction. This process is not particularly comfortable. Often individual members feel the discomfort of conflict and come away from their time together feeling unproductive and ineffective. They may think that the group is not getting anywhere, and with this increase in tension individuals sometimes feel like giving up.

While you may prefer to think you are part of a group situation that does not include seeking power or craving influence, the reality is that in all well-functioning groups the process of challenging leadership and establishing direction is vitally important. In the inclusion stage the real issues are not being raised. However, those who finally risk raising these issues help the group to move into a place of clarity about the work to be done. If the issues are not raised, the group stays in a place of avoidance by trying to be nice to each other. Avoidance is frustrating to everyone if it is allowed to go on for too long. You will feel personally ineffective if you play into this. You may feel equally frustrated by the arguing and bickering about how to proceed when moving into this stage. The good news is that this is a signpost for the control stage and is the first step to moving on.

How can you help the group move forward and at the same time garner the power and influence you need to feel personally effective? This is a time when your communication skills are critically important for success: clear, non-judgmental statements must form the foundation of any suggestions or questions to the group. Try to describe concerns using concrete language and avoid blaming and grand generalizations. For example, instead of saying, Why is this group spending so much time talking about what we all did on the weekend instead of getting down to work?, which is defensive and blameful, voice your concerns with observations and concrete suggestions such as, I am noticing that we are talking a lot about stuff happening outside of this group, and I am wondering if we could come up with an agenda during this session to help us proceed with the work. Recognize that while the second statement is more direct and neutral, it is still challenging the process and may not be well-received by others. However, it is an important part of group development because this kind of statement raises questions for the group about better ways of working together. If you are the person making the second statement, you may not experience the reaction you anticipate, but you have offered an honest and forthright contribution that serves to move the group during the storming stage.

Listening behaviour is equally important in this phase of group growth. When we feel challenged, we are often compelled to respond immediately with our own point of view rather than taking the time to clarify the meaning of the sender's message. Checking out messages does not come naturally to most people because we are usually quick to respond with a comment or opinion that contradicts the sender's message, repeats its meaning or simply changes the subject. Active listening is hard work, and includes the skills of paraphrasing and perception checking, both of which require conscious effort. If you are in a situation where arguing is dominating the group process, active listening can help reduce tension.

How do you gauge personal effectiveness at the storming or control phase of a group's development? Obviously the answer is as individual as you are. Accepting that storming is a natural part of group process will help you understand that any feelings of frustration and disillusionment are one part of a greater whole in terms of where the group is going. While communication skills help at this stage, it is a challenge to feel personally effective at a time when confusion, conflict and power seeking is the norm (see Exercise 3.6 on page 66).

Trust

Storming, control is the time when trust building occurs and is contingent on the quality and nature of communication amongst group members. The inability to communicate effectively and work through conflict issues natural to the storming or control stage inhibits the formation of trust and can contribute to a group becoming stuck in this phase. If members are able to listen to each other and accept the challenges of this stage, they will move through this phase.

Acceptance is the key. If you are able to accept others' risks in challenging the status quo and suggesting ways of structuring the power in the group, then you will show trust. If you are the one risking the questions and challenging the process, you must show the group that you are concerned with its overall success. You do this in a way that is open and not subversive, in other words, not as a product of some hidden agenda for personal gain. This displays integrity and in turn, trustworthiness.

At this challenging stage it is important to take responsibility for your contributions and to use language that reflects only your position. Speaking from your own position requires using phrases such as, "I am wondering about . . . .", "I think that . . . .", "I worry about. . . .", rather than negative blameful phrases such as, "Why do you always . . . .?", "It is obvious that everyone . . . .", "People aren't happy with . . . ." Using the latter phrases, the sender is incorrectly speaking on behalf of everyone in the group and opening the door to criticism, which in turn erodes trust.

Other trust-building behaviours important to moving through this time of storming or control include following through with anything you say you will do; refraining from gossiping in and out of the group context; and behaving in ways that are congruent with what you say you value.

Cohesion

In the storming or control phase, cohesion is lower than it is in the forming or inclusion stage. With people challenging each other, possibly bickering and arguing, the atmosphere is anything but cohesive. Recognize that this is an important time of role differentiation, giving group members an opportunity to get to know what each individual is capable or not capable of contributing to the work. This is the time to clearly identify each individual's role and the way the group will best structure itself. There is no potential for cohesion if these roles are not out there for all to see through the resolution of the storming or control stage. Again, as an individual at this stage you must communicate as clearly, honestly and openly as possible, so that others see what part you will play and how they can connect with you.

Productivity

There is little potential for task-related productivity during this phase. Because the goal of this stage is to determine how the group makes decisions and works together as a whole, the productivity is defined by less tangible outcomes like clarity of group structure, member roles and decision making. Productivity is focused on determining how the group will work together effectively, rather than on the concrete tasks it will accomplish at this time.

Transformational Change

Storming or control marks the beginning of the individual experience we have defined as transformational change. It is critical that as a student of group process you take the time to pull back from what is going on with the group during this phase and try to process the parts being played by all group members. Only then can you track any changes and possible movement toward power sharing and overall group comfort. Most of us have difficulty with conflict, and stepping back from the immediate experience of the group to take a more global look at what is actually going on helps us gain some awareness of our own values and beliefs, which in turn forms the foundation of transformation. As with forming or inclusion, groups can cycle in and out of the storming or control stage. Again, it is vital that you see this stage of disequilibrium as necessary to the effective functioning of the group.

EXERCISE 3.6 POWER LINE-UP

Objectives:

1. To explore others' perceptions of our power
2. To explore our perception of our power
3. To help understand the many ways group members define power

This exercise involves all members of the class. Place a mark on the floor to indicate where the most powerful person in the class should stand. Class members will arrange themselves in a line according to how powerful they see themselves in relation to the rest of the class with the most powerful person standing on the pre-determined mark. No definition of power will be given.

After the line has been stabilized, ask if anyone wants to move to a different location. Pause to ensure that everyone is where he or she wants to be, and take note of where everyone is.

The class then discusses the following:

1. Why did individuals place themselves where they did?
2. Does anyone think that someone should be in a different spot and why?

Move into your Base Groups and discuss any insights, revelations or feelings you had during this exercise.

Recall a time when any group you have been a part of was in the storming or control stage of development. How did this exercise relate to that experience?

Norming/Performing, Openness

Personal Effectiveness

When groups begin to shift out of the storming or control stage, a sense of settling in begins to permeate the interactions among members. There are fewer struggles for leadership and group members are more comfortable with established ways of doing business. Individuals feel useful and effective because there is a better use of each group member's skills and abilities as the work of sorting through differences begins to happen.

This change generates feelings of personal effectiveness. With a climate of openness, your contributions can be communicated in an accepting environment. The original term Schutz used for this phase was "affection" to describe the caring and compatible atmosphere that follows the hard work of the storming or control phase. Eventually the term "openness" was substituted to describe the interactive nature of this phase.

In the storming stage it was important for group members to focus on clear communication skills. In this norming or open phase, these skills start to become more natural. People express ideas and opinions freely and experience a high degree of receptivity from others. In this phase you will observe increased frequency in behavioural descriptions, personal responsibility for points made, more overall sharing of personal information and clarity of messages. Listening behaviours include consistent checking in on messages shared, perception checking and a climate of collaboration. Overall, you will feel a great sense of personal effectiveness because your contributions and your talents are being valued.

Trust

Part of the reason you feel personally effective and valued is that at this stage of group development there is an increased level of trust that has arisen from the work done in the storming or control stage. You have weathered the storms of challenge and disagreement. The disagreements were a kind of risking through member disclosure. Members have shared their issues and complaints openly, giving you insight into their wants and needs. Acceptance of open disclosure builds trust. If you are all able to stay together after the discomfort of the storming or control phase, you will be gifted with an increased sense of trust as a natural outcome of that process.

In the norming or openness phase there is a higher level of trust, yet still there is the need to slowly increase your own willingness to risk and enjoy the overall sense of comfort and acceptance. Of course you must continue to follow through with what you say you will do and behave in ways that are congruent with what you say you value.

Cohesion

In the norming/performing, openness phase, members have settled the issue of leadership. Whether leadership is structured or shared, there is a greater use of human resources within the group. The acceptance of each other's individual strengths and weaknesses is evident, and the goals of the work are generally clear. This moves the focus away from each individual's needs and wants toward what works best for the common good of the group. Some term this a sense of *groupness*.

As a group participant in this phase, it is important to understand and appreciate the contributions of other group members and to support the strengths of those with whom you are working. As well, you need to be aware of what you can contribute and, alternatively, what you may think might interfere with group process. Being mindful of your role in the group helps maintain a sense of togetherness. Even though this is a phase of comfort and cohesion, it is important not to simply sit back and become complacent.

Productivity

The norming/performing, openness phase is the time of productivity. Everyone is contributing in his or her own way, and the group has become goal-oriented. As work is accomplished, the group feels even more motivated because the goal of its existence becomes actualized. Those group members who are driven by task completion are increasingly satisfied as they see something actually happening.

With shared leadership and the ultimate use of each group member's strengths comes high-quality workmanship, regardless of the task. The organized people do the planning, the creative people have input into the product, the talkative people report on the process and the natural leaders support the direction of the work. Your contributions should utilize your energy and experience in pursuit of a quality product.

Transformational Change

Not all of your group experiences will lead to a sense of inner transformational change. However, as in the stage of storming or control, it is important to take the opportunity to step out of the group and assess your own change experience. Look for indicators of personal growth. This could be something as simple as a change in the perception you had about another group member or an understanding you had about certain subject matter. It could be complex, such as a new way of interacting with personality types or a newfound acceptance of certain ways of viewing the world. The shift may be immediately evident to you or may take a lot of in-depth reflection. Either way, it is important to remain open to the possibility of inner change while training and working in the field of human relations where the goal of self-discovery is central to effective practice.

Adjourning, Closure

Personal Effectiveness

When a group has really come together and functioned well, it is sometimes hard to accept that the work is done and it is time for the group process to come to an end. Promising to get together is often how groups handle this time of ending, yet these plans seldom come to fruition.

The energy of the group experience will dissipate naturally, but without a formal acknowledgment, endings often leave members feeling empty and somewhat lost. From a personal effectiveness perspective this is similar to a process of grieving. When grieving any transition, feelings have to be acknowledged and experienced. This is no less important during the adjourning, closure phase of group development. It is important to mark the success of the group's time together in a special way because only then can you witness, as a group, the completion of your experience together. With formalized "letting go" comes the healthy ending that leads to the next step in your own personal journey and whatever new group experiences await (see Exercise 3.7 on page 71).

Trust and Cohesion

The more trusting and cohesive the group, the more important the acknowledgment and celebration of closure. Obviously, the closer you feel to the group you have been a part of, the harder it will be to say goodbye. If the group has struggled throughout its existence, closure remains an important element and may be a time for reflection about what could have been done differently to enhance trust and cohesion.

Productivity

Productivity in this stage focuses on the plan for formalized closure. Your role in this phase is to acknowledge the ending and suggest scheduling and idea sharing around some kind of celebratory event. For the group that has not functioned well, this is a time for productive assessment, with a discussion of just what factors might have contributed to a higher level of function and task accomplishment. This is never easy, since it is human nature to move on, with little interest in revisiting a painful experience.

The president of a university college in transition to two separate institutions (a college and a university) wrote the following letter. It was addressed to all employees after months of turmoil and confusion, as the institutional work of separating took place. It provided the foundation for a positive closure experience that acknowledged an ending and opened the door for an optimistic new beginning. Along with the various celebrations came appreciation of the emotions all staff members were experiencing.

> Dear Colleagues and Friends,
>
> As you know, OUC Tributes Day will be held on Wednesday, June 22, 2005. I would like to remind you to send in your RSVP by this Friday so that we can get a handle on the numbers. Please respond whether or not you intend to attend the event. I want to personally urge you to attend this historic event, and I hope we will have a great turnout to send off OUC on a high note.
>
> I want you to come because this will be a unique opportunity to celebrate our successes and achievements as OUC and a final opportunity to meet as OUC colleagues and friends. The planned celebrations, commencing at 12.30pm, include:
>
>> A Convocation ceremony in which we will recognize the contributions of all OUC employees and volunteers over the years,

award honorary doctoral degrees to all of the former Presidents and Principals of OUC and its predecessor institutions, and award Distinguished Service awards to the former Chairs of the OUC Board of Governors;

An Employees Garden Party in which we will have the opportunity to mix and mingle with our colleagues from all across OUC;

A special OUC Graduation Cake to recognize the achievements of OUC and celebrate our "graduation" into UBC Okanagan and the new Okanagan College;

A special gift to all OUC employees to thank you for your contributions to the success of this institution and wish you well as you leave OUC and move on into the future.

In order that as many of you as possible can attend, I have authorized the closure of all OUC offices from 12 noon onwards, although this will take effect earlier in the regional campuses where we have arranged for buses to transport employees to North Kelowna for the celebrations. There will be some operations that will need to be maintained, but managers are attempting to keep these to a minimum so that the maximum number of OUC employees can attend.

I must point out, however, that if you choose not to attend and you do not have a prearranged leave or vacation on that day, then you will be required to work for that afternoon. The closing of offices is simply to allow the maximum number of employees to attend, and it is not a general "holiday" for OUC employees.

I know that this is going to be a great day, full of emotion and also full of pride at what we have achieved in building this wonderful institution. In celebrating our success to date, we also set a positive tone for moving forward into the new structure for post-secondary education in the region.

If I had a sentence to describe the OUC Tributes Day it would be: "Be proud of what we have achieved and where we have come from, so that we can be confident for the future."

Please RSVP by Friday, June 10, 2005.

I look forward to seeing you on June 22 for OUC Tributes Day.

Cheers,

Peter

Peter J. Ricketts, BA (Hons), PhD
President, Okanagan University College

(Courtesy of Peter Ricketts)

EXERCISE 3.7 CLOSURE EXERCISE

Objectives:

1. To experience the process of creating a plan for effective group closure
2. To reinforce the importance of planning for closure

In groups of four, think about times when you may have been part of a fun, successful group experience that has ended. Share these experiences with each other, discuss how these groups ended, and for any group that ended without acknowledgment, create a plan for closure that celebrates the group's success and prepares individuals to move on.

Share your ideas with the class.

Final Comment

As much as we can theorize about the factors that are at play as groups develop, it is important to recognize that groups are entities that, when formed, take on a life of their own. As all of the people, contexts, tasks, interactions and multifaceted details that contribute to any group begin to intertwine, there is really no certainty about what may happen. As explained in this chapter, there are patterns identified by researchers that are common to the evolution of many kinds of groups. With insight, awareness and experience we learn which behaviours will help a group move forward.

Summary

In effective groups, members work toward common, agreed-upon goals. There is open and respectful communication, appropriate structure for goal completion and acceptance of controversy. When participating in an effective group, members recognize that their contributions are meaningful, and they experience a sense of personal effectiveness. As well, there is a feeling of trust and cohesion amongst all group members as they build on each other's strengths and abilities in the completion of tasks. Time spent in any effective group results in some kind of personal transformational change in all participants. This transformational change is a result of questioning our perspective and gaining insight about others and ourselves as a product of being in a group situation.

All groups develop over time and progress through stages. The first stage of group development (forming or inclusion) is the exploratory time in any group. Members are testing out the impression they have of others in the group and the role that they might play within this new situation. Communication style is important in this first stage, as it provides the foundation for trust amongst group members. Productivity and transformational change are generally low as members of any group use this time to get to know each other.

In the second stage of group development (storming or control), group members test out their ability to influence each other and the structures the group will follow in accomplishing its task. Though a frustrating time for some, this stage is important to the development of any group, because it offers all participants the opportunity to clarify their issues, get to know each other and come to some conclusions about how members are going to work together. At times, groups become stuck in this stage, unable to work through individual disagreements and get on with the task.

In the third (norming/performing or openness) stage of group development, group members begin to work together utilizing each other's strengths, having worked through the control issues experienced in the preceding stage. Trust builds with the acceptance of each other's strengths and weaknesses, and working relationships feel more comfortable. This contributes to greater cohesion and productivity, because each group member plays an interdependent part in the accomplishment of the work.

The final (adjourning or closure) stage of group development is often not recognized or celebrated, yet is an important time for all group members to acknowledge their time together before moving on to the next group experience. Healthy endings help all members to acknowledge closure and reflect on the totality of their time together.

Key Terms

Adjourning *(p. 57)*
Cohesion *(p. 54)*
Control *(p. 59)*
Cooperative group development *(p. 53)*
Disclosure *(p. 51)*
Forming *(p. 57)*
Groupthink *(p. 54)*
Inclusion *(p. 58)*
Mediated discussion *(p. 51)*
Mutuality *(p. 53)*
Norming *(p. 57)*
Openness *(p. 59)*
Performing *(p. 57)*
Personal effectiveness *(p. 50)*
Productivity *(p. 55)*
Storming *(p. 57)*
Transformational change *(p. 56)*
Trust *(p. 51)*

Case Studies

The following case studies, taken from classroom, human service team and community contexts will help clarify the topics covered in this chapter, using real-world examples. These case studies focus on various stages of group development and will help to demonstrate both the behaviours that might be exhibited in various phases of group growth and the possible factors that contribute to these phases.

Case Study 3.1 Group Project Difficulties

CATEGORY: STUDENT

A group of six students (Turlough, Kelan, Alicia, Marie, Brittney and Talia) are working together on a classroom project. Because the task has several components, they have immediately separated into three working pairs, taking on different tasks

(Turlough and Kelan, Alicia and Marie, and Brittney and Talia). They have decided that they will simply do their own sections and combine them before they hand in the product. There is a group participation journal as a part of this assignment, but they are not worried about that because they think this arrangement will work out best. One working pair (Alicia and Marie) is highly organized and motivated to complete their section, and they do so very quickly. The group has class time to do the work, augmented by only a small amount of out-of-class time. Alicia and Marie begin to encourage the other two groups quite assertively to get their work done, as they hover over them at the computer-lab work station and continue to probe about when they will be finished.

The pressure builds as Alicia and Marie feel frustrated, and the unfinished groups feel pestered. Finally, all group members decide to go to the instructor for some help to clear the air because everyone is getting upset. The assignment is due in one week.

After airing their differences with the instructor, all group members leave the session feeling somewhat better. However, two days later Alicia tells Marie that Talia has been gossiping in the washroom that she (Marie) has not been doing enough work from the start. Then, Brittney comes to the group and accuses Alicia of gossiping about her and refers to an earlier project, saying Brittney never was a big participator in many group assignments.

There are tears from Marie and denials and defensiveness from Alicia as everyone begins to voice frustration. Turlough and Kelan are somewhat stunned by the fact that there was gossiping that they never knew about, and they voice their frustrations about being pestered to complete their project. There is no resolution during this meeting or afterward, and the group pairs simply complete their project parts and submit the assignment.

QUESTIONS:

1. Where is this group in its development?
2. What factors can you identify to support the conclusion that the group is in this phase?
3. What could this group do after their second meeting to move their process along in a more cohesive, trusting way?

Case Study 3.2 New Staff Member

CATEGORY: TEAM

There is a team of eight client support workers in an outreach community support program housed in a recreation centre. Each worker is trained in human service, community support or rehabilitation therapy. Their jobs vary and range from outreach support to rehabilitation therapy on site to a variety of program supports as deemed necessary and appropriate to client needs.

All eight team members are under the management of Linda, their program support worker. Linda facilitates bi-weekly meetings of about two hours, to review client goals, provide information and updates on the various programs, develop new intervention strategies and air issues. Staff members enjoy the opportunity to touch base on a regular basis and generally feel a sense of cohesion as a working unit, even though each member of the team works autonomously.

Most of the staff members have been together for a minimum of three years. However, Josie, a human service worker, has been with them for only three weeks. For the past few years, the bi-weekly meetings have had a clear structure with certain norms evolving naturally amongst all team members. There is a brief check in, setting of agenda, and time for discussion of all program areas. Linda facilitates the meeting and does not direct discussion. There is an exploration of issues and ideas and time is equitably shared amongst all participants. Everyone's point of view is sought out and suggestions are readily accepted by all. At each meeting all participants bring a toonie to contribute to coffee and goodies.

The first meeting attended by the new staff member, Josie, is generally non-productive — understandably so, since she required the necessary time to catch up on this new way of doing things. Linda clearly explains the way meetings have gone in the past. During the second meeting Josie is still asking questions, addressing all issues to Linda (to the exclusion of the other staff at the meeting) and reiterating concerns that make it evident that she wants to make sure her decisions are acceptable. She then asks the group if it would be a good idea if they alternate bringing snacks for the bi-weekly meetings, rather than donating a toonie.

QUESTIONS:

1. Where is this group in its development?
2. What could the members do to move to the next stage?
3. What behaviours might stop this group from moving on? Why?

Case Study 3.3 **Shift Communication**

CATEGORY: TEAM

A staff of six works in a group home for adults with disabilities. They work varying shifts, with three shifts structured over 24 hours. Four of the staff have worked together as a team for approximately four years, and two staff are fairly new, hired over the past three months.

Once a month the group gets together to discuss client needs and overall operational issues within the group-home context.

One of the new staff members, Faith, is a recent graduate of a college human service worker program and has come into the position with newly honed skills and high ideals. She is becoming irritated with the fact that when she arrives for the evening shift, issues that arose during the day with clients are not recorded or communicated in some way on a formalized, consistent basis. Faith begins to share her frustration with Tim, the other staff member on her shift, and eventually the complaining becomes more consistent, with regular sniping and gossiping about the sloppiness of the day shift.

One night Client A becomes very agitated because Client B is watching a television show. The agitation seems unnecessary to Faith, until she finds out that Client A had been promised another show in the same time slot. This was a promise made during day shift and not communicated to evening shift. This seems to ignite Faith, and she engages in a whole new tirade and announces to Tim, "This was not what we were taught in our training program! Things are supposed to be documented so this kind of stuff doesn't happen!" Tim, in a fit of frustration, defensiveness and annoyance at the constant complaining, says, "Lighten up, this is the real world, and this is just how things are done!"

Tim, who has been with the group home for a fairly long time, has shared Faith's frustrations with colleagues on the other shifts, and word is now getting around that Faith is putting down their work habits and professionalism. A couple of staff members are planning on bringing up this issue at the next staff meeting.

QUESTIONS:

1. Where is the staff team of two in their group development? How about the staff team of six?
2. What factors can you identify to support your conclusion that they are in this group phase?
3. How might this working team of six progress in their feelings of personal effectiveness and trusting?

Case Study 3.4: **Community Forum**

CATEGORY: COMMUNITY

Four people are meeting to finalize the details of a community forum on childcare issues. The forum's objective will be to hear issues on childcare relevant to parents, policy makers, support services, caregivers and politicians, and to create some direction for change locally and provincially in British Columbia.

Three of the people represent major stakeholder agencies linked to childcare and have partnered to get enough money to host the forum. Their names are Hans, Dana and Li. (A well-known childcare advocate from Vancouver is invited to speak at the forum, but will not arrive until the evening of the event.) The fourth member of this group is Susan, a local college instructor who has been asked to facilitate the sessions and oversee the process of grouping people at the forum and having them discuss issues and plans for change. There is a provincial election on the near horizon, and this forum is also seen as an opportunity to share issues with local politicians in hopes of influencing their electoral platforms.

The four members of this committee have worked together for a number of years in the community on many different childcare initiatives — Dana, Li and Susan, the instructor, for about 12 years and Hans for about one year. Initial meetings to set up the forum have been attended by the three stakeholder representatives who obtained the funding. Susan has been asked to the last planning meeting so that final details about the agenda and structure of the evening can be decided.

At this meeting the group of four has already discussed the number of people anticipated (about 60), how to get word of the forum out to the public, expectations of the special guest and some costs (the instructor is facilitating as a volunteer). Now the group is carefully going over the meeting format. The agenda will include a plenary with the guest speaker and then the grouping of participants for issue sharing and suggestions for change. Ultimately all groups will share their ideas, and the guest speaker will summarize the meeting. The instructor's role will be to facilitate the accumulation of ideas.

The conversation below is part of the interchange that occurs when the instructor suggests some changes to the initial meeting itinerary:

Susan: I am wondering if maybe we might discuss who introduces whom. I see that I am the one doing this, and I think it might be best if the person who has organized the arrangements with the speaker actually do the introduction. Not a problem for me — just a suggestion.

Dana: Hmmm . . . good idea. We just thought it might smooth out the evening a bit to have you do this, but that sounds more appropriate. Yikes, looks like I actually have to do something that night!

Hans: Now I am thinking that might change the order of things . . . . (At this point the group brainstorms a different way of introducing the planners, the guest and the audience, and makes a small change to the agenda.)

Susan: I see that the special guest speaks for about 45 minutes — great idea — because she will have lots to talk about!

Li: Yes, and this gives participants a chance to review issues before they engage in their own discussions.

Susan: Do you anticipate my pulling some ideas out during this time, or do you want to let the groups do that when they break up into discussion groups? If I pull some themes out of the speaker's presentation and the questions from the audience, this might make the process go faster. What do you think?

Li: So you are saying that the groups will work on the issues we pull out rather than reaching agreement on common issues while working in their own groups?

Susan: Exactly! I still see time being the enemy here! Remind me of exactly what the outcome of this forum might be — maybe this won't meet your objectives? (Active discussion about ways this might or might not work — then a review of the outcomes. The decision is made to do both — note common themes when the guest speaks and the audience ask questions; then have discussion groups add any themes they see have not been covered.)

Susan: Sounds great to me! Now, one last thing: How do you see the groups recording their thoughts and ideas? Do you want them to come up with a wish list of the ways they want issues about childcare to be handled? I see this as a listing on paper . . . .

Hans: (Interrupting with an apology). Actually, no . . . (standing up) . . . I have used concept maps for brainstorming ideas (shows on board next to meeting table). They inspire creativity and really work to get people thinking about issues and concerns.

Susan: Frankly, I wonder about concept maps in this kind of forum. My experience is that they confuse people who are linear thinkers. And most people do tend to think that way.

Hans: I have to disagree here (with a laugh) . . . I believe in the reverse . . . most people get their creative juices going with this way of recording their ideas. . . .

Dana: Hmmm . . . I disagree . . . they leave me a bit cold because I never quite know if I am doing them correctly . . . .

Susan: . . . and . . . we don't want people challenged by the "hows" and not taking the time to actually get to the issues . . . I'm not sure about what to do here . . . .

Hans: No problem . . . I understand . . . plus most of the time I use concept maps to help people create visions and goal setting . . . .

Susan: (Finishing his sentence) . . . not something as specific as the objectives of this forum. How about we just tell people to record their ideas in whatever format they like — with the task being to have both issues and a wish list of childcare thoughts and ideas?

Dana, Hans and Li: Perfect! Choice is good! (Meeting continues and format gets finalized . . . all is beginning to wind down.)

Susan: So, I hope I haven't been too pushy about the way to do things?

Hans:	Actually, I want to ask the same question! (Everyone laughs.)
Susan and Hans:	At least we were pushy at each other and not at Dana and Li — and we are used to that after our last project together (laughter continues).
Susan:	Dana, looks like, as usual, you have everything all written down and organized. I feel clear about what my role will be on that evening. Thanks for using my ideas today.
Li, Hans and Dana:	Thank you for volunteering your time that evening.
Susan:	No problem — just wait until you get my bill! (More laughter.)

QUESTIONS:

1. What stage is this group at in its development?
2. Offer some reasons why the group is at this stage, considering more than just the conversation.

Reflection Tool

What?

What stood out for you in this chapter? Describe a reading, exercise, incident, person's behaviour, etc.

So What?

1. Emotional impact?

2. Why do you think you had this emotional response?

3. What assumptions might you be making in this situation? What beliefs and values were touched off by this situation?

Assumptions:

Beliefs, values:

4. Write about the meaning this has for you. Some helpful questions might be:
Do you think your values might be clouding your interpretation of the situation? If so, how?

Have you been affected by similar situations in the same way? How have you responded?

5. Is it important for you to change your behaviour? Why?

Now What?

6. Based on the learning from this chapter, what other behaviours might you consider?

7. What might stop you from engaging in these new behaviours?

Objectives

What Questions Remain?

Chapter 4

Leadership and Group Roles

Objectives

In this chapter, the students will acquire the knowledge, skills and attitudes to:

1. Define components of leadership behaviour common in all group contexts.
2. Differentiate between task and maintenance functions of leadership.
3. Identify the need for leadership in a variety of group contexts.
4. Reinforce natural leadership roles in groups.
5. Develop functional leadership skills appropriate to the helping professions.
6. Define and respond to non-functional behaviours in group interactions.

Group Roles

In Chapter 2 we discussed how the elements, or dimensions, of groups significantly affect all aspects of their function and effectiveness. A group's size, the amount of time it spends together, where it spends this time together and who is part of the group are all concrete factors that interrelate and influence who does what during its existence. Less concrete dimensions, yet equally important to a group's level of function, are factors like norms, preconceived notions about the group's purpose, goals and a group's level of interdependence. Your role in all of these swirling dimensions now becomes a subject for more intense investigation.

As all of the group dimensions interrelate in unique and interesting ways, member roles can either adapt and continue to contribute to effective group process, or can become maladaptive and detract from the task at hand. Learning which roles move a group forward and how they match individual styles of group membership is vital to effective group function. For you, as group participants moving into the helping professions, this becomes the work of your practice. By identifying commonly known and highly functional group leadership roles and engaging in a process of self-awareness, it is possible to find a match between these identified roles and your own natural way of participating in groups. This match will improve the role you play in all group contexts and enhance your level of congruency and interaction in other areas of your practice.

Exercise 4.1 will help identify some **natural roles** you take in groups. It will help you to identify your natural interpersonal style in groups and provide a foundation for growing self-awareness. As well, this exercise should help you to roughly define the kinds of behaviour you engage in as you take part in a group with an expected task or outcome. The questions themselves suggest roles taken by group participants. What kind of role did you see yourself taking? Were you the one who made suggestions about how to make a decision? Did you appear a bit pushy with your ideas? Were you concerned about whether everyone was heard or how people felt about the way the decision making was going? Did you work with other members of your decision-making group to create a small team that advocated for some way of making the decision? All of these answers are significant to a definition of group roles, whether they are helpful or not to the group's progress or the quality of the decision made.

EXERCISE 4.1 NATURAL ROLES YOU TAKE IN GROUPS

Objectives:

1. To analyze group roles in common decision-making situations
2. To exchange feedback about the natural roles taken in groups
3. To lay the foundation for a discussion of effective group-leadership roles

It is important that each person in the class have the opportunity to take part in at least one decision-making process. As well, when groups are engaged in decision making, other class participants observe the process and answer the questions listed.

The students not taking part in the decision-making process split into five observation groups, using the questions provided below to direct their observations.

SET UP:

Eight to ten students sit in a circle, surrounded by class observers. They have 10 minutes to make one of the decisions that follow. Class observers will have pre-assigned behaviours to look for. They will share their observations immediately after each group has made its decision.

Once one group of students has had a chance to make a decision and hear feedback, that group moves into the observer roles and another group moves into the middle circle to work on the next decision.

Individuals receiving feedback must record the information in some way, for use in future exercises.

Decision #1: The class must choose a library representative to hold a two-semester term on the student library advisory committee for the college. Meetings are held once a month.

Decision #2: What should the class do with the pop cans and bottles left around after each class? It is a shame to simply recycle these when the refund money could be put to good use. If it is decided that a fundraiser will happen, who will organize this?

Decision #3: What kind of process should be put in place to say goodbye to students who leave the training program for any reason (e.g., failure, illness, family emergency or lack of interest)?

Observers will look for the following in order to offer feedback to individual group members.

Note: At least one-third of the class should be making a decision, with two-thirds observing:

Observation Group #1:

Who are the high participators in the discussion?
Who are the low participators?
Who seems to be influential (seems to be listened to, has suggestions that others follow, etc.)?
Who seems to have little influence (ideas are ignored or dismissed)?
Does anyone make a suggestion and no one responds?
Are there any shifts in participation during the 10-minute discussion?

Observation Group #2:

Did anyone decide on a topic to be discussed and immediately begin talking about it?
Does anyone seem to be trying to push an idea forward while ignoring others' input?
Does anyone check with others in the group when an idea seems to be moving forward?
Does anyone suggest that the group take a vote?

Observation Group #3:

Does anyone ask for or make suggestions about how to proceed?
Does anyone attempt to summarize what might have been said so far?
Who gives the most ideas, facts or opinions?
Who asks for others' ideas, facts or opinions?
Who keeps the group on track?

Observation Group #4:

Who helps others get in to the discussion?
Who checks to see how everyone is feeling about the way the group is working together?
Who acknowledges the group's progress?
Who attempts to reduce tension by making humorous comments?
Who attempts to ensure that all members are participating?

Observation Group #5:

Name any sub-groupings (cliques).
Is anyone looking left out?
Does anyone behave in ways that cause tension?
What is the general atmosphere of the group (work-oriented, sluggish or play-oriented)?
Who contributes to this atmosphere and how are they doing this?

Once the feedback is shared, individual class members should take the opportunity to internalize specific feedback by considering the following questions:

1. What were others seeing you do during the decision-making exercise?
2. Were these behaviours typical of your usual participation in groups?
3. Were there any surprises for you based on the observer feedback?
4. Are there any of your behaviours you would like to have changed in this decision-making exercise?

Share your personal insights either in your Base Group or with the whole class.

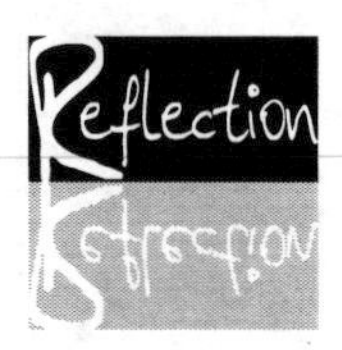

Reflect on any specific feedback you received during Exercise 4.1 about your style of interaction that may have been a surprise to you.

Assigned and Informal Leadership Roles

Assigned or formal designations are the most commonly understood types of leadership. Often when a group comes together for a task of some kind, roles are ascribed to particular individuals in order to accommodate the organization, time commitment and work involved in accomplishing the task. Assigned roles often include familiar positions like team leader, chairperson, secretary or recorder, time keeper, treasurer and heads of sub-committees, as well as the myriad other ways we frame the tasks for which someone must be accountable. Sometimes these assigned roles can be as unique as the essence of the task itself. For example, many of the groups involved in the helping professions include consultants or specialists who are expected to speak to their level of expertise when asked to attend a meeting or take part in a project.

Assigned roles automatically create an expectation from group members and seem to establish a comfortable norm for group participation, expectations and contributions to the task at hand. Depending on their importance to the work of the group, these roles have levels of authority built around them: the *formalized leadership structure* expected within the organization that created the group and any policy or procedure that supports those expectations. By **formalized leadership structure**, we mean the framework within which the assigned roles and expectations of people within that organization are defined. These assigned roles make the job of taking on that position easier in some ways because the expectations are often clearly outlined and the rules are there to follow.

Sometimes assigned roles can restrict our level of participation in groups. If, for example, you assume the responsibility for recording minutes, your participation is often consumed by having to write and listen for all pertinent information. This can become restrictive in terms of your ability to actively engage in the process of any meeting. Or, in some cases, if you are lucky enough to be one of those people whose role is not assigned, you may be tempted to think you can avoid a lot of participation because no one has any prescribed expectation about what you will say or do. This, of course, is not the kind of behaviour expected of a person who has a heightened level of understanding about the kinds of leadership roles each and every member of a group should take.

Of more importance to the discussion in this chapter are informal roles or expectations. These transcend an appointment or a position. Even if we have a formalized assigned role, we still have to take responsibility for participating in ways that move the group forward.

Leadership as a Group Role

The term *role* is defined as "a part played in a play, opera, etc; the leading role; a part played in real life" (Avis, Drysdale, Gregg, Neufeld, & Scargill, 1983). In any group, you play a part or role that affects its overall function. In Chapter 3, we discussed group development and the healthy, productive ways groups grow and succeed in the accomplishment of a goal. Integral to this high level of group development are the **leadership roles**, or functions, each of its members perform to a common end. The idea of seeing ourselves as leaders in all group situations is not something many of us consider. This means taking a look at the concept of shared leadership in groups and realizing that the responsibility for effective group function lies with each and every one of its members. Sometimes this means taking on roles that may not feel natural to you and yet fill a gap necessary to the group's effectiveness. As well, it means understanding that some of your natural leadership roles are helpful and that the work is to figure out just how and when your skills are going to be most useful.

Shared Leadership

If you take a closer look at Exercise 4.1 or other leadership questionnaires you may have completed in class, you will see that some questions focus on what the group is doing and others on how the group is working together. These two areas of group role identification have been described by Bales (1950) as functional to the ultimate success of all groups. Not only should groups be able to get the job done, they should do so in ways that satisfy their members and retain cohesiveness within the group. Bales defines the roles related to the content of the work as task functions and those roles that focus on the satisfaction of group members as maintenance functions. Both are leadership roles that can be shared by all group members. In this sense leadership is everyone's responsibility, and the role we play contributes to whatever a group might need at any given time, whether it is getting on with the work or making sure group members are all on board.

Every group has a variety of needs in connection with the completion of its task and the satisfaction or maintenance of its members. These needs are unique to its definition, its membership, its setting of goals, the task at hand and any other circumstances that affect its existence. With a thorough understanding of the task and maintenance functions that contribute to effective group development comes the ability to analyze what any particular group might need and how certain behaviours might meet that need.

Task refers to *what* the group is trying to achieve and *maintenance* refers to the process of *how* the group members work together toward the completion of the task. Remember that the ultimate goal, as discussed in Chapter 3, is a productive, cohesive, trusting and personally satisfying group experience.

Defining Task Functions

So what are the typical **task leadership functions** that contribute to the ability of a group to get the job done? Groups get together for a reason and that reason becomes the task, or work, they hope to accomplish. Even social groups have a task. It may be to re-connect or catch up on news or simply have a good time. If this doesn't happen, some group members feel a sense of dissatisfaction. In a group that has a specific job to accomplish and task needs are not met, that feeling intensifies and may be fear, annoyance or anger. Again, there is a continuum of task importance contingent on the reason for any group's existence.

What follows are well-known task roles necessary to the completion of the work of the group. Some roles are similar or operate in conjunction with another. These roles may or may not be performed by the same person. For example, an information giver may also offer an opinion, yet an opinion giver may not have the information to offer and so would not necessarily perform both roles. It is important to understand exactly what function each of these task roles fulfills in the objective of completing whatever work needs to be done by groups. By recognizing the role of each of these functions, individuals can identify which roles feel most natural and comfortable to them and can decide whether they can take on those roles when others are not performing them.

The following are descriptions of each of the task functions, with some examples of what they might look like. We also have included some cautions and suggestions in the "What to look out for" section for when these functions might detract from or enhance the success of the group.

Initiators

Initiators are those people who suggest ways of doing things, come up with new ideas, propose goals and look at new ways of approaching problems.

What this might look like: When was the last time you were in a group and someone said, "Let's get going on this. I think I have an idea about how this may work out."? Initiators not only get the ball rolling at the beginning of a task, they also find ways of moving through problems when groups get stuck, by suggesting new approaches to the process. These may also be the people who help create an agenda or a timeline to help the group move through the work. They may also be the ones who help keep the subject on topic.

What to look out for: Sometimes initiators become so focused on getting the job done that there is little room for any other kind of interaction among group members. The agenda or timeline become pressure points for those people with an overwhelming need to keep the work moving toward the goal. This can irritate other group members who need the time to talk problems through. As well, changing ways of attacking a problem is helpful, yet must be well-timed and respectful of the speed at which all group members process information. Initiators are vital to task accomplishment, and when we discuss maintenance leadership functions, we will suggest ways of ensuring that all group members are comfortable with the pace set by this task function.

Information Givers

Information givers offer facts, relevant information and experience that have to do with the task.

What this might look like: Obviously when the group is in the process of task accomplishment there is a great need for information to come to the attention of all participants. In formal groups where a consultant is hired or someone is researching a particular topic, the role of information giver is understood by all. In informal groups, any person who offers ideas or facts that are relevant to the topic is taking on the role of information giver.

What to look out for: The biggest issue with information givers is staying on topic and staying true to the task at hand. Sometimes it makes sense to have group members assigned to this role, researching and presenting important information. Depending on the goal or content of the project, the people with the most expertise should naturally take the responsibility of sharing their knowledge to the betterment of the task. They should also present information to other group members in ways that are understandable, easy to absorb and relevant.

Opinion Givers

Opinion givers state their beliefs in relation to whatever is being discussed in the moment. The biggest difference between opinion givers and information givers is that the opinion givers comment on how they feel about a topic or suggestion, in relation to what they value, and information givers are more objective in stating information and experience.

What this might look like: If you hear someone say, "I think that . . . ." or "I believe that . . . .", then an opinion is being offered. Sometimes an opinion comes veiled in a strong, emotional value statement. For example, a comment like, "Those programs got more money than they deserved!" may sound like a factual piece of information, yet is an opinion based on someone's judgment.

Opinion giving helps all group members get a better sense of where others are coming from, which can be particularly helpful during the storming or control stage of group development.

What to look out for: If opinion giving gets out of control (and we see this often), the task stalls due to lack of real information and the back-and-forth of unsubstantiated ideas that not everyone can agree on. If progress slows, and you are wondering why, listen for opinions and either ask for examples that clarify the statements (see the clarifier function discussed on p. 88) or comment on the fact that the group is stalled and there may be a better way of getting back on task (see the role of process observer discussed on p. 93).

Information Seekers

The role of information seeker is taken when someone requests facts, ideas or relevant information.

What this might look like: These group members want to know more about the content of the discussion. They may use questions or suggest that they will do the work of finding out more about certain topics. Remember that information seeking happens within the group context rather than individuals gathering data outside of the group context. Essentially, questions for more information help most of the other group members to better understand the topic. Well-timed questions for information help spur the creative process.

What to look out for: Some people need lots and lots of information in order to feel totally confident in future decision-making processes. Sometimes it can be overwhelming to others in the group and may seem like a waste of time, particularly when the information gathering is preventing the group from actually getting to the process of making a decision.

Opinion Seekers

Opinion seekers look for some clarification about the way group members feel about the content of the task or topic at hand. These people help the group by bringing out values and opinions that may be influencing the progress of the group, yet remain hidden until asked about.

What this might look like: Opinion seekers will ask either individual members or the whole group about what they may think about a particular discussion topic or suggestions for action. These are not the people who ask about how others might be feeling in general or how the group feels about the way the process is going (we discuss describers of emotional climate on p. 92). Opinion seekers are simply interested in moving the task forward by gauging what people think about the content being discussed. This moves the group forward by putting everything out on the table.

Remember that opinion seeking is beneficial at any time during a group's time together, because it increases the understanding the members have of each other in relation to the task.

What to look out for: If you find that the group is engaging in a long debate, asking others about how they feel about the actual discussion under way may help group members to clarify which values are important to them with respect to the topic. Often we become so embroiled in making our own point that the task function of opinion seeking is lost in the throes of a growing argument. The function of opinion seeking works with other task functions to break these often frustrating points of impasse.

Be careful not to overload on this function. Asking group members continually what they think or how they feel about a decision, task content or discussion topic can become downright irritating and prove to stall group progress as well.

Elaborators or Clarifiers

These people expand on ideas, clear up confusion and generally interpret salient aspects of the topic at hand. Not only do the elaborators or clarifiers extend the subject, they make connections that pull together information to help the group understand what needs to happen next.

What this might look like: Elaborators or clarifiers have a very important task function. These people offer examples or re-define the meanings of certain topics or ideas in ways that help other group members better understand the direction the task is taking. An example of something an elaborator might say would be, "So you are saying that the money being allocated for this budget item is really coming out of our travel account." This comment might clarify some information that may not have been a part of a budget conversation where group members have hedged or hesitated with their suggestions. In this example, the clarifier pointed to an inevitable example of what consequence certain monetary decisions might have. The clarifier got to the point quickly.

An example of elaboration would be something like, "If we adopt this proposal, I see lots of great opportunities for the clients in our care. Moving them out into the community will help us make connections with the parks board and the seniors group. We might even get the support of the City on this one . . . ." This person is openly envisioning the opportunities that a certain decision on a proposal would have. This kind of creative process is an energizer.

What to look out for: When in the role of clarifier or elaborator, it is important to watch timing and the tone of voice being used. Obviously if something is not clearly stated, the elaborator role is helpful. However, it can be most annoying if someone begins to paraphrase or clarify information when all the facts have not been presented. These roles work best when there is lots of information on the table and someone needs to sort out the pieces and clean up any confusion.

If not careful with wording and tone of voice, clarifiers and elaborators may come across as patronizing and all-knowing in their process of clearing up confusion. There must be sensitivity, respect and simplicity in the use of this task role function.

Summarizers

Summarizers pull together related ideas or suggestions and restate them back to the group members after they have discussed them. They may even offer an obvious conclusion or possible decision for the group to consider. Summarizing happens throughout the task and is helpful to those group members who have trouble attending to a lot of detail.

What this might look like: Summarizers look a bit like coordinators in that they seem able to take the many bits and pieces of discussion and decision making and come up with one or two sentences that describe what has been done up to that particular point in the task. This role is discriminated from the clarifier role in that its purpose is to condense, while the clarifier's purpose is to get to the point. When there is a lot of information and decision making happening and some group members are feeling lost in the details, summarizers help others by stating in very simple terms what has been accomplished so far.

What to look out for: Many groups suffer when members do not take the time to pull together the many fragments of work in progress in ways that focus the process. This role gets lost because, again, group members get drawn into information and opinion sharing until there is so much information available that the group gets bogged down and confused. Checking out what you think you have heard by summarizing during a given task will inevitably be helpful to someone in the group and begin the process of clearing up confusion.

Obviously, at the end of any meeting of a project group, summarizing helps group members to acknowledge achievements and accomplishments to date and sets the stage for the next meeting. See Exercise 4.2 and Table 4.1 on page 90.

In this discussion of task roles, are there roles that have helped you understand more clearly the way you function in groups? Are you comfortable with this new awareness?

EXERCISE 4.2 TASK-FOCUSED DISCUSSION

Objectives:

1. To experience the effects of task-focused decision making
2. To practise task leadership behaviours
3. To have some fun with task roles

The set up for this exercise involves a group of seven volunteers sitting in a circle surrounded by the rest of the class (observers). All class participants (both volunteers and observers) must familiarize themselves with the elements of task functions, as described earlier.

Volunteers will each receive one of the seven task functions discussed above (initiator, information giver, opinion giver, information seeker, opinion seeker, elaborator/clarifier or summarizer). Each member of the volunteer group will receive his or her task function written on a piece of paper and is encouraged not to share his or her role with the other group members. Using the text description, each volunteer must prepare to simulate that function during a decision-making task. It is important that each volunteer understand that he or she must use *only* that function during the discussion.

Each volunteer should choose one or two students in the class to observe his or her participation. Using the observation form (see Table 4.1 on page 90) these observers must record instances of task leadership behaviour, checking off each behaviour demonstrated. At the end of the exercise the observers will guess which function the volunteers were assigned.

Discuss one of the following issues in a 15-minute conversation:

1. Discuss some ways you can ensure that people keep your classroom clean by taking care of their own messes. Prepare a statement with a rationale to support your decision.
2. How much personal information do you think students should be expected to disclose in an interpersonal communications class? Prepare a statement with a rationale to support your decision.
3. Do you think friendships that develop amongst students contribute to the richness of classroom learning or detract from it? Prepare a statement with a rationale to support your decision.

When the decision is made, it should be shared with the whole class.

Volunteers then discuss with their observers exactly which task functions were noted. Did the observers correctly guess the task role being simulated?

After small-group discussion, the class is encouraged to debrief the whole experience of using only task functions to make a decision. As well, there should be discussion of how many volunteer decision makers actually performed only their role and whether another role that felt more comfortable was played, either in addition to or instead of the assigned one.

TABLE 4.1 Observation Form for Task Behaviours

Behaviour	*Demonstration of Skill*
Initiator	
Information Giver	
Opinion Giver	
Information Seeker	
Opinion Seeker	
Elaborator/Clarifier	
Summarizer	

Were there any reactions to this feedback? How did you feel in this task role, and did it match what leadership roles generally come naturally to you?

Defining Maintenance Functions

All of the task functions contribute to the actual outcomes or productivity of each group's time together. However, in our discussion of effective group criteria in Chapter 3, we discussed outcomes that transcend the product and speak to less tangible elements like cohesion, transformational learning and trust building. As you read through the task functions above, it is easy to see that they are product-oriented in that the outcome is the most important thing. The question remains, what functions contribute to those highly effective groups where individuals leave the group experience feeling satisfied, respected, involved, valued and generally transformed by the time spent with others? These types of groups place significance on **maintenance leadership functions** that serve to build a climate of mutuality and what some term *community*.

You may have participated in student-project groups or committees where you accomplished the work that needed to be done, but you left the experience feeling empty, dissatisfied and not totally trusting that the product of your efforts met your standards. More than likely, this group was so focused on the task to be accomplished that it failed to look after the sense of well-being and connectedness of the group members. The functions that are described below will help identify the ways group members can contribute to a more positive atmosphere. Again, as with task functions, some of these behaviours will feel natural to you, and some may feel awkward. All contribute to a more effective group experience and, ultimately, to a richer task outcome. It is up to each individual to notice the need for maintenance and, even if it feels awkward, perform that function to the betterment of the group's process.

The following are descriptions of well-known maintenance functions:

Gatekeepers

Gatekeepers is a term used to describe those people who invite others to participate when they notice that some group members are not getting involved in discussion. They may also suggest some kind of system where everyone gets a chance to have input.

What this might look like: This function is easy to spot. This person is the one who says something like, "I notice that some people have not said anything yet. Aiko, how do you feel about the issues we are having with this client?" They may suggest doing a round table, checking in to assess what everyone has to say about a topic. Gatekeepers want everyone to feel included and heard.

What to look out for: There is potential for this role to move into a caretaking stance, meaning that the gatekeeper begins to take a greater responsibility to ensure that an individual is being heard than the individual takes for himself or herself. In other words, gatekeepers must be careful that others not begin to rely on them for their air-time. This can also irritate those group members who are contributing and losing patience with non-participators.

Constant checking that everyone is having a say may also irritate group members because, if it is not done subtly, it can easily interfere with group process and task accomplishment. Groups handle non-participators in many different ways (see non-functional behaviours on p. 102). If gatekeepers are performing their function in sensitive and subtle ways, the group process will be inclusive and feel accepting for all.

Encouragers

Encouragers do just that, encourage. These people show acceptance of others' ideas and input, making it a point to notice their contributions with positive reinforcement. Encouragement is seen in both verbal and non-verbal behaviours.

What this might look like: Encouraging responses are natural, positive and accepting. When someone says, "I like that!" or "That's a good idea!", he or she is encouraging the contributor. This serves to reinforce that person's participation and to validate his or her input. Encouraging responses can also take the form of nods, smiles, open body language and an overall positive demeanour. All create a nurturing atmosphere for everyone and can be a powerful tool for group building.

What to look out for: As powerful as the role of encourager can be, if it is overdone or does not come across as sincere, it can become patronizing and demeaning. Body language is of particular significance here and affects the message of encouragement we may be sending. Body language must be congruent with verbal messages and appropriate to the interaction. If someone is responding to our message with encouraging comments, yet at the same time looking in another direction, writing or handing something over to another group member, the words lose their value. As well, uninvited, intrusive and overly sympathetic encouragement feels patronizing and somewhat irritating if it is not relevant or welcome.

You know you are being an effective encourager when others seem to respond easily and comfortably to your message. There may be a feeling of connection and appreciation in the moment.

Harmonizers

This function is very much like a mediation role. Harmonizers note conflict (some also call this a diagnosing role) and suggest opening up what they perceive to be tension through discussion or some other way of reaching a more mutually agreeable decision.

What this might look like: This role is natural to some individuals who seem to be able to sense when other group members might be feeling somewhat conflicted with where the group is moving with its decision making. They check on individuals and point out what they notice in a non-biased, non-judgmental way that supports others. They focus on the issue at hand and avoid pinpointing individuals. An example might be a person who says, "We seem to be stuck right now. Some of us are worried about playgrounds that are safe, and others want an environment that challenges children's physical development. Let's think out of the box here. Is there some way we can have a safe environment that is also creative and challenging?" Here the harmonizer may appear to be attempting to keep the group on task, yet is actually facilitating process by identifying the emotional climate. As well, the harmonizer is focusing deliberately on the issue of divergent ideas and not personalizing any disagreements.

What to look out for: You will know you have handled the harmonizer role successfully if other group members respond favourably to your comments or suggestions. They will readily accept suggestions about ways of exploring their differences and find commonalties that might resolve any tension or conflict. If group members rebel at the notion that someone has the gall to point out that they are in conflict with someone else in the group, you may have somehow evoked defensiveness. Some people do this through patronizing or pointing out the person rather than the issue when attempting to unearth what they believe to be uncomfortable tension. Sensitivity and respect is the key here, along with well-honed communication skills.

If no one is taking on this mediation role, conflict will move in very mysterious ways. It will either move underground until it erupts in ways that might stall the group permanently, or it will simply continue to brew and interfere constantly with the work of the group. If you find yourself in a group where there is continual bickering and sniping, then someone has to take the time to unearth exactly what the conflict is (or might have been). Often groups avoid working through basic ideological differences, and because they have not been identified early in the conflict, the original issue becomes clouded with other unrelated difficulties. In these situations, a strong harmonizer role could easily have prevented this discomfort.

Describers of Emotional Climate

These people describe the feelings they sense within the group. Describers of emotional climate take the time to ask group members how they are reacting to what is happening at various stages of group decision making. They often begin this process by sharing what is going on for them. By describing prevalent emotions, group members call attention to themselves and others in ways that open up the interpersonal climate. A lot of energy gets used up when people experience emotion and at the same time try to focus on the task. Once the emotion is labeled and there is the opportunity to acknowledge and discuss how everyone is feeling, that energy becomes freed up and available for more useful things like focusing on the task.

What this might look like: A description of the emotional climate might simply be a general comment about what someone is noting in the group at any given time; for example, "Boy, it feels like we are all drained after that hard work!" or "I feel frustrated, and it looks like others are, too. Let's get on with this." By openly acknowledging what emotions are evident in the group, group members might open up about what they are feeling about the task at hand. Even members who are not experiencing this particular emotion benefit from hearing what others are experiencing. This enhances cohesiveness and in turn leads to increased productivity.

What to look out for: Once again, style of communication, tone of voice, timing and all kinds of interpersonal nuances are factors that contribute to success in this role. Remember that the point of this role is to help group members to identify emotions that might be inhibiting their process at any given time. This function is not about talking about feelings with the sole purpose of becoming closer as a group emotionally. This might be a byproduct of the effective use of this role, but, again, the idea is to air the emotions so that group members can get on with the task.

Consensus Testers

Consensus testers pay attention to group discussions and when it seems that group members are close to making a joint decision, they identify the stage in the process and seek confirmation that the group is ready to close the discussion and make the decision. Even though this role appears to be task-focused, it is far different because of its attention to the process of the group rather than just the product of the work.

What this might look like: Some call the process of consensus testing "sending up a trial balloon". For example, a consensus tester might say something like, "It looks like we have all had a chance to talk about what we think about this issue. I am wondering if we are ready to make a decision about how to build this playground." Or the consensus tester might say something as simple as, "Let's vote!" to help focus the process of information sharing and encourage the group to move on.

What to look out for: As long as the consensus tester simply "tests" and is careful not to jump to decision making before the group can make an informed and helpful decision, this role is effective in calling attention to the process. Group members who still want to engage in discussion will not feel pushed unnecessarily when consensus testing is done with sensitivity and, again, focuses on the process and not the people.

When you have a group that wants to gather information and discuss all of the possible ramifications of a particular decision, the consensus tester plays an invaluable role in helping the group pay attention to its process.

Process Observers

Another role that appears to be task-driven, yet is really a maintenance function, is the process observer. Process observers observe and identify for the group exactly what they see happening in order to improve the way that the group works together. This is not necessarily an encourager role because these people notice what is not working and use their observations (hopefully) to strategize with the group ways to improve process.

What this might look like: Process observers comment on how the group is functioning. A process observer might say something like, "We have been going back and forth with this issue for 10 minutes now and getting nowhere. I wonder if there is another way we can approach this whole question." Notice that this person has paid attention to the way in which the discussion has been operating (time, amount of discourse and lack of progress) rather than blaming any particular person for the stalled process.

What to look out for: Be aware that a continual overview of the way in which the group is working could be perceived as intrusive. People may become irritated by too many process suggestions and simply refuse to consider new ways of working through the task. At the beginning of any task, process observers are important to creating effective structures that help unblock any difficulties. Once the task is underway this role continues to be important as a way of monitoring group member satisfaction with the process.

This is a very important maintenance function, and if it feels natural to you, use your powers of observation and sensitivity to the group's receptiveness when making suggestions for change.

Tension Relievers

Tension relieving is often accomplished through the use of humour. It also can be simply the suggestion that a group take a break or bring snacks and other goodies to meetings. It is a powerful maintenance function because it inspires cohesiveness and, even though it takes time away from the task, it usually serves to energize the group.

What this might look like: These people make humorous comments during a get-together of the group. These comments are usually linked to the task or process and may look like gentle sarcasm, puns or self-deprecation. How can one describe humour that is relevant to any particular group process? It is not just someone telling a joke, but rather a person making witty comments that strike group members as funny.

Often groups forget about the importance of taking breaks because they are worried about the time taken from task accomplishment. If you have ever experienced being in a group that scheduled short breaks and made sure all group members had a chance to re-energize, you probably remember that the task was still completed on time. On the contrary, if you have experienced long meetings without a break, that were completely scheduled around the task alone, you may remember loss of focus and increased irritability among group members that slowed down progress. Both group experiences may have produced the desired outcome, but the group that took breaks probably had increased cohesiveness and higher levels of personal effectiveness because group members looked after these important human-process needs.

What to look out for: Obviously humour is not funny to everyone in the same way. Sometimes when the group responds with laughter at our jokes or innuendoes, we keep going and others become distracted and annoyed. Too much humour can serve to detract from the group's enjoyment of being together rather than serve to enhance its process. Watch out for this.

Timing is important when considering breaks. You do not want to interrupt the momentum of the group, but you also want to ensure that some time is taken to re-energize. As well, consider the amount of time you are going to be together and plan accordingly. If you only have a very short time together (e.g., one hour), then you had best have your tea during the meeting. Common sense should prevail here. See Exercise 4.3 and Table 4.2.

Which maintenance roles have you seen yourself engaged in? Are you surprised that they contributed to group effectiveness?

EXERCISE 4.3 MAINTENANCE-FOCUSED DISCUSSION

Objectives:

1. **To experience the effects of maintenance-focused decision making**
2. **To practise maintenance leadership behaviours**
3. **To have some fun with maintenance roles**

The set up for this exercise involves a group of seven volunteers sitting in a circle surrounded by the rest of the class (observers). All class participants (both volunteers and observers) must familiarize themselves with the elements of maintenance functions, as described earlier.

Volunteers will each receive one of the seven maintenance functions discussed above (gatekeeper, encourager, harmonizer, describer of emotional climate, consensus tester, process observer or tension reliever). Each member of the volunteer group will receive his or her maintenance function written on a piece of paper and is encouraged not to share his or her role with the other group members. Using the text description, each volunteer must prepare to simulate that function during a decision-making task. It is important that each volunteer understand that he or she must use *only* that function during the discussion.

Each volunteer should choose one or two students in the class to observe his or her participation. Using the observation form (see Table 4.2), these observers must record instances of maintenance leadership behaviour, checking off each behaviour demonstrated. At the end of the exercise the observers will guess which function the volunteers were assigned.

Discuss one of the following issues in a 15-minute conversation:

1. Should students be evaluated with a Pass/Fail, or should they be evaluated with a traditional letter grade for practicum assessment? Prepare a statement with a rationale to support your decision.
2. Should there be a limit to the amount of class time instructors spend answering student questions about assignments? Prepare a statement with a rationale to support your decision.
3. Should post-secondary institutions have restrictions on calling instructors at home? Prepare a statement with a rationale to support your decision.

When the decision is made, it should be shared with the whole class.

Volunteers then discuss with their observers exactly which maintenance functions were noted? Did the observers correctly guess the maintenance role being simulated?

After small-group discussion, the class is encouraged to debrief the whole experience of using only maintenance functions to make a decision. As well, there should be discussion of how many volunteer decision makers actually performed only their role and whether another role that felt more comfortable was played, either in addition to or instead or the assigned one.

TABLE 4.2 Observation Form for Maintenance Behaviours

Behaviour	*Demonstration of Skill*
Gatekeeper	
Encourager	
Harmonizer	
Describer of Emotional Climate	
Consensus Tester	
Process Observer	
Tension Reliever	

Were there any reactions to this feedback? How did you feel in this maintenance role, and did it match what leadership roles generally come naturally to you?

Summarizing Task and Maintenance Behaviours

Both the task and maintenance functions are shared amongst all group members. Individuals may take on more than one function, as you may have experienced having now participated in Exercises 4.2 and 4.3. These exercises were designed to help you practise particular task and maintenance roles. You may have felt uneasy when restricted to only one role in a decision-making process because it is natural to take on a number of both task and maintenance roles.

Earlier in this chapter (Exercise 4.1), you explored some leadership behaviours that came naturally to you. These are likely the roles that you will move into comfortably without much conscious thought. Obviously, time and experience will serve to enhance, or fine-tune, those roles. However, there are times when you may have to move into one of the other task or maintenance roles in order to better support the group's process. Eventually, you will learn to recognize what task or maintenance function will best serve the group, to move out of your comfort zone and to take on that role. Ultimately, the more skilled all group members are in all of the task and maintenance roles, the more effective the group's process.

A balance of the task and maintenance functions is important to the quality of the group's experience. In the task-only exercise, Exercise 4.2, you may have easily come to a decision yet thought that something was missing in the process, particularly when the decisions were about human issues. In the maintenance-only exercise, Exercise 4.3, the decision was probably hard to achieve, as members were so busy focusing on process. These two exercises were purposefully designed to help you experience the impact of a lack of one set of leadership functions.

But is there a perfect balance of task and maintenance roles that ensures group effectiveness? No, there is not. There are too many variables that dictate whether task or maintenance factors dominate the process. For example, when a group is first getting together and trying to determine what they have to accomplish, task roles are prevalent and helpful to group members as structures are created. However, if a group is in the storming stage of group development, maintenance roles like process observer or harmonizer can help identify the emotions involved and move the process along.

Variables like the stage of group development, the group membership and other dimensions explored in earlier chapters significantly contribute to the unique task and maintenance leadership needs of any particular group. What we want to make clear is that *both* task and maintenance functions are important to all groups and that we can increase the effectiveness of groups by engaging in well-timed, appropriate use of these leadership roles. It is your responsibility to stay alert to imbalances and the need for a change of leadership direction (see Exercise 4.4A and Exercise 4.4B).

EXERCISE 4.4A BALANCED GROUP LEADERSHIP ROLES

Objectives:

1. To experience the effects of both task and maintenance leadership roles in decision making
2. To practise assigned task and maintenance roles
3. To practise the timing of task and maintenance roles to maximize their effectiveness

The set up for this exercise involves a group of seven volunteers sitting in a circle surrounded by the rest of the class (observers). Each volunteer chooses one or two observers. Each observer has a copy of the Observation Form for Task and Maintenance Behaviours (see Table 4.3 on p. 99) and records the number of times his or her assigned volunteer demonstrates specific task or maintenance roles.

Volunteers will each receive one of the seven maintenance functions (gatekeeper, encourager, harmonizer, describer of emotional climate, consensus tester, process observer or tension reliever) and one of the seven task functions (initiator, information giver, opinion giver, information seeker, opinion seeker, elaborator/clarifier or summarizer). Each member of the volunteer group will receive his or her task and maintenance functions written on a piece of paper and is encouraged not to share his or her roles with other group members. Using the text descriptions, each volunteer must prepare to simulate those functions during a decision-making task. It is important that each volunteer understand that he or she must use only those functions during the discussion.

Discuss one of the following issues in a 15-minute conversation:

1. Instructors are considering having a dress code for this program. Provide input on what that dress code should be. Prepare a statement with a rationale to support your decision.
2. When a student dresses provocatively in class (not in practicum), is it up to the instructor to give him or her feedback? Prepare a statement with a rationale to support your decision.
3. To what extent should a college or university program accommodate a student who has had an illness that has resulted in lengthy absenteeism? Prepare a statement with a rationale to support your decision.
4. Is it the student's responsibility, or is it the instructor's job to monitor and address side talking? Prepare a statement with a rationale to support your decision.

When the decision is made, it should be shared with the whole group.

Volunteers then discuss with their observers exactly which task and maintenance functions were noted? Did the observer correctly guess the roles being simulated?

As a class, share the experience of participating from a more balanced leadership perspective. As observers, how easy was it to determine the roles being played?

TABLE 4.3 Observation Form for Task and Maintenance Behaviours

Task Behaviour	*Demonstration of Skill*
Initiator	
Information Giver	
Opinion Giver	
Information Seeker	
Opinion Seeker	
Elaborator/Clarifier	
Summarizer	
Maintenance Behaviour	*Demonstration of Skill*
Gatekeeper	
Encourager	
Harmonizer	
Describer of Emotional Climate	
Consensus Tester	
Process Observer	
Tension Reliever	

EXERCISE 4.4B BALANCED GROUP ROLES

Objectives:

1. **To experience the effects of both task and maintenance leadership roles in decision making**
2. **To practise the timing of task and maintenance roles to maximize their effectiveness**

The group of seven volunteers from the previous exercise will choose another one of the discussion topics from Exercises 4.2, 4.3 and 4.4A. Observers will continue to use the Observation Form for Task and Maintenance Behaviours (Table 4.3 above) to document the functions observed.

The volunteers will engage in a discussion and reach a decision within 15 minutes using whatever task or maintenance functions seem natural to them. After completion of this decision-making exercise, observers will share feedback noting the functions they observed and any functions that seemed to be missing. Members of the decision-making group will discuss the difference between using assigned roles and having the freedom to choose the roles that felt most comfortable.

All members of the class are encouraged to take the opportunity to engage in a similar decision-making group in order to practise the skills of effective task and maintenance leadership roles.

Leadership Issues in Groups

There are times in groups when members focus too much on the task or pay much too much attention to the process, to the detriment of the work to be done. Some examples have been noted in the "What to look out for" sections of the task and maintenance function descriptions. Imbalances in the focus on task or maintenance can take many forms, and it is next to impossible to identify all the ways in which groups may get off track. There are, however, some subtle indicators that signal the need for a change in process.

Was there a leadership role that you found most natural to you? If so, has it been observed as effective?

Too Much Task

The following symptoms may be an indication of too much focus on the task:

- Group members are taking a lot of time to discuss the timeline and the way they will structure their work.
- There are too many changes in the way the group approaches its task.
- The work timelines are too structured and inflexible.
- All group members seem to be offering opinions and information and do not seem to be getting anywhere.
- Someone is always directing the discussion toward the task with little opportunity for taking a break or for humour.
- Little attention is paid to group members who seem frustrated or dissatisfied with the process.
- Momentum seems to be totally task-driven, and members who seem unable to stay involved are ignored.
- Only the people who actively contribute to the job get attention.
- Little acknowledgment is made of the importance of group member satisfaction.
- Group members feel rushed, and something seems to be missing during their time together.

This listing, though not exhaustive, has the overwhelming theme of getting the job done, whether through consistent attention paid to the work or through a need to find methods that will make that work go faster. The tension will build in this kind of unbalanced process because group members become obsessed with the best use of time. They do not see the value of investing time in the more human components of working together.

Again, there can be many symptoms that arise from groups that focus too much on task completion. If you feel frustrated, rushed or irritated by the lack of opportunity to relate on a personal level to other group members, take the time to observe what is going on in the group. Is anyone taking on a gatekeeper role and checking that all group participants are being heard? Is there someone lightening the atmosphere (tension reliever) or commenting on the feelings they perceive existing in the group (describer of emotional climate)? Experiencing the feelings listed above might signal a need for increased attention to maintenance leadership functions. This will serve to acknowledge feelings, support contributions everyone is making and inevitably improve cohesion, trust and, ultimately, the productivity of the group.

An unbalanced focus on task is common in groups required to complete projects or make decisions. Task leadership helps set goals, structure the work, delegate responsibility and generally ensure that all group members are contributing toward the final outcome. Unfortunately, groups seem to forget the human needs in their zest to organize and be productive. Without attention paid to process through maintenance functions, the quality of any task or product will suffer.

Too Much Maintenance

The following symptoms may be an indication of too much focus on maintenance:

- The group is spending a lot of time socializing or sharing what they have done since they last met.
- The work is not getting accomplished, and group members are feeling frustrated and worried.
- There is a lot of joking around and side talk.
- It takes a long time to get the work started when the group gets together.
- People are constantly checking in on how others feel about developments.
- There is little structure to the work, and nothing feels organized.
- Often the group gets off topic, but no one helps the group get back on task.
- There seem to be many people talking about impressions of how they feel about the task, yet no real progress.

If you participated in Exercise 4.3, you experienced the frustration of going around and around in a discussion without any outcome or sense of productivity. An over-abundance of maintenance is actually rare in any kind of project group. Sometimes, though, when groups have been together for a long time, they temporarily lose sight of the work and lapse into periods when they spend more energy on personal discussion than on task completion. As well, particularly in the helping professions, you may find yourself in a group with others who, due to the nature of their work, have a natural tendency to focus on people and give less attention to the importance of the task.

If you find yourself involved in a group that is strongly focused on maintenance you may experience similar feelings to those that resulted from too much focus on task. The difference is that the frustration is coming from lack of accomplishment and achievement. In unbalanced task-focused groups, you feel rushed and overwhelmed in the drive to get the job done. In unbalanced maintenance-focused groups, feelings of anxiety arise from the lack of movement toward goals that have been set. You may even feel irritated when ideas move off topic, and the conversation is not contributing meaningfully to the work.

Again, you must look out for an obvious lack of task leadership in the group. Is anyone getting the group started at the beginning of each get-together (initiator)? Are thoughts and ideas that are relevant to the task being presented and noted (information giver and opinion giver)? Is someone pulling together related ideas and drawing conclusions for the group (summarizer)? These roles will help keep group members engaged in the task and help to counteract any unbalanced attention to process.

There may be a misperception that groups in the helping professions must operate totally within a framework that pays 100% attention to the human needs of its members. Remember that even in the helping professions where the job is focused on people, it is necessary to discriminate between process and content and to ensure a balance of each.

Non-Functional Behaviours

It is inevitable in a group's work together that difficult situations or dynamics arise. We label the behaviour of individuals who actually impede the progress of a group as **non-functional behaviours**. Recognize that defining a non-functional behaviour is a highly subjective and interpretive process. This means that we have to be aware of our own values, beliefs and attitudes as we take note of the behaviours listed below and respond in ways that bring the group back on track. All these behaviours occur periodically during group work. It is when they persist or happen regularly that they become non-functional.

We may interpret someone's aggressive style of questioning or offering an opinion as disruptive (and maybe even a bit frightening), yet this person may be contributing effectively to the task in the only way he or she knows how. This is an important place for reflection-in-action, as you consider whether certain behaviours are interfering with the overall progress of the group, or whether your reaction to that behaviour is clouding your judgment of that person's contributions. Your reaction may come from a value about ways people communicate verbally. For example, if you grew up in a family that spoke quietly and rarely challenged each other, you may view an assertive, loud communicator as someone exerting his or her own power rather than contributing to the process. If you grew up in a family where you had to be loud in order to be heard, you may view the assertive, loud communicator as a helpful group member. There are, however, instances when individuals engage in behaviours that are downright irritating, regardless of your interpretation.

When non-functional behaviours develop, it is a sign that the group is not meeting the needs of its members. This is not to say that it is not frustrating to experience the kinds of difficult dynamics that prevent full group participation. It is just that there is the risk of simply blaming an individual for his or her behaviour rather than facing the fact that the group itself has to take responsibility for the existence of this behaviour. This is another opportunity for shared leadership.

What follows is a description of some significant non-functional behaviours and suggestions of ways groups can respond:

Blockers

What this might look like: Blockers impede group process in a number of ways. They might argue or question in ways that stall the group. This may become personal and persistent. Blockers often move the group off topic with unrelated, personal stories that interfere with the ongoing work.

Blockers may also behave aggressively by attacking other group members, interrupting others and demanding attention. Again, this may present itself as a personal attack on others, their ideas and their value systems.

What to do about it: Try to avoid reinforcing this behaviour by attending to it with arguments, answering the questions or competing with your own input. These people need attention and are getting it in the only way they know how. Responding to the actual behaviour and satisfying these attempts for recognition will only intensify the blocking. As difficult as it may be, this is the time for a gatekeeper (maintenance function) to re-direct attention to other group members who are less vocal. If other members participate more, blockers will have less airtime.

If a blocker becomes aggressive and engages in personal attacks, then bullying is taking place and must be addressed. Individual group members affected by the bullying behaviour can either use the group forum to share the impact of that behaviour or choose to do so one-on-one, outside the group. This is a highly complicated and very difficult situation to respond to. Factors that will affect the timing and location of your response are countless. You may choose to confront the blocking within the group immediately. This may feel safer than confronting the person alone, yet may become an argument and reinforce the behaviour. Your communication ability, your level of confidence and your own values about confrontation are considerations that will affect the success of a one-on-one encounter. This will be discussed more thoroughly in Chapter 6.

Jokers

What this might look like: Jokers are tension relievers (maintenance function) taken to the extreme. While occasional joking can be a welcome relief in the midst of hard work, constant joking and "goofing around" disrupts the concentration of group members and gets in the way of concerted efforts to focus on the task at hand. Joking becomes non-functional when individuals stop contributing to the forward movement of the group and spend the majority of their time being witty or sarcastic, or engaging in side talk. This means they are no longer participating constructively in the group's process and are likely preventing others from doing so as well.

What to do about it: Be careful about giving these people too much attention. Responding with laughter or joking back obviously reinforces the message that this behaviour is welcomed. If many of the group members are responding to the joking around and the work is getting lost in the jocularity, there is the high probability that there is the need for a break. If you find that goofing off happens regularly in your meetings, it may indicate that deeper issues exist. For example, group members may be losing commitment to the task in its current format and will only get back on track with some discussion about whether or not the goals of the work are still valid for everyone. The task leadership role of initiator or the maintenance role of process observer can help check this out and lead the group in a review of why and how the work could progress.

Competitors

What this might look like: Competitors are loudly vocal, pushing their thoughts forward at the expense of hearing others' ideas. These people want to look good in the eyes of the perceived or assigned leader. They believe the way to achieve that goal is to put forth as many ideas as they can and to increase their visibility by contributing as much as possible to discussion, even if it means interrupting or overriding other group members.

What to do about it: Responding to the competitor is similar to responding to the blocker. Gatekeepers requesting input from others have an invaluable leadership role with competitors. A task leadership role that complements the gatekeeper role is the role of initiator, who might suggest a different structure for hearing all members' contributions.

Competitors can be very difficult to deal with at times, when they have stories or examples that tend to go on and on. You might be at a loss about how to curb their contributions. You also might feel frustrated and unheard. If so, you might feel inspired to send a direct "I" message about how you are feeling. Be clear about exactly how you feel and what it is you want when you send this message, and recognize that you are risking confrontation.

Sympathy Seekers

What this might look like: Sympathy seekers try to gain support from other group members by discussing personal problems, putting themselves down and making self-deprecating comments. At first, other group members usually respond supportively to these comments, but as this conduct continues over time, the non-functional behaviour seems to suck the energy from the group, and others lose patience, often sighing, rolling their eyes or ignoring the person altogether.

What to do about it: Sympathy seekers often want group members to take care of them by making some kind of allowance for what they perceive to be their special circumstances. Sympathy seeking is troublesome because most people feel initial empathy for those who are struggling. When the behaviour interferes with the work of the group because these people are either taking up time or not able to contribute fully, then empathy is replaced with irritation. The role of process observer is helpful here as this person can identify that the group is getting off track.

Special-Interest Pleaders

What this might look like: Special-interest pleaders are the people who lobby for specific events or projects that they may be involved with. These people are quite easy to identify because they use group time to lobby for whatever special interest they might have. It is quite amazing that, no matter what kind of group they are a part of, they use this forum to express their point of view. An example might be a person who has strong dislike of a college instructor and uses group time to gain support from others. Community groups can often be contexts for special-interest pleaders who use this forum to represent their own political or advocacy-oriented cause. As important as it is to have representative community committees, special-interest pleaders can block significant progress on issues if they consistently return to their own agenda.

What to do about it: Special-interest pleaders and sympathy seekers are similar non-functional roles. They both take the group off track by introducing topics that are not relevant to the group's work. The leadership role of process observer can serve to identify the unbalanced focus of the group and suggest ways of redirecting the process.

In community committees, special-interest pleading can be limited if groups create a very clear structure for proceeding during meetings. When the group is very focused on its goals and meeting tasks, there is little opportunity for extraneous conversation.

Withdrawers

What this might look like: Withdrawers disengage from active participation in the group's process. This might take the form of daydreaming, passing notes, whispering to other members or simply sitting quietly, not participating in conversation or in any work being done.

At first glance it might not seem like a big deal that a member is not engaging in the process. However, lack of participation from any group member limits the creative potential of the group as a whole. Lack of participation may also be an indication that the process has become stagnant, for example, uninteresting or covering ground that has already been addressed. Some group members withdraw when the process has become extremely task-oriented with other people taking on so much of the work that there is little left over for them to do.

What to do about it: It is important to discriminate between quiet group members and those members who are withdrawing from the process. It is easier to spot withdrawing when someone has been a high participator and then appears to lose interest in what the group is doing. It is more difficult to ascertain when quieter group members withdraw from the process. Gatekeepers encourage participation by asking the quieter members for their input. Process observers notice when people withdraw and check to see if everyone is still comfortable with the way the group is progressing. Sometimes it is helpful to break into smaller groups (if the initial group is large) to encourage the participation of all members.

On a cautionary note, some withdrawers (and quiet participants) are given a lot of power in groups when members pay too much attention to trying to include them in the process. If you find that you are continually deferring to the quieter members of the group every time a decision is being made, then you have set up a situation where these members are not taking responsibility for their own contributions.

Exercise 4.5 on page 106 offers the opportunity to observe non-functional behaviours and their effect on group process.

Are you seeing yourself in any of these non-functional roles? If so, how are you reacting?

EXERCISE 4.5 | DYSFUNCTION IN THE GROUP

Objectives:

1. To practise ways of handling non-functional behaviours in groups
2. To experience task and maintenance leadership abilities in groups

A group of seven students chooses one of the topics not yet discussed in Exercises 4.2, 4.3 or 4.4A. The rest of the class will observe the group decision-making process and may use the Observation Form for Task and Maintenance Behaviours (Table 4.3 on p. 99) to focus their observations.

The instructor will prepare seven slips of paper, five of which will be left blank and two of which will have a non-functional behaviour inscribed. Each volunteer will pick a slip of paper, and the group will have a few minutes to ready itself for the decision-making discussion. The group will have 15 minutes to discuss the topic and reach a decision.

When the discussion is complete, the observers are asked to share who they thought were non-functional participators. The decision-making group is then asked to share the experience of how they dealt with these behaviours, with input from observers on alternative strategies.

The whole class may want to debrief the experience together.

Formal Leadership Roles

Our discussion so far has focused on the natural and adapted leadership roles each individual can play in all kinds of group contexts. Being aware of your own leadership role and how it contributes to effective group process is, to us, of the utmost importance to the success and failure of all groups. There are, however, ascribed, **formalized leadership roles** that are more traditionally understood as the leaders who are assigned the responsibility for task completion or who rise to the occasion as the popular candidates to lead a particular group.

In most Western cultures, societal structures with singular leadership authority are the norm. These structures are based on frameworks of accountability that ensure that someone will see that the work gets done. No matter how noble the concept of collaboration and teamwork might be, even in the helping professions, it seems that we continue to create those structures that culminate with some kind of ascribed leader. We call them chairpersons, team leaders, managers, directors, shift supervisors, and a number of other titles with the ultimate goal of assigning them some kind of formalized leadership role.

What kind of people do we prefer in these roles? The authority roles implicit in assigned leadership positions are as unique as the styles of the leaders themselves. Often people find themselves in leadership positions that demand a skill set that does not always suit their style of interaction. They may be administrative marvels who can manage all tasks in a timely fashion, yet find that they are simply not able to connect with the people they are managing. Popular, traditionally defined leaders are generally well-rounded individuals able to manage the details and also contribute to an atmosphere of trust and cohesion in the people who work for them. Competent managers do not always make great leaders. We have already looked carefully at the results of unbalanced task and maintenance functions in groups, and it is easy to see that someone totally focused on accomplishing the work does not always take into consideration the human process needs of those individuals doing their part.

There is an abundance of rich research on the styles, preferences and definitions of well-regarded, formalized leadership traits. If you find yourself in an assigned leadership position, it would be to your advantage to explore the wider variety of resources available. Ultimately, the success of any assigned leadership role is affected by such factors as group membership, the context of the task to be completed and the timing and importance of the work itself. Regardless of these and other factors that make assigned leadership situations unique, ultimately there has to be a match between the style of authority and the people being managed.

Some assigned leaders slip into a controlling role of authority due to their need for power, their need to please authority or simply their need for an outcome that meets their own standards for quality. This kind of leader can significantly affect those group members who either fear authority or reject it at all costs. In groups where the assigned leader becomes all-powerful, the result is dissatisfying to group participants because they experience a loss of personal significance. On the other end of the continuum, there are leaders who refuse to bring some kind of structural power to the group. Often the kinds of leaders who engage in this kind of misguided leadership style fear their own sense of authority, value complete autonomy or are unsure of their own ability to adequately lead a group. Again, if the assigned leader fails to create some sense of trust in group members in their ability to lead the process, then there is little direction, chaos and sheer disgruntlement.

The bottom line is that if all group members become aware of the task and leadership roles important to balanced, effective group process, the role of assigned leader seems somewhat redundant. This takes us to a fairly obvious conclusion: if the structures that support our group work with teams, families and the community require assigned, formal leaders in order to meet the needs of organizations, then the best kind of leader is one who assures, nurtures and facilitates a balance of leadership roles in the groups he or she leads. Only then will group members build upon their own natural leadership abilities to the betterment of the group.

Summary

All group members take responsibility for the effectiveness of the group's function by taking on a diversity of roles. These roles are called leadership functions and are either assigned or shared and build upon the natural roles we all bring to group situations.

Assigned or formal leadership roles are ascribed and structured in some way helpful to whatever organization created that particular position of responsibility. Shared leadership roles are those roles all group members take in accomplishing the work to be done, while ensuring that everyone participating in the group is satisfied with the way they are working together. A balance of both of these leadership roles is vital to effective group function.

The leadership roles that contribute to the ability of a group to get the job done are termed *task functions*. Those who take on these roles may initiate ways of tackling the work, offer opinions and information, ask others for their opinions or seek information from group members. This leadership function also includes elaborating or clarifying the ideas or opinions others bring to the task. Finally, those performing task leadership functions also contribute to overall group productivity by summarizing the work on an ongoing basis to enhance clarity and overall group decision making.

The leadership roles that enhance the process of how a group actually works together are termed *maintenance roles*. Maintenance builds a group's trust and cohesion and helps all group members feel satisfied and respected during the task. Those who take on maintenance leadership roles encourage all group members to participate, encourage everyone's contributions, suggest ways of settling conflicts that may arise and help others pay attention to the overall emotional climate of the group's process. These are also the people who pay close attention to the group's readiness to make decisions or contribute to overall cohesiveness through humour or attending to such things as snacks or coffee breaks.

Too much focus on the task or too much attention paid to maintenance can impair group cohesiveness and productivity. When the needs of all group members are not being met, certain individual non-functional behaviours may develop and stall group progress. These non-functional behaviours include blocking with arguments or other nuisance actions, too much joking, competitiveness, withdrawing, lobbying with individual special interests or seeking sympathy through self-deprecating behaviour.

Knowing how to deal with non-functional group behaviours and learning which leadership functions will help contribute to more balanced task or maintenance roles is vital to all effective group development.

Key Terms

Formalized leadership roles *(p. 106)*
Formalized leadership structure *(p. 84)*
Leadership roles *(p. 85)*
Maintenance leadership functions *(p. 90)*
Natural roles *(p. 82)*
Non-functional behaviours *(p. 102)*
Task leadership functions *(p. 85)*

Case Studies

The following case studies, taken from classroom, human service team and community contexts will help clarify the topics covered in this chapter, using real-world examples. These case studies focus on individual task, maintenance and non-functional leadership roles and their impact on group process. There is also an opportunity to suggest leadership functions that might improve group effectiveness.

Case Study 4.1 **Classroom Issue**

CATEGORY: STUDENT

A class of 25 students has been in the same college course for about eight weeks into a 16-week semester. The course they are taking in human development is part of their community support worker certificate program and is one of the first semester foundation subjects. The instructor for this course has been teaching in the program for about 15 years and teaches using lots of experiential exercises and group discussions.

Nyla is a mature student who is returning to school after having worked at a number of jobs throughout the country. At first, she seemed very interested in the subject matter in class and had many comments and questions to contribute to the discussion. Nyla and a small group of students in the class have begun to socialize out of class and now sit together on one side of the classroom. The desks have been moved into small discussion areas and form a "U" shape around the instructor. As time has progressed in the human development course, the quieter, less vocal students have gravitated to one side of the classroom, with the more vocal students over with Nyla.

Nyla has appeared to become irritated with the experiential exercises and has commented to the instructor that she would like to see fewer group activities and more lecture material in the class. As the sessions progress, her questioning becomes more frequent and often she confronts the instructor or argues with him about components of the exercises or other areas she believes are ambiguous or unrealistic. As well, she side talks and jokes around with friends nearby during the class.

The instructor has answered the questions asked and managed to clarify points of contention with Nyla. He is also seemingly paying little attention to her side talking. A group of six students have arrived at his office to ask him what they can do about Nyla's interruptions. They are seriously concerned about how much time is wasted on Nyla's behaviour and are irritated by her side talking. Interestingly enough, this group of students includes two of the people Nyla socializes with out of school and sits with during the class.

QUESTIONS:

1. What is happening here, with reference to the content of Chapter 4?
2. How should the instructor respond to the group of students?
3. What might the rest of the class do, in terms of leadership behaviours? Discuss the timing, the setting and the objectives of this response.

Case Study 4.2 **Project Work Group**

CATEGORY: STUDENT

Melina, Carlos, Callum and Brodie are all fourth-semester diploma students in a community college early childhood education program. Melina, Carlos and Callum generally obtain high marks on assignments. They are excited to finally work together on a project. Brodie was assigned to their group, and no one really knows what kind of marks he usually achieves. The assignment is worth 40% and is the culmination of all of their course work in this class.

Melina and Carlos have completed projects together before, but Callum and Brodie have never worked with any of the others. They have received the criteria for their big project and have been told they have some class time to complete their assignment (though they will certainly have to work out of class as well). They are having their first meeting together:

Melina: Well, it looks like we have to get organized. I think we should book time out of class right away so we know exactly when we can get together. I'd also like to make sure we make the best use of our time. Carlos, you remember how well we did on that assignment in Mr. Bellow's class? We worked really hard, eh?

Carlos: Yeah, I agree. We should get going on a timeline right away. I'll write it all down. What should we get accomplished this class?

QUESTIONS:

1. If you were part of this group, how would you automatically feel about the comments made by these two people?
2. What might your response be?

Callum: Are you saying that we need to meet outside of class time? I work part-time, and this is going to be a problem for me. My schedule is really tight. I really want to do well on this project, but I'm feeling a bit pressured here about having lots of meetings.

Brodie: Me, too. I work Monday, Wednesday and Friday nights and all day Saturday. Sorry, but maybe you should just give me stuff to do, and I can get it done on my own. Hey, it's coffee time, and I have to have a cigarette. See you in 15!

Callum: Geez, looks like getting together might be tough. How does everyone else feel about the scheduling thing? Looks like it might be a problem.

QUESTIONS:

1. Identify the role Callum took in this interchange.
2. How about Brodie's comments?
3. How do you think Melina and Carlos would respond to Brodie? How might others react to their response?

Carlos: I don't feel like a break, but now that Brodie's gone, does anyone know what kind of work he does? I'm not going to carry him through on this project, and I don't trust him to do the work himself. Geez, why did he have to be in this group? I want this project to get me an A+, and I see that slipping away! I'm applying for that job with the Boys and Girls Club, and this will look good on my resume.

QUESTIONS:

1. Identify the role Carlos is taking here.
2. How might you respond? What reactions might Carlos have to this response?
3. Now that you have a sense of the potential challenges this group might be facing, what leadership roles might help this group stay on task, enhance group trust and ensure a high-quality product?

Case Study 4.3 **Staff Meeting**

CATEGORY: TEAM

Ten staff members working in a day program for adults with disabilities have been feeling quite disillusioned about the cutbacks in funding that have been taking place over the past six months. There have been rumours of layoffs and increased ratios. They are not only feeling the pressure of possible layoffs, they are also experiencing the frustration of not knowing exactly what the administration of the facility has been doing to advocate for their needs. The mood is sombre and somewhat irritable as staff members continue to do the work under this stress. The supervisor of the facility has called a meeting for Saturday morning. Staff members are led to believe they will have a chance to vent and perhaps even hear about what might lie ahead for them.

The group gathers on Saturday morning at 10:00. The room is set up with small tables (for groups of three of four), a chart with the agenda (structured with specific time allotted for specific topics) and paper and pens on each of the small tables. The supervisor begins the meeting by explaining the agenda and immediately asking the staff to work in teams of two or three to come up with action plans for specific improvements to be made in programming, shifting off and overall operation of the facility.

QUESTIONS:

1. What leadership role did the supervisor take here?
2. What does this staff need?
3. How do you think the staff might respond in this situation?
4. If you were one of the staff members, how might you take a leadership role in this situation? How might others react to this?

Case Study 4.4 **Staff Coffee Meeting**

CATEGORY: TEAM

Five staff members (three caregivers and two childcare workers who support the inclusion of children with special needs) are meeting with their supervisor to discuss one child with challenging behaviours who is new to an after-school centre. The supervisor is concerned that two of the staff members do not want to include this child due to the seriousness of her behaviours. She plans a coffee meeting for the staff to decide how they might integrate this child. She begins by praising everyone and then asks that all staff share what is really going on with them. As each staff member shares, she adapts her tone of voice and body language to communicate understanding and encourages them to fully explore their feelings.

After about an hour of checking in, she brings up the subject of the child and asks staff to brainstorm ideas for inclusion. She enthusiastically agrees with each idea and writes them all on chart paper for everyone to view. She thanks each person for his or her input and praises the group for being such a dedicated, committed team. Two hours go by. The meeting ends with the supervisor asking everyone to consider the options and come back the next week prepared to discuss how he or she feels about each idea.

QUESTIONS:

1. What's happening here? Label the leadership functions.
2. How might staff members respond during the lengthy sharing, checking in and brainstorming?
3. Are there any imbalances in leadership? If not, why? If so, what leadership functions might be changed during this meeting?

Case Study 4.5 Community Forum

CATEGORY: COMMUNITY

We return now to the community-based case study from Chapter 3 (Case Study 3.4). Four people are meeting to finalize the details of a community forum on childcare issues. The forum's objective will be to hear issues on childcare relevant to parents, policy makers, support services, caregivers and politicians, and to create some direction for change locally and provincially in British Columbia.

Three of the people represent major stakeholder agencies linked to childcare and have partnered to get enough money to host the forum. Their names are Hans, Dana and Li. (A well-known childcare advocate from Vancouver is invited to speak at the forum, but will not arrive until the evening of the event.) The fourth member of this group is Susan, a local college instructor who has been asked to facilitate the sessions and oversee the process of grouping people at the forum and having them discuss issues and plans for change. There is a provincial election on the near horizon, and this forum is also seen as an opportunity to share issues with local politicians in hopes of influencing their electoral platforms.

The four members of this committee have worked together for a number of years in the community on many different childcare initiatives — Dana, Li and Susan, the instructor, for about 12 years and Hans for about one year. Initial meetings to set up the forum have been attended by the three stakeholder representatives who obtained the funding. Susan has been asked to the last planning meeting so that final details about the agenda and structure of the evening can be decided.

At this meeting the group of four has already discussed the number of people anticipated (about 60), how to get word of the forum out to the public, expectations of the special guest and some costs (the instructor is facilitating as a volunteer). Now the group is carefully going over the meeting format. The agenda will include a plenary with the guest speaker and then the grouping of participants for issue sharing and suggestions for change. Ultimately all groups will share their ideas and the guest speaker will summarize the meeting. The instructor's role will be to facilitate the accumulation of ideas.

The conversation below is part of the interchange that occurs when the instructor suggests some changes to the initial meeting itinerary. Pay close attention to this conversation with a focus on the task and maintenance roles being taken throughout this meeting. The meeting has been segmented into three sections with questions specific to each section.

Susan: I am wondering if maybe we might discuss who introduces whom. I see that I am the one doing this, and I think it might be best if the person who has organized the arrangements with the speaker actually do the introduction. Not a problem for me — just a suggestion.

Dana: Hmmm . . . good idea. We just thought it might smooth out the evening a bit to have you do this, but that sounds more appropriate. Yikes, looks like I actually have to do something that night!

Hans: Now I am thinking that might change the order of things . . . . (At this point the group brainstorms a different way of introducing the planners, the guest and the audience, and makes a small change to the agenda.)

Susan: I see that the special guest speaks for about 45 minutes — great idea — because she will have lots to talk about!

Li: Yes, and this gives participants a chance to review issues before they engage in their own discussions.

Susan: Do you anticipate my pulling some ideas out during this time, or do you want to let the groups do that when they break up into discussion groups? If I pull some themes out of the speaker's presentation and the questions from the audience, this might make the process go faster. What do you think?

Li: So you are saying that the groups will work on the issues we pull out rather than reaching agreement on common issues while working in their own groups?

Susan: Exactly! I still see time being the enemy here! Remind me of exactly what the outcome of this forum might be — maybe this won't meet your objectives? (Active discussion about ways this might or might not work — then a review of the outcomes. The decision is made to do both — note common themes when the guest speaks and the audience ask questions; then have discussion groups add any themes they see have not been covered.)

Susan: Sounds great to me! Now, one last thing: How do you see the groups recording their thoughts and ideas? Do you want them to come up with a wish list of the ways they want issues about childcare to be handled? I see this as a listing on paper . . . .

QUESTIONS:

1. What role is Susan taking up to this point in the meeting?
2. How has this role affected the group's process?
3. Label the maintenance comments.

Hans: (Interrupting with an apology). Actually, no . . . (standing up) . . . I have used concept maps for brainstorming ideas (shows on board next to meeting table). They inspire creativity and really work to get people thinking about issues and concerns.

Susan: Frankly, I wonder about concept maps in this kind of forum. My experience is that they confuse people who are linear thinkers. And most people do tend to think that way.

Hans: I have to disagree here (with a laugh) . . . I believe in the reverse . . . most people get their creative juices going with this way of recording their ideas. . . .

Dana: Hmmm . . . I disagree . . . they leave me a bit cold because I never quite know if I am doing them correctly . . . .

Susan: . . . and . . . we don't want people challenged by the "hows" and not taking the time to actually get to the issues . . . I'm not sure about what to do here . . . .

Hans: No problem . . . I understand . . . plus most of the time I use concept maps to help people create visions and goal setting . . . .

Susan: (Finishing his sentence) . . . not something as specific as the objectives of this forum. How about we just tell people to record their ideas in whatever format they like — with the task being to have both issues and a wish list of childcare thoughts and ideas?

QUESTIONS:

1. What has happened here?
2. What communication skills are evident during this segment of the interchange?
3. Label the task or maintenance roles you see affecting the way the group functions at this point and discuss what impact they have had on the group's process.

Dana, Hans and Li: Perfect! Choice is good! (Meeting continues and format gets finalized . . . all is beginning to wind down.)

Susan: So, I hope I haven't been too pushy about the way to do things?

Hans: Actually, I want to ask the same question! (Everyone laughs.)

Susan and Hans: At least we were pushy at each other and not at Dana and Li — and we are used to that after our last project together (laughter continues).

Susan: Dana, looks like, as usual, you have everything all written down and organized. I feel clear about what my role will be on that evening. Thanks for using my ideas today.

Li, Hans and Dana: Thank you for volunteering your time that evening.

Susan: No problem — just wait until you get my bill! (More laughter.)

QUESTIONS:

1. Label the task or maintenance functions in this segment.
2. Comment on the balance of task and maintenance in this entire interchange, discussing how it contributed to the process of decision making.

Reflection Tool

What?

What stood out for you in this chapter? Describe a reading, exercise, incident, person's behaviour, etc.

So What?

1. Emotional impact?

2. Why do you think you had this emotional response?

3. What assumptions might you be making in this situation? What beliefs and values were touched off by this situation?

Assumptions:

Beliefs, values:

4. Write about the meaning this has for you. Some helpful questions might be: Do you think your values might be clouding your interpretation of the situation? If so, how?

Have you been affected by similar situations in the same way? How have you responded?

5. Is it important for you to change your behaviour? Why?

Now What?

6. Based on the learning from this chapter, what other behaviours might you consider?

7. What might stop you from engaging in these new behaviours?

Objectives

What Questions Remain?

Chapter 5

Power in Groups

Objectives

In this chapter, students will acquire the knowledge, skills and attitudes to:

1. Recognize the importance of power dynamics in every relationship.
2. Understand the link between power and group dynamics.
3. Connect dependency to perceived power in groups.
4. Define empowerment within the context of the helping professions.
5. Reflect on the origins of their own power.
6. Use power in groups in productive, cohesive ways.
7. Note power shifts in groups and respond in ways that contribute to balanced group function.
8. Distinguish between constructive and destructive power in groups.
9. Correlate power with leadership.

Power in Groups

In Chapter 4, there were many opportunities to practise the task-focused and maintenance-focused skills that define leadership roles in groups. As you participated in the exercises in Chapter 4, you gained some insight into how much influence you have when working with others. You also had the opportunity to experience the influence others around you have in group situations. Critical to a fuller understanding of effective group leadership roles is an exploration of the concept of power.

The term **power** is commonly understood as influence or authority that is often seen as assertive, strong or forceful. In group situations, individuals have their own sense of power or influence in the presence of others. As well, they have perceptions about the power and influence of other group members. Therefore, in any group situation, there is a mix of personal power and perceived power that has the potential to create a dynamic interplay of influence and control.

To better understand how groups are affected by power interplay, we look to the source of power, how it originates in us and how we come to believe it exists in others around us. In highly effective groups, power is shared, and all group members have the ability to exert positive influence. In less effective groups, power imbalances are evident and create a context where some members have authority and others feel overpowered. Absolutely balanced power amongst all group members is rarely possible or realistic as a group goal. What is possible is developing the ability to recognize shifts in power and to deal with those shifts in ways that help the group function more effectively. Dealing with shifts in power involves the use of refined communication skills coupled with sensitivity to the ways others appear to be responding to your input.

Power is a good thing, unless it is used in ways that destroy trust and cohesion in groups. The word *power* comes from the Latin term *podere*, which means *to be able*. When thought of in this way, power becomes a productive, assertive and helpful element in group interaction. Some of you may have to work hard to shift your view of power

EXERCISE 5.1 PAST EXPERIENCES WITH POWER

Objectives:

1. To revisit experiences with power
2. To distinguish elements that contribute to positive or negative feelings about power
3. To create an initial foundation for further discussions of the concept of power

MATERIALS NEEDED:

- Chart paper
- Felt pens

Individually

Write down one example of a time when you observed or experienced power being used in a positive and productive manner. You may have observed this in person, on television, from afar, or actually used your own power in this way. After you note this experience, write down what it was about this experience that caused you to remember it as productive and positive?

Then, write down one example of a time when you observed or experienced power being used in a negative, disrespectful or destructive way. Again, this may have been power observed or experienced in person, on television, or from afar. Note what caused you to remember this experience as negative.

In Your Base Group

Share the details and reactions to both of these experiences. On one piece of chart paper, collate the elements that comprised positive experiences. On another piece of chart paper, collate the elements that comprised negative experiences. Each Base Group will share its thoughts and listings with the whole class and then post the papers on the classroom wall.

As a whole class, discuss whether the positive or the negative experiences have influenced your current views of power and why that might be.

from that of being controlling, authoritarian, forceful and harmful. Your childhood experiences with power will affect whether you view it as a negative or as a positive influence. Later in this chapter we will discuss how these views of power might develop over the lifespan.

Power takes many forms, some of which remain unrecognizable until groups find themselves in the throes of **power struggles** (when two or more people attempt to influence others without considering their views) or stalled productivity. Sometimes power can be passive, allowing some group members to control the group in quiet, yet highly impactful ways. Developing the skills to distinguish destructive power patterns in group interaction takes time and experience. Analyzing the components of this often-misunderstood concept called power will begin this process (see Exercise 5.1).

Having completed Exercise 5.1, think about your personal view of power and how that might influence your behaviour with others.

The Concept of Power

When we link power to influence, the first thing we think about is how much capacity one person has to influence the behaviour of another. There is a rather convoluted mix of influences in this process of interaction: there is our perception of others' ability to influence us; there is their perception of their ability to influence us; and there is also our willingness to be influenced. This sounds very confusing, yet it is integral to understanding the way power works. Implicit in the mutual influence exchange are the concepts of *perception* and *dependency.*

When you look at the well-known descriptions of forms of power that follow, you will see that there are some kinds of power that are assigned and formalized, that is, the person has power by virtue of his or her position. These forms of power are not as affected by perception as some of the other less-structured categories. Like assigned leadership roles discussed in Chapter 4, these positions of power come with norms and expectations that are clearly defined by organizational policies and procedures. However, there are other kinds of power that are a product of our perceptions.

Perception

Throughout our day we interpret or give meaning to what we experience. We call this process **perception**, and often our perceptions (interpretations and meanings) are not accurate. Our perception of someone else's power is affected by our view of that person and how we think that person can influence us in some way. This is a result of our own early experiences with power and the beliefs and attitudes we have developed over time. Early experiences include our family structure, our culture, our society and the history of the interactions we have had with that person.

As we visit issues of power, think about the fact that you have some control over the way you view others. Your perception of someone else's power affects how much power you allow that person to have. Be careful of this, because you can put yourself into a position where you believe others have influence over you when perhaps that does not need to be the case. For example, in Case Study 4.2 (Chapter 4, p. 109), Melina and Carlos immediately tried to organize the project group and set parameters for when the group would meet. If you were part of this group, you might go along with their suggestions because you think they are smarter than you, and you also want to get a good grade, or you really like one of them, and you want him or her to like you. These are both perceptions you have of the situation, and your decision to go along gives those group members some power based on your perceptions. There is no right or wrong here about allowing others to have influence over you. The important message is to increase your awareness of those times when allowing others to have power is helpful (or not helpful) to you or to the task.

Dependency

Dependency is another factor in the concept of power. The more dependent we are on another person, the more influence that person has over us. The reverse is also true; the more someone is dependent on us, the greater our ability to influence him or her. The degree of dependency has to do with the availability of whatever it is the dependent person needs. This may be something concrete like information or money, or it may be something emotional like affection, attention or nurturing. The greater the availability of that resource, the less power is given to the person meeting the need. For example, if you are a single person with very few friends, and you meet someone you like and want to know better, you may find yourself agreeing to do things that person likes as a way of spending more time with him or her. Automatically, you are giving that person a degree of power because he or she is filling a social or emotional gap.

Dependency is sometimes real and sometimes a function of our perception. Real dependency is relatively easy to identify. However, when dependency is linked to perception, it is more difficult to determine how it yields power in our lives. An example of students' real dependency might be their source of funding in order to attend college. This gives power to their bosses, their parents or the people in financial aid who distribute student loan packages.

A more complex example that mixes perception and real dependency might be one where a student in a program of studies that ends with professional certification perceives an instructor as having influence over the way he or she write reports. The student wants to pass the program and so asks many questions in order to meet the instructor's preferred style (as well as criteria) for particular assignments. The student perceives that in order to pass the courses, he or she has to please the instructor.

The instructor's sense of power and the student's sense of power contribute to the level of dependency, whether real or perceived. What this means is that the instructor may or may not believe he or she has power over the student, and the student has some feeling that his or her grade is dependent on his or her ability to impress the instructor. Either way, there is an interchange of real or perceived power that affects the amount of influence that instructor has on the student. The outcome is situational and obviously unique to the individuals involved, yet it shows how any discussion of power must include reflection on how we are affected by the mix of dependence and perception (see Exercise 5.2).

EXERCISE 5.2 PEOPLE IN OUR LIVES

Objectives:

1. To link real-life experience to the concepts of dependency and power
2. To identify power influences in our lives

Pick five people in your life you think you are dependent on in some way. List them on paper.

Rate your level of dependency on a scale of 1 to 5, with 1 being *very slightly dependent* and 5 being *very dependent.*

Once you have rated the five individuals, indicate what need they may be meeting for you (this may be emotional, financial or concrete in some other way).

Are some of the needs more concrete than others?

How much influence do you allow each of these five people to have in the way you live your life? (For example, if you are counting on your parents for funding, how much influence do they have on the way you make decisions in other areas of your life?)

In your Base Group, debrief this guided reflection and discuss how much power you believe these five people might have in your life. Discuss as well how much power you think you have in your life.

When you were considering the people who have power in your life, were there any revelations about how they influence you?

Forms of Power

French and Raven's Bases of Power

French and Raven's (1959) explorations of power influences on social interactions remain relevant today. They discriminated among five bases of power and defined these bases with consideration of the factors of dependency and perception. French and Raven identified the base or origin of each of these five forms of power and how much that power has influence over any social interaction. The five forms of power are reward power, coercive power, legitimate power, referent power and expert power.

Reward power is the power we give to a person or thing that has something we want and will strive to obtain. We work so we can obtain a paycheque; this gives the organization we work for reward power. We study hard in order to be rewarded by high marks and the potential of a better career. If we are the people with reward power, we can ask others to do things for us and even withhold rewards if we believe they are not merited. Some parents make good use of this kind of power when special treats are offered for good behaviour and withheld when rules are not followed. Our perception of someone's ability to reward us is key to how much power we see in that person.

Coercive power can also look like reward power if the threat of no reward becomes part of a process of manipulation. When we coerce people, we are influencing them to do something against their will. Often this power takes the form of punishment for non-compliance. There are negative components to this kind of power. They might be threats that incite fear of some kind, bribes, physical force, withholding of reward or any other number of negative psychological influences.

With coercive power it is easy to see how the factors of dependency and perception play a role in the effect that levels of coercion can have on individuals. Many of us have difficulty recognizing coercive power, particularly when it overlaps with reward power. It can be subtle, almost unrecognizable at times, or it can be obvious and punishing. Subtle coercion is in direct contrast to forceful threatening coercion, yet no less powerful in many ways. In some situations we give a person power by doing what we think he or she wants, even though we may not be sure there will be any repercussions. We allow coercive power as a way of alleviating guilt or regret for previous, sometimes unrelated situations. For example, you may feel the need to agree to a fellow student's request to take notes while he or she is absent because somewhere in the past that student helped you with your homework. You may not want to do this, but you do it anyway. In this situation the person asking for help is not necessarily using coercive power. You are allowing a certain degree of coercive power to operate because you would feel guilty if you refused to help.

Legitimate power is what French and Raven have termed "socially prescribed" and specific to a given role or position. This type of role has power that has been reinforced and legitimized by history, norms or culture. The impact of legitimate power is affected by the way it is used and the way it is regarded by others. If we do not regard a position as one of legitimate authority, then the influence of any person in that position on our behaviour will be lessened. How people play out a legitimate power role is also a factor in how influential they are in that role.

Examples of legitimate power are not just prescribed, assigned leadership roles. Often categories like age, experience, wealth, professional status, intelligence and

EXERCISE 5.3 LEGITIMATE POWER IN YOUR LIFE

Objectives:

1. To reinforce the concept of legitimate power
2. To share reflections on how a form of power from our past might influence us today

Think about someone in your family of origin who holds some kind of legitimate power role, based on your culture or family customs. This person's opinions are highly regarded, and he or she is called upon as a force and is consulted in any kind of large family decision.

- Are some in your family resentful of this power?
- What happens when the family does not consider this person when making decisions?
- If there is no one with legitimate power in your family, who has the final say in important decisions?
- How does that feel to you?

Discuss the answers to these reflections with someone in the class.

physical characteristics are considered the bases of legitimate power specified in some cultures. For example, in many family structures that exist in Canada today, certain family members hold legitimate positions of power based on their age. This often gives these older family members the right to influence others with respect to the ways they make decisions in their life. Again, those in valued legitimate power roles can prescribe how others should behave (see Exercise 5.3).

The processes of identification, attraction and association form the bases of **referent power.** We want to be like people we admire and associate with them as closely as possible. We may strive to retain any relationship we have developed with a particular person or group of people and take on their values, beliefs and attitudes. This gives that person or group referent power as we change our behaviour to closely model the behaviours we admire in them. We also want these people to admire us. As with all of the other bases of power, the behaviour changes may be minimal and almost indiscernible, or they may be overwhelmingly obvious. Fashion changes in adolescents are a great example of how referent power given to teenage idols or to the latest craze can affect the ways young people dress.

The risks of strong identification with people we admire and want to associate with might be social exclusion or the use of rewards or coercion by those people to exert their power over us. However, if we feel some sense of satisfaction through this association or identification, then giving these people referent power helps us in some way.

You have **expert power** if you have more knowledge, expertise or experience than someone else, and it is useful or necessary to others. This is a common power base in organizational structures that require special competence in certain areas. When an organization makes full use of information technology in its day-to-day business, the computer technology experts hold a lot of expert power. The perceptions we have of the extent of someone else's level of expert power affect its usefulness to us. In many cases we learn what we need from the person with the specialized expert power and then become less dependent on their knowledge or experience base. When you first entered your program of professional studies, you relied on the expertise of your instructors. When you graduate, you will rely on your own learned expertise to a greater degree.

A base of power added later by Raven (1965) that is somewhat similar to expert power, is **informational power.** People who seem to know what they are talking about and are able to articulate themselves clearly and logically exert informational power. If you have ever changed your mind after hearing a well-presented argument, you have been influenced by informational power. Other group members sometimes hold those with informational power in awe. This may prevent those members from contributing due to feelings of inferiority. If you have informational power, be aware of this potential block to full contribution by others, and take some responsibility for asking others for input.

Mayer's Categories of Power

Mayer (2000) differentiates amongst other forms of power, extending some of French and Raven's work. Categories that apply to the helping professions include nuisance power, habitual power, sanction power and personal power.

Nuisance power comes from the ability to annoy or irritate someone else. Children use this form of power by engaging in behaviour that we as adults would rather not deal with. We ignore their behaviour or make decisions based on this behaviour that often serve to reinforce its occurrence. Nuisance power is given to people or things that you find annoying. It could be someone biting his or her nails or eating sunflower seeds during a meeting or someone whose voice is difficult to hear. The attention you give to this distracts you from what you are doing and ultimately influences your behaviour. As well, any attention paid to that form of power will increase the probability that it will not go away.

Habitual power comes from the comfort of maintaining the status quo rather than experiencing the discomfort of adapting or making changes. For example, in organizations it seems easier to allow board members or current leaders to stay in their positions for many terms than it is to recruit new members or employees and orient them to those positions. This staying with the status quo gives a lot of power to those well-entrenched in positions.

Sanction power is the ability to prevent or interfere with someone's course of action through the use of legitimate or coercive power. A perfect example is the funding source for social service agencies. A social service agency must comply with the funding agency's criteria in order to receive financial support. If this compliance does not happen, the agency can easily pull the funding. Another example is the power wielded by the government ministry overseeing children in foster care.

The list of characteristics that contribute to someone's **personal power** is endless. It includes physical attributes and skills, the ability to articulate thoughts, a sense of humour, confidence and the ability to empathize. These characteristics and others contribute to the individual's perception of his or her power, as well as others' perceptions of the individual's power. This kind of power described by Mayer is significant to the overriding theme of this chapter. When individuals know that others respond to certain aspects of their personality, they use these characteristics consciously to influence others. Sometimes people are not aware of their personal power and do not realize the influence they have on others. Our life's work is to understand the way our power is perceived (see Exercise 5.4).

EXERCISE 5.4 TYPES OF PERCEIVED POWER

Objectives:

1. To identify individual sources of power
2. To receive feedback from others about perceived power
3. To anticipate how forms of power might affect future practice

On your own, think about the kinds of power you have with reference to the categories described in this chapter. List them and give at least one example of a situation when you used each kind of power.

In your Base Group, discuss your list and any additions based on insights from other group members.

How do you think you might use these forms of power in your practice?

How might they pose challenges for you?

Empowerment

In the helping professions, the term *empowerment* has become well-used, yet not always well-understood or agreed upon. Empowerment is a term that became popular in the 1980s and 1990s primarily through two different movements. Grass-roots advocacy groups worked to improve the living conditions of marginalized groups of people by attempting to change the way they viewed themselves and the way society viewed them. Through a number of supportive strategies (funding, education and advocacy) the goal was to help these marginalized groups not only feel good about themselves, but also take on more responsibility for meeting their own needs. This was viewed as building power in others through teaching and support, that is, *empowering* others.

As this idea of empowerment became more well-known, businesses and corporations embraced the concept and began to shift their organizational structure to reduce the amount of middle management and increase the responsibility of employees. By increasing the amount of responsibility given to employees, there was the need to also allow them a heightened level of influence or authority. This was seen as empowering for the employees.

Even though there are many different definitions of **empowerment**, they share some elements implicit in this term. When we feel empowered, we feel some sense of authority about our ability to make a difference. We also feel confident and appreciated for our individuality. We feel heightened self-esteem and are clear about what we are capable of and are willing to do. In a group we feel heard, influential and valued.

When we empower others, we support their development in some way. We recognize someone's abilities and build on them. Obviously this is an important goal in the helping professions, as our work with others focuses on supporting people in ways that facilitate their own independence. By helping to remove existing challenges (through advocacy or direct support), empowering people involves helping others to see their own potential and be the best people they can be.

We can look at empowerment from either the individual perspective or from the viewpoint of a group of people working together. From an individual perspective, empowerment is about personal growth and a feeling of competence and self-confidence. It is sometimes termed **power-from-within** and is reliant on the individual's perception of his or her own ability. This is in contrast to the traditional view of power as coercive, controlling and manipulative, sometimes termed **power-over**.

From the perspective of working with others, empowerment is closely related to our discussion of shared leadership roles in Chapter 4. Empowerment is most often thought of as the ability of the group and/or employees to make decisions and have a degree of direct control over their work environment. Individuals, in cooperation with others, take responsibility for ensuring that the work gets accomplished. In order for groups to feel empowered there must be a sense of commitment, dedication and confidence that they have the authority to make a difference. Empowered groups exist within an organization that has moved from the traditional view of power-over to one characterized by collaboration, sharing and mutuality. The sense of empowerment that comes from this kind of cooperative context has been termed **power-with**.

Our role is to support people in finding their own healthy power when working with clients, whether they are young children and their families, people with disabilities or community members. We practise power-with, using group contexts, communication skills and respectful interactions to model appropriate sharing of power. This in turn creates a context of empowerment for all. As much as there are elements that seem mutually understood in any discussion of empowerment, there are also questions that merit deeper consideration. These will be explored in Exercise 5.5, below.

Are there outstanding questions about empowerment based on your readings so far?

EXERCISE 5.5 MORE QUESTIONS ABOUT EMPOWERMENT

Objectives:

1. To explore issues implicit in the concept of empowerment
2. To critically reflect on values and beliefs about empowering others
3. To discuss in some depth common elements of empowerment

The following questions are designed to help you fully explore the concept of empowerment as it pertains to the helping professions. These questions are also meant to inspire a deeper understanding of the many meanings of empowerment.

In four groups, discuss the following questions and offer examples to substantiate any conclusions. As well, consider the implications these questions might have for your professional practice. Be prepared to share your discussion, examples and implications with the entire class.

Discussion Group #1: Why is a discussion of empowerment important to understanding power? Illustrate your points with examples of group situations where empowerment was evident. What implications might the use of empowerment have in your work environment?

Discussion Group #2: Is it possible to give power to someone else? If so, how might this happen? When is it okay to give power to someone else, and when is it not a good idea? Offer some examples to support your discussion. What implications might giving power away have for your work environment?

Discussion Group #3: Empowerment is a term often used in the helping professions because one of the goals of caring for others involves supporting them in ways that move them to independence. How do you think you can facilitate someone else's power in your work environment? Is this something you would want to do? Offer some examples to support your discussion. What implications does the goal of empowerment have for your work environment?

Discussion Group #4: Is there such a thing as true empowerment in a work situation where you must be accountable to some kind of authority? Is this a realistic goal? What examples might you have experienced where empowerment was the goal, yet there was still a sense of power from some kind of authority? What implications might a goal of true empowerment have for your work environment?

Developing Power Through the Lifespan

How do we grow into the kind of people who have power-from-within, are respectful of others' power and are able to influence others in ways that do not impinge on their power? Addressing this question requires a quick look at the effects of early experience on personality development. This will help to clarify the origins of power and how individual differences in the use and perception of power develop over time.

Researchers interested in the development of social-emotional skills look closely at the origins of self-concept and self-esteem when discussing how a healthy sense of self develops. This healthy sense of self includes the way we feel about our power, use our power and react to others' power. Delving into early childhood offers some clues as to how individual personalities are shaped. This is the critical period during which first relationships are experienced. The nature of these first adult-child relationships creates a foundation from which later experiences grow.

An interplay of forces exists, involving inborn temperament and a host of environmental factors (including parenting style) that contribute to the growth of self-esteem and self-efficacy. **Self-esteem** is generally defined as the opinion we have of ourselves and our own feelings of self-worth. **Self-efficacy** is the sense we have that we are capable human beings, and, when necessary, are able to achieve what we want to achieve. Our sense of our personal power is a significant component of both our sense of our self-esteem and our feelings of self-efficacy. These feelings of personal power are a product of an interplay between the environment and the growing child. Our personal power grows during those vital early years, when influenced by those experiences that either nurture and bolster our sense of self or erode it in some way.

A baby may come into this world with an irritable temperament, yet be born into a family that is easygoing, generally functional, and financially comfortable. An assured parenting style will be as much affected by this irritability, as the irritability will be affected by the parenting style. The myriad systems that surround this developing family (economic, familial, cultural, societal and global) will make this dynamic process that much more complicated. Whatever way this process unfolds is a product of all of these factors and affects the development of that baby's individual sense of self. The complexities are so numerous that it is no wonder more and more attention is now being paid to the critical periods of early childhood that shape individual personality growth. A closer look at the parent-child relationship in the early years offers some explanation of how the stage is set for the development of a healthy sense of personal power.

Baumrind's (1978) research offers the most comprehensive overview of common parenting styles as related to the development of social competence in children. Baumrind identifies three kinds of parenting styles: authoritarian, permissive and authoritative. With each defined type of parenting there are certain predictions about the child's growing sense of independence, confidence, control and sociability. All of these characteristics contribute to a child's feelings of personal effectiveness and personal power.

If parents overpower their children with a punishing, forceful and restrictive style of interaction, there is little room for independence. Children with such **authoritarian** upbringing may become so subordinate to their parents that they lose their sense of autonomy. Authoritarianism is not always outwardly punishing or aggressive. It may be the opposite, with parents creating a context of co-dependency through over-protectiveness.

In all cases of authoritarian upbringing, there is so much dependence on the authority of parents that children do not develop self-reliance and always doubt their own decision making. Developing in an environment where power-over is a daily experience robs most children of their self-esteem and self-efficacy. There is potential for either rebellion in defiance of this parental power or compliance and low sense of self. Rebellious children hold on to whatever power they can find and take power from others, modeling what they have experienced from their parents. Children with a low sense of self need power as well, and it will be their life's work to develop the autonomy to find that either in themselves or from others in less healthy ways. In both instances, the stage is set for seeing power as a valuable commodity that might have to be taken from others in order to feel a heightened sense of self.

Permissive parenting, in contrast to authoritarianism, is a style that holds children totally responsible for their own decision making. Permissive parents are accepting and pose few restrictions on children's behaviour. Some permissive parents feel caring and high regard for their children and believe that allowing them complete freedom is the right thing to do. Others are simply taking the easy, less responsible path through parenthood. Children from permissive upbringings tend to be even less self-reliant than children from authoritarian upbringings, because they have grown in an atmosphere where there is little structure and expectations are unclear. This means that there is also lack of clarity about their self-regulation. Without some sense of right and wrong, personal power has few limits, and there is potential for lack of self-control.

Baumrind's preferred parenting style is labeled **authoritative**. Authoritative parents set structures and expectations in ways that are rational. Rules are there to be followed, yet are negotiable. In this context, children become well aware of the expectations of their parents, yet feel valued for their individuality and their input into the structures that support the family. Both parents and children have a sense of power in this arrangement. With a healthy development of autonomy, the power base is shared naturally. Children develop a healthy regard for others' power, comfortable with their own sense of authority and able to negotiate with a power-with perspective.

This quick glimpse at the impact of three generalized parenting styles that contribute to growing self-esteem and ultimately to one's own sense of power is in no way meant to over-simplify the link between early experience and the origins of power and personal effectiveness. It does, however, identify some of the factors at work as we look at ways we all develop opinions about ourselves and our personal power as members of any group. A large body of research on *attachment* and early socialization has also contributed to our understanding of the development of social competence.

The term **attachment** refers to the emotional tie that forms between infants or children and the adult in their lives (Landy, 2002). Researchers John Bowlby (1958) and Mary Ainsworth (1978) defined the kinds of attachment evident in observational studies of parents and their infants and young children. This work created the foundation of current research on the effects of early attachment on later personality formation. The most important finding is that the kinds of relationships we experienced with adults at critical periods in our very early years continue to affect the kinds of adults we become. This happens because we internalize the early relationships, affecting not only the way we perceive ourselves, but also the way we perceive others in our social world.

If we have experienced predictable, consistent, genuine and sensitive care from adults in the early years, then we will have formed what Ainsworth terms *secure attachments* with those adults. Securely attached children develop trust in the adults around them because they quickly learn that those adults will be there for them when they need them. Securely attached children establish social competence and a sense of personal power from this kind of consistent, positive early relationship building. As well, with the early experience of secure attachment comes the development of healthy autonomy, the self-confidence that we are capable of accomplishing things on our own. We bring this kind of personal power to all of our later social interactions.

Insecure attachments are the product of less predictable, non-responsive and sometimes neglectful care in the early years. Ainsworth points out three types of insecure attachments (avoidant, ambivalent and disorganized), all of which are the result of irregular, often negative parenting responses to the infant's and young child's needs. Children who have developed insecure attachments during this early, most critical time in their development have the potential for difficulty in establishing healthy social relationships in later years. They may have poor social skills because they lack confidence from an over-dependence on the adults in their lives. They may also be socially aggressive with lack of control in frustrating situations. Each type of insecure attachment outlined by Ainsworth has predictable adult outcomes that are directly linked to the type of insecure attachment experience in the very early years. These outcomes have a significant effect on how adults who developed insecure attachments perceive themselves and others in their social world. This perception also affects their level of personal power and the power they perceive others have in their lives (see Exercise 5.6).

> Working models of attachment — or the ideas that people internalize about themselves and other people — influence how individuals see the world, particularly other people, as well as how they perceive themselves. Children who are securely attached are more likely to perceive and remember events positively and to view their role and that of others in ambiguous situations as benign and unintentional. Children who are insecurely attached see that same event and the children involved in it as being rejecting and hurtful. (Landy, 2002, p. 158)

This quick overview of the origins of our power and others' power offers a glimpse at how we each come to regard our own feelings of self-esteem and self-efficacy and the

EXERCISE 5.6 LOOKING BACK

Objectives:

1. To identify how early experiences have contributed to origins of personal power
2. To discuss with others ways that these experiences may affect perceptions of power in others
3. To discuss how these early experiences can contribute to the ways you use power in class and in future practice

In your Base Group, revisit the questions in Exercise 5.4 with reference to where or how these kinds of power may have originated, based on your early childhood experience. Be aware of your personal boundaries around the information you share in this discussion.

As each Base Group member discusses links to his or her early childhood experience, others help that person make connections to his or her sense of power now by offering observations or suggestions. Use the objectives listed here to guide your discussion.

effects this has on our role in current social situations. The most recent research on personality development indicates that parenting styles and the socialization role of early attachment have a critical impact on our behaviour in adult social situations. As discussed in Chapter 3, personal effectiveness (in this case, our personal power in groups) is a factor that affects the dynamics of any group situation.

Do you have any insights into how the way you were parented connects to your view of your own power?

Communication Skills and Power

The way that we communicate with others is the primary demonstration of how we use our own power and how we respond to others' power. There are two ways in which power is experienced in group contexts: by the person who exerts influence on others and by the person being influenced. In both cases effective communication skills will affect whether the use of power has a positive or negative outcome. A positive outcome would be one in which people come away feeling good about the interaction. A negative outcome would be one in which people come away feeling controlled, uneasy and resentful.

In this chapter we talk about power as the ability to influence others. In many cases we influence others regularly without thinking very much about how we do it. This happens when influence is exerted in a way that is received well and responded to easily. In reality, people exert power all the time. Many of us have been brought up to view power in a negative light, and for that reason we do not see situations in which we have been willingly influenced as ones that involved the use of power. It is doubtful in these situations that the level of emotionality was very high.

Usually, when we think of power in a work context, we imagine an uncomfortable emotional climate in which we feel controlled by someone who is trying to get us to do something we do not want to do, using a type of coercive power described earlier. Power often goes hand in hand with conflict, and when most of us are involved in a conflict, our emotions become elevated. When this happens it is much more difficult to think clearly and communicate effectively. However, it is at precisely such a time that these skills become crucial.

When Influencing Others

It would be impossible to list the various situations that might arise in your work environment when you would want to influence others or the way things are done. Program changes, the way in which staff members respond to clients, what to spend money on, how best to support families — all of these and many more potential decisions provide the foundation for you to shape the environment in which you work. The question is, how do you explain your ideas in a way that others are likely to respond to favourably? The answer of course is to use clear, effective communication skills. It is beyond the scope of this book to treat the topic of communication skills with any real depth. We will, however, discuss some basic skills that will help you put forth your thoughts with a healthy use of power in a positive, non-threatening manner.

If you remember that using power is essentially influencing others, this implies that there will be some sort of change occurring. People often resist change because the future (with the change in place) is more uncertain than the present. When people resist, they usually exhibit some form of defensiveness. **Defensiveness** is the emotional response we might have to feeling threatened by another person. It can take many forms, from complete silence to shouting personal insults and is our way of protecting ourselves in interactions where we feel uncomfortable. Individuals' personality and level of communication skills will affect how they express defensiveness. It is helpful to bear in mind that what you are saying may seem threatening to some people, so avoid, as much as possible, taking their defensive comments personally. If you want to minimize the potential for defensiveness, then you will want to pay careful attention to how you frame your comments.

It is very important to be clear about what you want (the outcome) and to use language that is as factual and accurate as possible. In other words, you want to avoid language that implies judgment or blame. Take time to reflect on the situation before presenting your ideas and ask yourself:

- What is going on? What is the situation as I see it?
- How do I feel about what is going on?
- What would I like to see done differently and why?

Coming up with objective answers to these questions will help you to be clear and non-judgmental when the time comes to discuss the situation with others.

When you present your ideas, pay attention to your body language. It is important to face the people you are talking to, but if your emotions are high, you might lean in quickly or move in ways that others might interpret as aggressive. Even though you might feel nervous, take care to minimize any jittery body movements you might make. Your tone of voice is also considered in the realm of body language. Again, the more calmly and objectively you can verbalize your point of view, the more likely it is that it will be received non-defensively.

People rarely like being told what to do by a colleague or teammate. When you want to suggest change, it can be helpful to frame your idea tentatively as a suggestion or a question. Finally, remember to phrase what you say from the "I" position, taking responsibility for your thoughts and ideas as your own, rather than speaking for others.

For example, say you work in a recreation program supporting youth with special needs, and you have a client who frequently spits at people. Currently, she gets a 10-minute time out in which one staff person must take her to the time-out area and sit nearby until the time is up. You think there is a better way to handle this behaviour and want to suggest it at the next staff meeting.

Choose the best way to put your ideas forward:

1. Putting Chelsea in time out is not working. We're just wasting our time if we keep doing that. It would work a lot better if we all just walked away and ignored her.
2. You guys are way off track using time out with Chelsea. It's obviously not working, and I think we should try something else.
3. I think we should stop the time outs and ignore the spitting.

4. I've noticed that Chelsea smiles a little bit on her way to time out. For whatever reason, she seems to like going there. I was wondering about ignoring her when she spits, walking away from her without saying anything.

Statement 1 is speaking on behalf of others, Statement 2 blames others, and Statement 3 tells others what to do with no discussion of why change is necessary. Statement 4 gives some background information and tentatively offers a solution. This statement is the least likely to evoke defensiveness in others (see Exercise 5.7).

Responding to Others' Power

When someone is trying to influence you, your response will depend on their level of communication skill as well as your general perception of that person. It is easy to respond when you agree with what the other person is saying. The focus of this section is how to respond when you disagree or feel threatened or intimidated.

One of the most useful skills you can develop is to become aware of how you feel right in the moment so that you can make a conscious choice about how to express yourself.

EXERCISE 5.7 COMMUNICATING POWER

Objectives:

1. To practise ways of communicating needs with a healthy use of power
2. To practise a variety of communication skills to meet your needs in various situations

On your own, write down how you might communicate the following messages in a way that minimizes defensiveness in the person (or people) you are talking to:

1. You have had feedback from parents that they do not like the way your colleague is communicating with their children. Because you are the supervisor, you must give feedback to your colleague. You have chosen to meet in a quiet and appropriate location. What might you say to begin this conversation?
2. You have to tell the parents of a youth with behaviour challenges that you can no longer cope with their child's behaviour in your recreation program. How might you communicate this?
3. You have a colleague who continues to offer suggestions about how you are doing your job. This has become irritating, and you want to ask that person to stop trying to change you. How might you communicate this?
4. You are at a staff meeting and are aware that an issue about some people taking longer coffee breaks than others is not being discussed. You want to bring this topic up for discussion. How might you communicate this?
5. You are working on a project with two other students, and it is due in two days. The other two students are friends. One of these students is late for project meetings, never has his part of the work completed and frequently talks about unrelated topics during work time. You decide that if you don't say something soon, you will be doing all the work, and this person will benefit unfairly by getting the same mark as you. How might you communicate this?
6. In class you sit next to a good friend. It is the second week of the course, and you find that she is side talking to you during the class. It is uncomfortable, embarrassing and irritating because you are having trouble concentrating on the material being presented. How might you communicate your concerns?

   Save your answers to use in Exercise 5.8

This sounds obvious, yet many people are unable to identify their feelings when they arise and are unaware of the physiological responses that indicate pleasure, discomfort, anger or any of the many emotions that can be experienced. The result of this lack of awareness is to react to a situation rather than respond to it. When you react, it is as if you operate on automatic pilot, saying or doing the first thing that comes to mind. When you respond to a situation, you are aware of how you feel and what triggered your emotions, and you are thoughtful about what you say or do.

In order to make the move from reacting to responding, you must be able to distinguish your internal experience from the external situation. In other words, you must recognize that your feelings and interpretations are your own and are not caused by anyone else. To illustrate this idea look at the following scenario and determine what is the internal experience and what is the external situation.

You work in a group home with another staff person who checks everything she does with you before doing it. This is the comment you make to another co-worker: "Shayna is driving me crazy. She is so useless. She can't do anything on her own and needs me to hold her hand the entire day. I can't believe she got a job working with people when she obviously has no idea how to relate to others."

The external situation is that Shayna checks with you first before completing a task. "Driving me crazy, useless, can't do anything on her own, needs me to hold her hand, obviously has no idea how to relate to others" are all part of your internal experience. They are feelings and judgments that reside in you and have very little to do with Shayna. Operating from these kinds of interpretations increases the likelihood that you will blame Shayna for how you feel (react), rather than take steps to clarify what you've observed and what you hope might change (respond).

Notice the difference if in the above situation you were to say to yourself, "It's starting to bug me that Shayna keeps asking me if it's okay to do what she is thinking of doing. I was flattered at first that she thought I was smart enough to help her, but now she checks with me so often that I can hardly get my own work done. I think I need to talk to her about it." In this example you have distinguished between Shayna as a person and what she does. You have recognized that this is your problem and have taken at least partial responsibility for creating the situation in the first place (usually if we feel flattered by something, we behave in ways that encourage the behaviour to continue). In addition, you haven't brought a co-worker into the situation, which avoids setting up uncomfortable or hurtful working relationships.

The previous example involved regular work issues and not necessarily any use of power (unless you decided to influence Shayna to change her behaviour). The skills that need to be developed in order to respond in such an objective manner require a concerted effort at reflection, and practice in stepping back from the situation and looking at it in a broader perspective.

Now imagine how much more challenging responding would be when faced with a highly emotional situation in which someone is attempting to persuade you to do something you are uncomfortable with. The level of emotionality would increase, and you would be faced with direct questioning and persuasion. For example, you are in a planning meeting that is organizing your upcoming graduation, and a small group of students is pushing you to take on the role of class valedictorian. You can feel your heart start to beat faster, and you are aware of growing tension within your body. These physical signs are your first indicators that you are having a reaction (becoming defensive) to what is going on.

Tuning in to your biological state can help you become more conscious of times when you might react to a situation in a manner that results in defensiveness from others, which prevents them from being receptive to your comments. Recognizing when you are becoming defensive provides you with a choice point in terms of your behaviour.

The first thing you have to do is interpret what your body is telling you in this kind of situation. It could be excitement, enthusiasm, anger, fear or any other emotion. Ideally, the next step would be to verbalize those feelings in a way that helps others understand what you are experiencing. You have to be careful when describing your feelings not to blame others in the group for your response. For example, one response to the above situation might be, "I am feeling really scared right now that I might get pushed into doing something I don't want to do." This statement acknowledges your internal state without placing the responsibility on others. A less-than-helpful response would be, "You guys are forcing me into a situation that I want nothing to do with!" The second statement could leave other group members feeling defensive and somewhat confused, particularly if they expected that you would have liked this opportunity. The difference between these two responses is subtle, yet the first response is likely to limit any defensiveness that might occur.

In most group contexts it is extremely difficult to step back for a moment and take the time to reflect, identify feelings and avoid reacting. However, this is exactly what you will need to do if your goal is to respond in ways that maintain a positive working relationship instead of an unhealthy exchange of power and control. Again, there are a number of ways of responding in any interaction. The level of comfort and safety you feel in any group will determine your willingness to share your feelings. The important point is to strive to recognize those internal reactions (hence the need to practise reflection) and make choices about how you respond, rather than react without thinking.

There is no one right way to communicate with others. The expectation here is that you become aware of power, know how it is being used around you and respond in ways that increase your ability to work together with others. There is *never* the expectation that you always respond directly and correctly in all interactions; this is just not natural to any of us. Sometimes we simply want to sidestep situations that pose difficulties for us, take a breath and decide whether we want to invest the time and energy to get our needs met through direct communication. Sometimes the answer to that is "no". Recognize that the choice is yours and that there are consequences to every choice you make (see Exercise 5.8).

EXERCISE 5.8 COMMUNICATION PRACTICE

Objectives:

1. To identify immediate emotions in response to powerful communications
2. To practise responding non-defensively to powerful communications
3. To debrief possible changes to communications that might lessen defensiveness

Working in pairs, take turns communicating your responses created in Exercise 5.7. Divide the responses in half (three each).

One of you reads his or her previously written response (communicator), and the other (responder) responds in the way that feels most natural. Once that is completed, the responder identifies his or her initial feelings in response to hearing the message and together you discuss any changes that might be made.

Take some time to debrief responses with the whole class.

Did you have any particular difficulties creating the communications in Exercise 5.7? Was there any emotion evoked in Exercise 5.8 that relates to your own sense of personal power?

Power and Leadership Roles

In Chapter 4 you had the opportunity to explore the many leadership roles necessary to healthy group process. Any time you take on one of these leadership roles you are using power and influence in some way. Exercise 4.1 (p. 82) offered a first glimpse at your style and ability to influence others in decision-making situations, that is, the way you express your power in groups. With consideration of the current chapter's discussion of power, how might you now better understand your natural style of influencing others? Exercise 5.9 will help you to look at how influential you perceive yourself to be and to identify the style of power you tend to use most naturally.

EXERCISE 5.9 YOUR POWER IN GROUPS

Objectives:

1. To link power and influence to natural leadership abilities
2. To reflect on the congruency between feedback from others about the way you use power and your own perception of how you use power
3. To identify when and how others are using power and influence in decision making

In Exercise 4.1 (Chapter 4, p. 82) you were part of at least one decision-making group and received feedback on your style of interacting with others. Retrieve the feedback you received in that exercise and answer the following questions:

1. How would you rate your level of influence in the decision-making group you worked with?
   a) Not very much influence (others seemed to ignore you; you sat silently)
   b) Some minor influence (a couple of suggestions seemed to be responded to; you had input and seemed to be acknowledged, but it was not necessarily used in the decision made)
   c) Lots of influence (others looked to you for ideas; every time you said something others responded enthusiastically; your input was definitely used in the decision)
2. If you believe you were influential in some way, what behaviours did you engage in that contributed meaningfully to the decision that was made?
3. Looking back on the decision-making process in Exercise 4.1, look closely at the feedback you received from others. What did others see with respect to your use of power and influence?
4. With consideration of the kinds of power described in the current chapter, what type of power did you use in this decision-making exercise (reward, referent, coercive, legitimate, expert, informational, nuisance, habitual, sanction or personal)? Consider both your perception and the feedback received from others.
5. Does your perception of your influence match the feedback you received? If there are some differences between your sense of power and influence and the feedback you received, what do you attribute those differences to? What questions does this bring up for you, and how could you resolve them?

With either the whole class or the original decision-making group from Exercise 4.1, share any insights you may have about the use of power and influence during that exercise.

Exercise 5.9 has helped you take a closer look at the ways you and others perceive your level of power and influence in groups. The next step is to increase your ongoing awareness of the overall use of power in group situations by all members. There will be times when you will recognize the need for influencing group process and will feel unsure about how to proceed. Looking at power with respect to leadership roles provides a framework for assessing how you might successfully influence the group in helpful ways. It is important to identify uses of power, appreciate power dynamics being used by all group members and recognize when power shifts are not helpful to group function.

If your work in the helping professions is based on building power through teaching, modeling and support, then it only follows that you operate from a place of power-from-within, with the objective of creating a context of power-with in all group situations. Consideration of the objective of power-with is the foundation for any task or maintenance role you take and should be the starting place for how you use power and influence to maintain positive work relationships.

Power in Task Leadership

The melding of task leadership roles with the kinds of power explored in this chapter creates a dynamic interaction between personal style and the perceptions of others. Personal power is the determining factor in how successful you will be in leadership roles and the kind of power that others perceive you to have (legitimate, referent, coercive, informational or others discussed earlier in this chapter). Personal power involves your communication style, your own sense of self-confidence and the endless list of characteristics that comprise who you are and how you present yourself to the world.

For example, if you are a person who wants to be seen as knowledgeable and articulate and have just joined a new group, then it is likely that you will take on the task leadership roles of initiator or information giver. Your style will draw attention because you will show enthusiasm and confidence, and there will be an element of wanting to be recognized for the knowledge you have. You will likely want others to perceive that you have informational, expert power. In this example you are focused on getting your own needs met and risk setting up a competitive atmosphere. This is not an altogether negative way of participating, because others may react positively to your enthusiasm and automatically feel more motivated and appreciative of your expert power. It does, however, have the potential for slowing down the group's task progress, depending on how others in the group react to your style of contribution.

In the same scenario, what if you are knowledgeable about elements of the task of the group, yet do not have the same desire for recognition? In this instance, both you and others will perceive your personal power differently. If the group appears to be able to accomplish the task at hand, it is likely that you will be comfortable and participate as necessary. When the group becomes stalled, you may offer your suggestions with the goal of helping the group to continue its work. Other group members may eventually perceive you as having a kind of informational power. In the second instance you are focused on helping the group maintain its momentum. Your responsibility is to make sure you do not miss the opportunities to offer information when it is most helpful. In both of these scenarios, personal style has affected how you and others perceive your power in leadership roles. The task will be accomplished either way, yet the experience will be quite different as the power shifts amongst the group members.

The remaining task leadership roles (opinion seeking, information seeking, clarifying and summarizing) are also affected by your style of influence. For example, when clarifying information during any task, your communication style can be perceived either as threatening or helpful, depending on your tone of voice, the wording used and your body language. Notice the difference between saying, "I don't get it! I don't understand what you're saying because you are using big words. Could you please explain this in simple terms?" and saying, "I am not sure I understand. Can you give me an example so I can figure this out?" Both of these are asking for information that helps clarify the topic being discussed. The first comment is confrontative and may evoke defensiveness. The second comment puts the responsibility on the person trying to understand, rather than on the person sharing the information and comes from a power-with perspective. Communication skills are an aspect of personal power that will affect the way in which others perceive your use of influence.

All of the task leadership roles you take on in groups are significantly affected by the personal power you bring to any group experience. Again, there is no right or wrong style of influence. The way in which others perceive your power is beyond your control. In other words, you cannot be responsible for others' perceptions. What you are responsible for is meeting the leadership goals you hope to achieve and assessing whether you are being successful in reaching those goals. If you are not reaching those goals, take a close look at how you are using your personal power when trying to influence others, and consider what kind of change might be more effective. This is also important to the way you use your personal power in maintenance leadership roles.

Power in Maintenance Leadership

Just as with task leadership roles, personal power significantly affects the way we are perceived in maintenance leadership roles. Maintenance roles are not linked as easily as task roles to the kinds of power described earlier by French, Raven and Mayer. In general, maintenance is about improving the ability of group members to work together.

The goal of maintenance leadership is the creation of a comfortable and positive atmosphere and may not commonly be associated with the use of power. In essence, maintenance leadership is about creating a power-with working atmosphere. Therefore, the objective is to use one's personal power in a way that encourages, harmonizes and supports the group members and the overall process of the group. However, as noted in Chapter 4, there are times when the style of communication can be construed by others as patronizing and insincere, interfering with the process rather than contributing to it. When this happens, the feeling of shared power becomes lost as the influence shifts from a helpful, power-with approach to the use of what could be perceived as nuisance power (see Exercise 5.10).

EXERCISE 5.10 POWER IN MAINTENANCE LEADERSHIP ROLES

Objectives:

1. To link maintenance leadership roles to defined types of power
2. To consider how to use power in ways that best support group process
3. To analyze ways that personal power could most effectively be used in all maintenance roles

Create seven groups, with each group assigned one of the following maintenance roles, as outlined in Chapter 4:

- Gatekeeper
- Encourager
- Harmonizer
- Describer of emotional climate
- Consensus tester
- Process observer
- Tension reliever

Each group plans two simulations. In one simulation, the group acts out an effective use of power with their assigned maintenance role. In the other simulation the group acts out an ineffective use of power with that role. (Groups can come up with their own theme for the simulations or refer to earlier decision-making exercises for ideas.) Please note that it is not necessary for each member of the group to take on the role, but that there can be more than one person acting out the maintenance function.

When debriefing the simulations, the whole class will consider:

- Any links to French, Raven and Mayer's descriptions of kinds of power?
- What aspects of personal power contributed to either the positive or negative effect of the maintenance roles observed?

Coping with Destructive Uses of Power

We define **destructive power** as any style of influence that is used in ways that prevent groups from either accomplishing the task or maintaining a balanced work relationship amongst its members. This power can be expressed in many ways, including the non-functional leadership roles described in Chapter 4. Destructive uses of power can be either overt and easily recognized or subversive and less obvious. It is important to learn how to identify unhealthy uses of power and to respond in ways that help you and other group members maintain a level of respect within the group.

Overt uses of power include such things as coercion, bullying, the nuisance power of annoyance or irritation, complaining, sarcasm, whining and competing. You can most likely add other forms of overt, destructive power to this listing based on your personal experience. Overall, the effect of this kind of power is that individuals feel overwhelmed, annoyed, uneasy and uncomfortable. The person wielding the destructive power often becomes the focus of attention and, if not confronted in some way by other group members, gains even more power and momentum from his or her behaviour.

Dealing with bullying, competitive behaviour requires the ability to keep your emotional reaction under control while maintaining your position. Bullies evoke fear in most of us, yet it is important to acknowledge that this behaviour is unacceptable. The context (face-to-face, telephone or email), the dependency you have on the harassing person, and past history you have with that individual affect your response. Clear, well-timed and non-blameful statements that reflect your thoughts and feelings serve to de-escalate the interaction and send the message that you will not be intimidated, regardless of your relationship with that person. Take the time you need to decide how you are going to word your response and avoid getting caught up in a verbal battle that only reinforces the bullying behaviour. Though there is no fast rule about how to word any kind of response, simply remember that this person's power is effective only if others give in to his or her style of control.

Annoying, sarcastic, rude and whining behaviours also garner power and attention if they are not addressed in some way. If you are in discussion and find that someone in the group consistently uses these harassing tactics, it will be very difficult for you to ignore such behaviour and avoid using an equally sarcastic response. However, the most effective way of handling this behaviour is to simply put what you are saying on hold and somehow find out from that person what it is he or she is trying to say. One way of responding without sarcasm involves a communication that shares that you have noted what the person is saying and that you would welcome his or her comments. An example of a response might be, "Sounds like you don't agree with what I am saying. Can you tell me a bit more about what you are thinking?" The effectiveness of this statement is completely dependent on your tone of voice and your body language. If you are able to say this in a sincerely inquiring manner, it can be very effective in diminishing the destructive power.

Subversive, passive power that is used in indirect ways is difficult to spot. It will eventually become apparent as you look back at the dynamics of your group's interactions and realize that there is some kind of power imbalance you just cannot seem to pinpoint. There are many ways this type of power might present itself. Some of these include offering to take on responsibility and not following through, blaming others for whatever issues may have arisen in the group, consistently resisting others' ideas or suggestions, or outwardly agreeing to others' ideas and suggestions and then passively resisting them. A person may even subversively sabotage the work of the group by purposefully holding back information in order to gain a sense of control over other group members or the task itself. In some cases this kind of power is termed *passive-aggressive* in that the individual's goal is to somehow get another person to become so angry that he or she loses control. The power comes from the satisfaction of having this kind of control over others' behaviour.

How do you respond to this kind of power? You will feel irritated and manipulated by the use of subversive, passive power because it often falls just within the parameters of socially acceptable behaviour. You may even ask yourself whether a response is necessary. If you have to deal with a group member's subtle use of passive-aggressive power tactics, remain calm and describe the behaviour you have observed (whether it is not following through on tasks, blaming others, resisting ideas, etc.). After clearly describing the behaviours observed, it is important to explain the consequences for the group (mentioning that the group is behind on its work, clarifying that this was work that the individual had promised to do and acknowledging that the group seems stuck and cannot move forward). Both components of this communication are important because if you do not explain the consequences of the individual's behaviour, your comments may be confronted with arguing or other forms of resistance. This calm response also lets the person know you will not be manipulated into an angry outburst.

Overt and subversive destructive power can destroy a group. It is challenging to deal with this kind of power, and it is experienced in different ways by each individual. Self-control, reflection and clear communication are necessary in dealing effectively with these difficult situations. Reflective practice and experience over time is really the only way of learning how to respond successfully.

Power in Formal Leadership Roles

In Chapter 4 we discussed aspects of formal leadership roles that best support groups over which assigned leaders have authority. When you are in an assigned leadership role, you have legitimate power, and in order to be most effective you have to become comfortable with the power that comes with directing others. Essentially you have been assigned a power-over position, and factors of personal style, organizational need, dependency and others' perceptions affect the success you will experience in this role.

The most successful assigned leaders accept the power of their position and create an **egalitarian** atmosphere that empowers those within their team. Along with this power-with approach comes the acknowledgment that these individuals hold organizational responsibility for decision making. That is, they are straightforward about accepting the accountability inherent in their position. When individuals are comfortable in their assigned roles as leaders, they work on establishing trust and respect the roles of those over whom they have authority. In this way, the reality of a power-over position is tempered with a power-with style. The ability to create this positive, respectful work environment comes from the assigned leader's own healthy sense of self-confidence and power-from-within.

What we have just described is the ideal state of affairs in any situation where there is an assigned leadership role. Obviously environments exist where people in formal leadership roles use coercive and controlling power to force employees to work in specific ways. Unless the organization in which you work has a formalized process (sanction power) that helps employees deal with difficult working conditions, there is very little you can do in situations where you are being unfairly treated by an assigned supervisor, director or manager. If you have explored all avenues for giving feedback and attempts at working through better, more reasonable ways of working together, you are then faced with the decision of whether this is the right place for you to work. Otherwise you may run the risk of behaving in ways that are in conflict with your values and beliefs and your natural way of interacting with others.

Final Comment

Issues of power are implicit in every one of our interactions. Remember that the extent of the power we wield or the impact of the power we witness is a function of the way those around that power respond. Even the most destructive, coercive power will gain its strength from the way it is responded to by others. Learning to recognize the use of controlling, negative power offers you the opportunity to think about how you can respond in ways that do not reinforce its strength. The more you feel a healthy power-from-within, the easier it will be to engage in communication strategies that will restore balance to the trust and productivity of the group. Again, feeling your own power and recognizing how you allow yourself to be influenced by that power used by others develops with time and experience.

Summary

A discussion of how we use our power and how we respond to others' power helps us better understand the effective, balanced use of group leadership roles. In interaction with others, our perception of their power (whether or not it is accurate) affects the amount of influence they have on us. As well, the more dependent we are on another person, the more influence they may have over us. Both dependency and perception influence the power balance amongst group members.

Other power influences in social interactions include reward power, coercive power, legitimate (prescribed) power, referent power, expert power and informational power (French & Raven, 1959; Raven, 1965). These bases of power are ascribed, earned or perceived by group members. Nuisance power, habitual (status quo) power, sanction power and personal power (as described by Mayer, 2000) are also relevant to an understanding of forms of power that affect group process.

In the helping professions, the concept of empowerment includes the personal power we develop in ourselves (power-from-within) as well as the power we help build and support in those we work with (power-with). Developing healthy personal power begins in the very early years and is a product of our early relationships. Our own feelings of self-efficacy and self-esteem affect the kind of power we share with others.

In all interactions, our communication style is the primary indicator of how we demonstrate our power to others. Clear, respectful communication (when influencing others or responding to others) indicates a healthy and non-threatening use of power. Learning how to pay attention to our behaviour in all interactions helps develop our ability to work with others in ways that share power and improve cohesiveness. This awareness of our use of power also affects the impact of our task and maintenance leadership roles in group situations.

As with non-functional leadership roles, there are certain destructive uses of power that can threaten group trust and stability. Ways of dealing with these kinds of difficult behaviours serve to de-escalate the impact of threatening, unhealthy power and stop its momentum.

Key Terms

Attachment *(p. 128)*
Authoritarian *(p. 127)*
Authoritative *(p. 128)*
Coercive power *(p. 121)*
Defensiveness *(p. 131)*
Dependency *(p. 120)*
Destructive power *(p. 138)*
Egalitarian *(p. 140)*
Empowerment *(p. 125)*
Expert power *(p. 123)*
Habitual power *(p. 124)*
Informational power *(p. 123)*
Legitimate power *(p. 122)*
Nuisance power *(p. 124)*
Perception *(p. 119)*
Permissive *(p. 128)*
Personal power *(p. 124)*
Power *(p. 117)*
Power-from-within *(p. 125)*
Power-over *(p. 125)*
Power struggles *(p. 119)*
Power-with *(p. 125)*
Referent power *(p. 123)*
Reward power *(p. 121)*
Sanction power *(p. 124)*
Self-efficacy *(p. 127)*
Self-esteem *(p. 127)*

Case Studies

The following case studies, taken from classroom, human service team and community contexts will help clarify the topics covered in this chapter, using real-world examples. These case studies offer the opportunity to view the effects of power in group situations. As well, there is an opportunity to identify how power affects others in groups and explore ways that power can be confronted or responded to.

Case Study 5.1 **Power in a Small Group**

CATEGORY: STUDENT

It is now the third semester of Reza's community support worker diploma program and the instructor has announced that she would like to assign work groups on a project worth 50 percent of the overall course grade. The assignment is part of her Programming for Adults with Disabilities course, and the student groups must create a program plan for a group of clients in a group-home context. Being part of an assigned group works well for Reza, because whenever the students in her class create their own groupings, Reza feels somewhat left out. It seems to her that when the students get to form their own groupings, the others are quick to find people they enjoy working with, and she and a couple of other students are left over to work with each other. Reza has two very young children, a husband who does shift work and so much responsibility outside of class that she has not had the time or energy to get to know the other students on a social level. Because of this, she feels somewhat isolated most of the time. As well, Reza has made it clear to the whole class over the past couple of semesters that she cannot stay after class, and during lunch hours she heads over to the college daycare to visit with her children.

The assigned group for the big project has been given class time (four afternoon sessions) to work on their task. This is enough time to get most of the work done, though there will be the need to meet outside of class, as well. The other group members (Maria, Skylar and Ewan) seem excited about working on this programming task, and during the first two class working sessions they take a strong leadership role in structuring what has to be done. As well, they are making sure everyone is comfortable with the process of working together. During the first work session, Reza is fairly quiet after telling the rest of the group that she is having a tough time with her little ones, she is tired all the time and that getting together after class may not work for her. During the second session, the others notice that she becomes even quieter, removes herself a bit from the group and has not accomplished much of the homework she had promised to do after their last session together. Maria, Skylar and Ewan move on with their sections anyway.

During the third meeting together, Reza is still behind on her portion of the work, and the piece she has accomplished is confusing and poorly organized. As each group member checks in and shares his or her homework on the project, Reza continues to complain about the fact that she has so many responsibilities that she cannot get her work done. The three others listen attentively, yet appear to be getting a bit impatient with her excuses. She then turns quiet, crosses her arms and looks down, withdrawing from the process as the other three continue to work on their group task. As far as Reza is concerned, she is feeling left out yet again. The work session feels uncomfortable, as the other three attempt to include her in the work by asking for her ideas and attempting to figure out some way that they can arrange meetings outside of class to keep up with the project work.

QUESTIONS:

1. What kind of power do you see having influence here?
2. How has the power shifted over the first three work sessions?
3. If you were a member of this group, how might you create a more balanced, productive situation? What might you communicate to all group members about how things might improve?

Case Study 5.2 **Dealing with Power**

CATEGORY: STUDENT

A group of 22 students has been in a human service diploma program for almost two semesters and are doing course work in preparation for their intercession spring practicum. They have three different instructors in this program. As is usually the case, each instructor has a different style of teaching and brings his or her own expertise to the content.

One instructor has different expectations from the other instructors, and now that the program has been underway for almost two semesters, the students have become increasingly irritated by the way he treats them in class. He is extremely well-versed in the subject matter he teaches and has published many research papers over the many years he has taught in human service programs. However, he tends to make subtle, off-hand, derogatory remarks to students when they do not agree with him on certain issues and has actually become outwardly impatient with those who do not seem to understand the logic of some of his rules about assignment expectations or due dates.

As time goes by in the program, he seems to be getting more and more rigid and inflexible, and many of the students are finding the class atmosphere very uncomfortable. Students begin to compare him to the other two instructors and, outside of the college context, share more and more anecdotes and gossip about how they are feeling about the way they are being treated.

Finally the situation comes to a head when the instructor refuses to give extensions to five of the students who have been feeling pressured about the assignment load before practicum and asked for those extensions a bit later than they should have. The rule is that you can only be granted an extension if you request one two days before it is due, and these five students asked the day before. Depending on how long it takes to complete the assignment, they will either fail the course or have to rewrite that assignment in order to continue into practicum. The rest of the student group finds out about this situation and decides to meet out of class and discuss what has happened. They are all feeling frustrated and angry about the treatment of these five students.

QUESTIONS:

1. What kind of power do you see having influence here?
2. Do you think the students should confront the instructor? If so, how should they do so, and what might be the consequences? If they do not confront the instructor, what might be the consequences?
3. How might the factors of dependency and perception affect the student response in this situation?

Case Study 5.3 **Parent Participation Preschool**

CATEGORY: TEAM

Kira has been working as a supervising teacher in a Parent Participation Preschool (PPP) setting for two years. Prior to Kira being employed by the parent board, the supervising teacher (Angelina) had been in the position for about 15 years and was well-loved by all families in the PPP. Kira is an experienced early childhood educator and has worked in childcare for approximately 10 years in a daycare environment. She came to the PPP with great excitement and excellent references.

Because all PPPs in the province are governed by local parent boards (within a provincial network), Kira has to work within the mandate of the overall structure of this parent-run organization. Although Kira is responsible for daily programming decisions having to do with the children, all administrative functions are governed by the parents. Kira works daily with four parent assistants who must take monthly education opportunities in order to learn the appropriate skills necessary to meet the provincial licensing criteria. As the months have gone by, Kira has become increasingly aware of a small group of parents who have had children in the preschool for an average of three or four years and hold executive positions in the parent board. One parent has been president for three consecutive two-year terms and another has been treasurer for two of those terms. They appear to be friends, as well.

Now that Kira is preparing for her third year in the PPP, she is hoping to make some changes to the program and is preparing to present these changes to the board at the June meeting. As well, during the second year of her employment, she has noticed that there are a number of new parents entering the program, and she is hoping to convince those parents and the more experienced parents that these changes would be helpful.

She has tentatively discussed some of these changes in the months prior to the June meeting and senses some resistance to her ideas from the board members. As well, at the monthly parent meetings Kira has noticed that new parents say very little and those parents who have been with the PPP for some time seem to take over the meetings. If a vote is taken, new parents appear somewhat afraid to vote against any of the issues suggested by the existing board.

QUESTIONS:

1. What kind of power do the board members have?
2. How might this organization ensure that new parents feel empowered to voice their ideas and get their needs met?
3. What challenges do you see Kira facing here? What opportunities?
4. How might Kira voice her ideas and get her needs met in a way that is non-confrontative and lays the groundwork for her own place of influence in the PPP?

Case Study 5.4 Power in Workplace Supervision

CATEGORY: TEAM

Michael, Sasha and Miguel have been working as recreation therapists in an extended-care unit of a large hospital. The unit head that they have worked with over the past ten years has recently retired and has been replaced by an RN, Chantel, who has worked in public health for about 20 years. She is fairly new to the community and has a lot of experience with seniors and with the issues associated with planning for multiple geriatric needs.

For the first six months of working under Chantel's management, Michael, Sasha and Miguel have enjoyed her enthusiasm and her energy in making positive changes in the facility. As the recreation therapy team leader, Miguel has had a number of meetings with Chantel and is hopeful that the issues they have discussed about new and innovative plans for clients will finally be resolved. As well, Miguel represents Michael and Sasha at unit meetings with all other team leaders supervising the other factions of the extended-care facility. As time goes by it becomes quite evident that Chantel is very popular with the hospital administration and many of the team leaders. At the same time, Chantel's interest in meeting the recreation needs of the seniors in care has waned somewhat, and at their upcoming one-on-one meeting Miguel will ask why the plans they had discussed in the past have not been implemented.

The meeting gets cancelled at the last minute, so Miguel calls Chantel about this one issue, since Sasha and Michael are becoming quite frustrated about the lack of progress. He begins by inquiring about the progress of their new planning ideas. As the phone conversation continues, Chantel becomes quite irritated with Miguel, raises her voice and begins to accuse him of being unnecessarily impatient and non-supportive. As well, she accuses him of talking about his frustrations with others and engaging in unprofessional behaviour. Miguel is not sure what to say because he is shocked that Chantel would over-react to his asking why certain project plans have been put aside. He apologizes to Chantel and defends himself by explaining that he has only talked to the other therapists in his team about the issues. He is quite taken aback by the accusations, Chantel's tone on the telephone and her unexpected outburst. He decides perhaps she has simply had a bad day and lets it go.

There is a meeting of all team leaders planned for the following week. At this meeting Miguel cannot help but notice a rather cool response from Chantel as the team leaders all gather. He is now becoming a bit agitated by all this, takes a breath and settles into the meeting, deciding to keep fairly quiet. About a third of the way through this meeting, Chantel reports on a new policy she has developed pertaining to client care. Part way through her report, she looks up, points a finger at one of the other team leaders (not Miguel) and screams, "What kind of an expression is that?" as the team leader reacts to her report with a scowl on her face. All team leaders look down, and the person Chantel has screamed at turns red and sits quietly for the balance of the meeting. Miguel is now quite perplexed and unsure about what to do, given that he has witnessed behaviour that is both surprising and disrespectful, with the potential of seriously affecting him and the people he works with.

QUESTIONS:

1. What kind of power do you see having influence here?
2. What implications does this use of power have for the workplace and client care?
3. How might you be feeling in this situation if you were in Miguel's place?
4. What options does Miguel have in this situation? For each option consider both short-term and long-term consequences.

Case Study 5.5 **Long-Term Board Members**

CATEGORY: COMMUNITY

Nadir is the supervisor of a group home run by a non-profit organization that is governed by a board of directors. The board consists of seven to ten members comprised of parents and community members. Terms of office are two years with elections held accordingly.

Nadir has worked for the group home for 12 years and has watched the gradual transformation of the board. When he first started working for the organization, the board was vital and enthusiastic, working efficiently together to ensure that decisions were made quickly to support the work of the employees with their clients. The president of the board had strong values about client-centred service and was very eager to ensure the group home offered a quality program. Other board members noticed this commitment, and when it came time to elect new officers, the same president was elected again.

Two years later the same president was re-elected again. Now in his fifth year as president, he is very familiar with important community contacts and government agencies that assist his organization. He speaks easily of the history of the group home and is knowledgeable about its needs for future growth. When board members have questions, they seek out the president for answers.

In the middle of this term, however, some of his enthusiasm starts to wane as other life commitments become important. He makes less effort to stay on top of critical issues and delays decisions, which affects the ability of the employees to provide quality care. There seems to be a decline in the president's commitment to and excitement in completing the necessary tasks of his office. He is vague about timelines, paperwork is lost, and contact with employees is minimal. Nadir is affected by the fact that issues are not responded to in a timely manner and that he cannot get the answers he needs in order to best facilitate program development.

Despite the awareness of other board members that perhaps it might be time for a new president, at election time no one wants to suggest he step down. Others are reluctant to run for the office of president, and he is elected again.

QUESTIONS:

1. What kind of power does the president hold? What are the effects of that kind of power?
2. What factors led to that power?
3. How could this kind of power be guarded against?
4. Is it ever positive to have this kind of power? Why or why not?
5. Is there anything Nadir might do about this situation?

Reflection Tool

What?

What stood out for you in this chapter? Describe a reading, exercise, incident, person's behaviour, etc.

So What?

1. Emotional impact?

2. Why do you think you had this emotional response?

3. What assumptions might you be making in this situation? What beliefs and values were touched off by this situation?

Assumptions:

Beliefs, values:

4. Write about the meaning this has for you. Some helpful questions might be:
Do you think your values might be clouding your interpretation of the situation? If so, how?

Have you been affected by similar situations in the same way? How have you responded?

5. Is it important for you to change your behaviour? Why?

Now What?

6. Based on the learning from this chapter, what other behaviours might you consider?

7. What might stop you from engaging in these new behaviours?

Objectives

What Questions Remain?

Chapter 6

Decision Making from a Shared Understanding

Objectives

In this chapter, students will acquire the knowledge, skills and attitudes to:

1. Define the concept of shared understanding.
2. Identify factors that affect the process of decision making.
3. Distinguish the most effective ways of problem solving when decision making is blocked.
4. Understand how negotiation, controversy and confrontation link to conflict.
5. Identify when disagreement becomes conflict.
6. Appreciate the role of conflict in group development.
7. Reflect on their own and others' conflict styles and the impact of these styles on resolving issues that block group progress.
8. Use models of conflict resolution in ways that enhance group effectiveness.

A Context of Shared Understanding

When working in group situations, we have to make decisions of all kinds. Sometimes these decisions come easily and consensus is reached without too much effort on the part of all group members. Then there are the times when some members do not agree, tension builds and an uncomfortable feeling overrides the group, blocking decision making and ultimately stalling group process. In earlier chapters of the text we identified how the stage of group development, leadership, or power and influence can affect group productivity. In this chapter we will focus on how certain problem-solving and conflict-resolution approaches can be used in ways that help groups deal with stalled progress while reaching a heightened sense of group cohesion. For us, the expression "reaching a shared understanding" describes the framework that supports this process of making decisions.

One of the best descriptions of the term *shared understanding* comes from human development researcher Dr. Michael Guralnick. Dr. Guralnick's work on the social integration needs of young children describes the importance of shared understanding to successful attempts at learning the skills of healthy interaction in the early years. His definition of the term **shared understanding** is also relevant to the group development needs of adults. For Guralnick (1993):

> . . . unless both the child and his or her peers have a shared understanding of the task or activities at hand, a common awareness of prevailing social rules, and agreed upon patterns of interaction, coherent, connected, and relevant exchanges are not likely to occur. (p. 6)

This also holds true for adults who engage in the process of decision making. In order to achieve an outcome that is satisfying to all group members, there must be a foundation that supports a willingness to engage in discussion and a willingness to explore disagreements. This foundation is created when all group members are clear about the goals of their task and have established an atmosphere where open communication is the norm. In this context, shared understanding is achieved because group members are willing to listen to each other and strive to appreciate each other's point of view. Within this atmosphere, interactions are "coherent, connected, and relevant" with all group members working together to reach a decision that meets the needs of all involved (Guralnick, 1993, p. 6).

Guralnick's definition of shared understanding does not imply that every good decision is made only through consensus. What it does imply is that group members may disagree, yet have the capacity to come to a decision that meets the needs of all those involved even when they have different perspectives. This chapter will explore how group membership, the stage of group development and communication styles affect this capacity. There are models of decision making and conflict resolution that support a group's goal to meet the needs of all its members.

Methods of Decision Making

There are several ways of reaching decisions, not all of which come from a place of shared understanding. We believe it is important to be aware of some of the more common decision-making styles in order to make informed choices about which methods are most useful in specific circumstances. The following exercise will help you experience the impact of these styles of decision making before you take a close look at their definitions (see Exercise 6.1 on page 152).

When you make the decisions in the following exercise, consider, based on your past experience, whether there is a particular style of decision making that you either like or dislike, and explore the reasons for your decision.

EXERCISE 6.1 METHODS OF DECISION MAKING

Objectives:

1. To experience the impact of specific decision-making methods
2. To more clearly understand how decisions are commonly made in groups
3. To reflect on how certain well-known methods of decision making can affect members' feelings of personal effectiveness, trust and cohesion in groups

This exercise will require a fair amount of time, because the whole class will be engaged in a large decision with components that build upon each other. As well, many of the decision components require the involvement of the instructor in preparation for the particular process.

The class will be engaged in creating a graduation celebration plan. This exercise can either simulate the process of planning graduation or can actually be the time when the class explores some concrete plans. Either way, it is important to the objectives of the exercise that the group follow the directions of the decision-making style carefully. Each component of the graduation celebration will be decided differently. As well, the whole class must be involved in each component.

After the decision has been made for each component of this exercise, students record the following (for later discussion and reflection):

1. What their role was in the decision
2. How personally effective they felt about the role they played
3. How committed they felt to implementing the decision
4. Their impressions of the quality of the decision made
5. Any impressions about the group cohesiveness during the decision-making process

Decision #1: The instructor explains that there will be a celebration and that its location has to be determined. The class sits in a circle, and the instructor asks each student where he or she thinks the graduation party should be held. As each student offers an opinion, it is recorded on paper for all to see. The most popular opinion will decide the location. There is no interaction among students, although the instructor can answer some basic clarification questions one-on-one as each student proffers an opinion. After the decision is recorded, students take time to note their reflections.

Decision #2: The instructor chooses someone in the student group to be the decision maker. This decision maker decides exactly what the dress code for the event will be. There is no consultation with the other students. Once the dress code is determined, it is recorded for all to see. After the decision is recorded, students take time to note their reflections.

Decision #3: The instructor explains that the students have two options in a decision about who can attend the celebration: (a) students only or (b) students and their families or friends (unlimited). Class members are then asked to vote for their choice. The majority choice wins the vote. If (b) is the majority choice, the instructor asks the class to vote again for the following two options: (a) no limits to number of family or friends or (b) limit to partners, mother and father. All majority choices are recorded for all to see. After the decision is recorded, students take time to note their reflections.

Decision #4: The students discuss who among them has a lot of experience with catering, restaurant work or cooking. As a group they must choose the person who has the most expertise about matters of menu planning and food selection. That person is then asked to decide what kind of food the celebration should include. Once that person has made a decision, it is recorded for all to see. After the decision is recorded, students take time to note their reflections.

Decision #5: The instructor appoints a group of four students to decide the entertainment for the graduation event. This group forms a small circle inside the larger student circle and discusses what they think the entertainment should be. Once they reach a decision on entertainment, it is recorded for all to see. After the decision is recorded, students take time to note their reflections.

Decision #6: The instructor chooses one member of the group to be the leader who has the responsibility to decide what the maximum charge should be for each person attending the graduation celebration event. This person's job is to decide the maximum amount each person will have to pay in order to meet the costs of Decisions 1 through 5. It is important that this person also ask all other group members what they think. After listening to everyone's opinion, he or she must make the final decision about cost. Once the decision is made, it is recorded for all to see, and there is no more input from other group members. After the decision is recorded, students take time to note their reflections.

Decision #7: The class breaks into five groups. Each group is asked to work out some kind of schedule for the graduation celebration. The small groups are encouraged to take the time they need to agree to a schedule that meets each group member's needs.

Once all small groups have created a schedule, one student from the class offers to facilitate discussion as each small group shares its ideas with the whole class, posting all the schedules around the room for everyone to see. As well, each small group should be prepared to share a rationale that supports its schedule.

All five groups listen to each other's schedules and rationales and engage in a discussion about the pros and cons of each other's ideas. If there are differing opinions they are discussed openly. No matter how long it takes, the group reaches consensus on a schedule that meets the goals of all five groups. The schedule is then posted for all to see. After the decision is recorded, students take time to note their reflections.

As a whole class, discuss your impressions of this exercise. Share any frustrations you experienced while using the various decision-making processes before you read about them in this chapter.

Johnson and Johnson (2006) have clearly defined the methods of **decision making** (coming to conclusions as a group) experienced in Exercise 6.1. Each of these methods has its strengths and weaknesses and is appropriate to specific situations. As well, each of these methods offers challenges and opportunities that will clearly affect group members' feelings of personal effectiveness, trust and cohesion during the decision-making process. Leadership style and the use of power are defining factors that affect all group members differently, depending on the kind of decision-making method used.

Decision by Authority Without Group Discussion (Exercise 6.1: Decision #2)

This type of decision making occurs when the person who has some kind of legitimate power in any group makes an autonomous decision without any input from other group members. Time constraints and the content and importance of the decisions being made affect the usefulness of this kind of decision-making process. If the supervisor of a large adult-care facility has to make a quick decision about what kind of paper towel to order when the vendor has said that there is a sale of paper goods that will end soon, then this kind of decision making is very effective. It is quick, it is timely and chances are others do not want to be bothered by this kind of decision. If the assigned leader of the organization is trusted and group members feel confident that these kinds of decisions will be in their best interest, then autonomous decision making makes sense.

This method will erode trust and cohesion in the group when the assigned leader continues to use this style to make decisions that would benefit from the resources available through discussion with all group members. Then this becomes a very powerful, power-over leadership style that diminishes group trust and cohesion. When members lack the opportunity to have input into the decision-making process they experience a loss of power, feel less committed to the outcome and may feel resentful if the decision goes against their values and beliefs. The opportunity for creative solutions that meet the needs of everyone is severely limited when only one person is making the decisions.

Decision by Expert (Exercise 6.1: Decision #4)

Just as we concluded in our Chapter 5 discussion about expert power, sometimes specific decisions are best made by the group member with the most expertise in a particular content area. This kind of decision making is helpful when group members are very clear about who has the expert knowledge that benefits a particular decision. The level of trust in that person is high, and other group members are willing to accept whatever the result of the decision making might be. It can be time-consuming and frustrating when it is not clear who has the expertise in the group, or when someone thinks he or she is the expert and others disagree. The person with expert power may not be the assigned leader, yet plays a strong task leadership role when taking responsibility for the decision-making process.

As with decision making by authority without discussion, decisions made by the expert also lack input from others and therefore involve the loss of creativity from whole-group interaction. If there is any lack of trust in the expert, there will likely be lower commitment to the decision and possibly resentment from others, resulting in diminished group cohesion.

Decision by Averaging Everyone's Opinion (Exercise 6.1: Decision #1)

This method of decision making is similar to taking a vote, except that there is a chance that a decision might be made by fewer than half of the total number of group members. For example, consider the scenario where a team of 10 early childhood educators is asked by their director to choose amongst three options for moving their program to a different location. The director calls each of the team members and asks him or her to choose which option he or she prefers: the room with lots of storage, the room with great lighting or the room with easy access to the parking lot. Four people choose the room with storage, three people choose the room with good lighting and three choose the room with easy access. As you can see, the room with the most storage is the most popular opinion, yet only four of the nine team members made this choice. If the director uses this method to make her decision, the decision will be based on the choice of fewer than half of the team members. This method accesses common (average) opinion but not majority opinion and may exclude the needs of most of the group.

This may be an appropriate process when accessing opinions on less important issues or when time is a factor and not all group members can meet to make a decision. However, as you can see from the example above, the risk of group dissatisfaction and lowered trust is high when the decision is important.

Decision by Authority after Group Discussion (Exercise 6.1: Decision #6)

If you work in a hierarchical organization and are represented by an assigned leader, then you will probably find that this is a common way of making most decisions. Usually the leader meets with the group and asks for input on specific questions or issues. Once the input is given, the leader then makes the decision. He or she may have to represent that decision to an even higher authority. With this style of decision making the onus is on the leader to make the best use of input from others, while taking responsibility for the impact of the decision itself. As in our earlier discussions of assigned or formal leadership style, there is the potential here for open and meaningful participation by all group members if the leader is willing to accept all input and accurately reflect that input in the decision made.

Potential challenges to this decision-making process might be that group members feel:

- distrust from not knowing exactly what the leader may be doing with the input.
- lowered group commitment because the leader may ask for input but not represent the needs of the group in the final decision.
- disempowered from lack of personal effectiveness and real authority.
- the need to compete with each other to gain attention.

Unless there is high trust and cohesion in a group represented by an authority responsible for ultimately making decisions, this style of decision making may result in group members feeling resentful and somewhat irritated if asked for input that may ultimately be ignored in the final outcome. If the leader can create a shared understanding amongst all group members that he or she is committed to using the group's input and is willing to reflect everyone's needs (as much as possible) in the making of decisions, then this arrangement can be effective. Obviously this requires extremely sensitive leadership.

Decision by Minority (Exercise 6.1: Decision #5)

In some large groups there may be situations where an assigned, representative group or committee makes important decisions. Examples include a student union association in a college or university, a parent advisory executive committee in a public school or a board of directors for a non-profit society. In these contexts, decisions are made by a very small group contained within a larger group. This system of decision making poses many challenges, because this small group is assigned to take responsibility for decisions that will affect a large, often changing, population of group members. Usually these **minority** groups are given the authority to make decisions without having input from members of the larger group. This precludes much hope of creating a process of shared understanding because decisions are made without the requirement of seeking input from the larger group.

Within some large groups a committee may be elected to research a specific issue and to make a decision based on the results of their investigations. In this example, expert power is given to a few group members, and there is enough trust in their ability that any decisions made will be accepted and utilized. Again, only when group members feel trusting of each other and cohesion is high, will this kind of decision making represent a context of shared understanding.

Decision by Majority Vote (Exercise 6.1: Decision #3)

This seems to be a very popular way for groups to make decisions. Decisions are looked at as a choice among options, and the option that gets more than half of the votes wins. We have been conditioned to believe that as long as a **majority** of the group agrees with something then that is the way the decision will have to be. Many people like to use this method because it is fast and easy, particularly when discussion becomes stalled; there is an impasse that has to be overcome with a decision, and group members just want to get on with the task.

Quick and easy does not necessarily work for everyone. Whenever there is a majority, there is also a minority, and in some cases the latter group is of a significant size. If there is a minority left behind, then there is the potential for dissension and resentment. As well, by avoiding taking the time to work through issues, there is a significant loss of creative input, personal effectiveness for all group members and group cohesiveness. When you think back to our earlier discussion of task and maintenance leadership roles, there is the potential for task-focused group members to hurry along decisions by calling for a majority vote. Reaching an impasse usually means that there are differing opinions amongst group members that are not easily resolved. Avoiding confrontation for the sake of time and energy by calling for a vote will only mask problems. Unfortunately taking a show of hands and voting for a majority opinion when groups are stuck has become a common way of overcoming stalled progress.

Decision by Consensus (Exercise 6.1: Decision #7)

Decision by **consensus** involves the active input of all group members in order to reach a solution that everyone can support. There is a shared understanding that the time will be taken to explore everyone's point of view in order to meet all group members' needs as closely as possible in the final decision. In other words, there may be members who do not fully agree with the final outcome but are willing to support it because they have a full understanding of the rationale that underpins the decision. By its very nature, consensus involves the open discussion of everyone's ideas. As a result, the potential for conflict increases as group members share ideas that others may disagree with. It is important to accept this conflict and explore differences of opinion rather than be intimidated or worried that the differences of opinion will escalate into unresolved conflict and hurt feelings. This process is supported by group trust and cohesion, which grows with each opportunity to resolve conflict and reach consensus.

For consensus building to occur, there should be structures in place that ensure that all group members have the opportunity to share their perspectives. In the case of Exercise 6.1: Decision #7, your class size was likely to be somewhere between 15 and 30 people, making it necessary to create a structure that allowed each of you to have a small-group forum to share ideas before representing them to the whole group. In a large-group forum the process of idea sharing can easily become unwieldy. It is our experience that when a large group tries to make a decision, some typical behaviours occur. Some group members just keep moving along by blurting out ideas and opinions; some people shut down in fear of having to express a different opinion and face possible conflict; and some become irritated by a discussion that seems to go in circles. If you take a look at the structure of Decision #7 you will see that small groups offered a less-threatening context for initial ideas to be shared before moving into the larger group. This provided more time for each group member to explore ideas and differences of opinion. When the rationales for these differences are shared, it becomes less arduous to reach some level of mutual understanding before settling on one decision.

All of the rules about open communication, sharing of power and balanced leadership are obviously important to consensus building. As well, there are other basic ground rules that will contribute to your success in working toward consensus.

Consensus begins with the exploration of a variety of ideas and possibilities. Remember to present your thoughts clearly and to invite the ideas of others in order to allow all group members to present their points of view. This allows for even less-obvious suggestions to be aired for consideration. It may be that one aspect of such suggestions is that they provide the creative energy that moves the group toward a solution that works for everyone. Some term this *thinking out of the box.* By brainstorming all possible solutions to a decision and then taking components of a variety of ideas, there is more potential for success. All group members then feel heard, power is shared because all contributions are considered and **synergy** (a heightened feeling of cohesion and productivity) grows from the process of interaction.

There is a fine balance that must be taken into consideration once group members have clearly described their ideas or advocated for their positions. On the one side, group members want to be clear and assertive about their positions, and on the other side, they cannot stay so rooted in these positions that they block progress. Flexibility and openness does not mean that group members yield their positions too easily or too quickly. What it does mean is that group members are open to listening to each other's perspectives and seeking out the reasons for their beliefs. This process often "dissects" components of the decision made and helps all group members to more carefully process those components. Some term this *unpacking the question,* which literally means that all of the components are laid out for everyone to consider. This is a valuable process with creative outcomes, once these components are then "repacked" into a decision that all group members can live with.

If group members advocate their positions and clearly identify their perspectives about a particular decision and still cannot come to a successful conclusion, then the process becomes stalled because of lack of flexibility on the part of certain individuals. The only way this process can be unblocked and consensus can occur is to take the time to look at the way in which the group is operating. The maintenance role of process observer can help by noting that the group is stalled and there is a need to clarify what the goals of the decision are and how the suggestions that have been made might fit with those goals. For example, a person might say, "We are really stuck here and it sounds like we aren't getting anywhere. What is it we are trying to achieve again? It looks like we may have lost our initial objective. Can we re-visit that?" This helps clarify the goals and can lead into a renewed discussion about possible solutions to the problem. It also helps shift any group dynamics that are contributing to stalled progress. This reminds us once again of the importance of certain leadership roles in the decision-making process (see Exercise 6.2).

EXERCISE 6.2 COMPONENT OF CONSENSUS BUILDING

Objectives:

1. **To practise a component of consensus building**
2. **To engage in communication skills that clearly express thoughts and ideas**
3. **To engage in listening skills that clarify and accept other perspectives**

This exercise is designed to help you engage in perspective sharing. This is one of the most important components of consensus building.

In groups of five, prepare for discussion by carefully reading the following guidelines:

1. All group members must have the opportunity to share their perspectives.
2. When a group member is not clear about something that is said, he or she asks for clarification or re-phrases the message to confirm that he or she heard it correctly.
3. All perspectives are listened to.
4. All group members must share their rationales for believing what they do about the issue.
5. Differences of perspective are explored openly, with respectful questioning.
6. Group members must work together to summarize perspectives shared.

Once all group members understand the guidelines, the task is to prepare a statement that summarizes the overall group perspective on the issue that follows, using the questions provided as guidelines for discussion.

This statement must also include reference to the rationales shared by group members. One person in the group should be chosen to read out the agreed-upon summary to the whole class.

In recent years there has been a tragic loss of life as a result of natural disasters like the tsunami in East Asia and the hurricanes in the southern United States. Canada has responded with varying degrees of support to the people affected by these disasters. The support has included fundraising, military service, human resources and a number of material supplies sent directly to the sites affected. As well, many people have felt the need to contribute personally to organizations that provide services to those affected by such disasters.

These disasters have also been fraught with controversy, as many question the appropriateness of the use of such resources when there are people suffering in our own communities and the possibility of fraudulent fundraising for funds that end up somewhere other than in disaster relief.

Discuss this issue and present your personal views to others in the group with reference to the following questions:

1. Should Canadian tax money be used to support disaster relief in other countries? Why or why not?
2. Do you feel obligated to donate money to disaster relief in other countries as a personal contribution to global responsibility? Why or why not?

Each of the five groups completes this exercise by sharing their statements with the whole class.

After all of the statements are read, members of each of the five groups debrief with each other how well they felt represented and listened to during the process of composing their statements.

Consensus is not always the best choice for some decision making. If time is a factor or if an organization has created authority structures that preclude decision making that involves all group members, then consensus is not a workable option. However, if consensus is the decision-making style of choice, then the backbone of this process is the willingness to see that a decision is taken to its conclusion and the determination not to give up by resorting to styles that resolve the issue quickly, yet leave group members feeling personally ineffective and dissatisfied (see Exercise 6.3).

EXERCISE 6.3 **BASE GROUP DISCUSSION OF DECISION-MAKING METHODS**

Objectives:

1. To increase self-awareness of your effectiveness in decision making
2. To discuss with others certain personal reactions to the various decision-making methods

In your Base Groups, revisit your answers to the discussion and reflection questions listed directly before Decision #1 in Exercise 6.1, on p. 152.

Discuss the following with Base Group members:

1. Did it seem to you that everyone in the class was happy about the decisions made (this refers to the commitment and quality questions)?
2. How personally effective did you all feel about the part you played in the process of decision making?
3. What other impressions did you have about the way the whole group worked together during each of the decision-making methods (this refers to the cohesiveness question)?

Consider the times when your role was limited by authorities making decisions without considering the value of your perspective in Exercise 6.1. Have you had similar experiences in the past? If you had the opportunity, would you make any attempts to shift the decision-making styles as you re-visit these experiences? If so, how?

Factors That Affect Decision Making

Certain factors can negatively affect the quality and efficiency of decisions being made if not addressed by the group during the decision-making process. These factors have been classified into three categories by Patton, Giffin and Patton (1989, p. 131): *procedural problems, process problems* and *personality problems*. Taking a closer look at factors that fall within these categories will help to draw together earlier discussions of group elements, leadership skills and the use of power into a context of decision making and ultimately conflict resolution.

Procedural Problems

As discussed in Chapter 2, there are certain preconceived notions we bring to the group experience that affect what we expect of others and ourselves as we begin to work together. If the group does not work quickly to clarify roles and create some kind of system that helps all group members understand how decisions are going to be made, then progress will stall. **Procedural problems** can occur when the norms need to be clear to all group members in order to provide some structure that allows them to trust that there is some methodology being used to move the group forward. When group members know that they will have enough airtime and all aspects of the decision will be actively explored, there is greater potential for effective group process.

Clarity about one's role in the group is a bit more difficult to define when shared leadership is the norm. When we work in a group that has a formalized leadership position, with someone to record the proceedings and other members having defined responsibilities, we generally feel confident about what the expectations are for us and for others we are working with. However, when shared leadership is the expectation and all we have is a task to be decided, role differentiation is less obvious and confusion may arise as to who is leading the group and how members are expected to provide input. This is the time to remember those important leadership roles that seek out structures that will support decision making. As discussed throughout Chapters 4 and 5, this process builds cohesion and empowers group members. It does not feel quite as comfortable as predefined role clarification and is a factor that affects decision making.

Process Problems

As we explored in Chapter 3, there is a developmental continuum that groups experience in their time together. The stage that any group is in has a direct impact on the ways members interact and ultimately make decisions together. Mix this with other factors of group size, group goals and the time that a group has to accomplish a task, and it is obvious that the way in which these variables present themselves will affect the ability of the group to make decisions. These variables are referred to as **process problems**.

When groups make decisions in the forming or inclusion stage of development, it is likely that there will be little deep exploration of people's perspectives, and decisions will be made at a rather superficial level. Members will be avoiding tension and potential conflict because they are still getting to know each other, and there is little trust or cohesion. Coming to quick decisions may serve the group when the decisions are of low impact on the people involved. If decisions are important ones to the group or organization involved and members are avoiding confrontation, then the result is usually a decision made with too little information. As well, staying at this stage of inclusion and engaging in the less confrontational process of coming to a decision will not help the group progress to its next stage of development and may lead to unresolved issues and hidden dissatisfaction with the decision made.

At the storming or control stage of group development, groups experience the discomfort of opposing views and the power struggles for perceived leadership. Because conflict is now surfacing and disagreements are more often verbalized, group members may begin to feel defensive and somewhat afraid that if the tension persists, a decision will never be made and relationships amongst the group members will be damaged. To avoid this, decisions are sometimes made hastily, with the use of majority vote to hurry the process. As discussed earlier in the text, this is a common solution in the avoidance of discomfort and does not make for informed and effective decision making. If a group is formed that will be working together on an ongoing basis (e.g., a team or staff grouping) and has the goal of becoming a cohesive, trusting group, then the uncomfortable processes experienced in the storming, control stage must be worked through. Only then can the next stage of productive, open interactions that lead to collaborative decision making be reached.

In the stage of norming or openness, groups feel a higher level of trust and cohesion, resulting in reduced fear when differences of opinion are expressed. There is a greater willingness to explore issues in depth, to take the time to hear everyone's perspectives and to retrieve whatever information is necessary for informed decisions. Power and control issues may arise, yet members trust each other enough to confront these issues when necessary. Be aware that when a group reaches this stage, there is the potential for groupthink as described in Chapter 3. One of the ironies of too much group cohesion is that group members support each other and have the potential of moving to decisions without considering alternative possibilities because everyone in the group is on the same page.

As you consider the groups you are a part of, be aware that the stage the group is at will affect your process of decision making. Your awareness of this as a possible problem area is the first step to understanding and overcoming what might be stalling or hurrying the decision making, allowing you to take corrective measures.

Personality Problems

Obviously the dynamics of decision making are affected significantly by the varying personality types in any group. There are some people in this world that each and every one of us finds hard to work with for a variety of reasons. We may perceive these people as hard to understand and frustrating to work with because we cannot identify with their style of interaction or simply because they are difficult for any number of reasons. As discussed in Chapter 2, personality types that comprise a group have an impact on the dynamics and effectiveness of that group. In decision making, the quality of the process and the product of the decision is affected by the ways personality types mix in a particular group. Personality types that have an adverse effect are often described as **personality problems**.

The earlier descriptions of non-functional leadership behaviours and destructive uses of power touch on the ways we work with uncomfortable dynamics in groups. But what about those times when we feel the frustration of working with someone whom we perceive as downright difficult?

Remember again the role of your perception in defining those people you may find challenging to work with. The person may be triggering something in you that others do not experience. It is always important to reflect on these situations and look carefully at what responsibility for the interaction resides in you as opposed to the other person. For example, say you enter a group situation and there is another group member who has the same strong organizational skills as you, yet seems to be much more assertive about the way he or she wants the work to be done. Your style is much less forceful, yet you are aware that doing things your way may take more time, and the group will benefit from a more organized process. However, this person is much more outgoing than you and takes over the task without allowing much input from others. You perceive this person to be somewhat of a bully, yet other group members seem content to let him or her take a strong task leadership role, making decisions expediently with less work for the group. The question you have to ask yourself is whether you perceive this person as a bully because he or she is pushy and disempowering or whether you are just upset because the process is not going the way you would have liked it to go. In this case, the challenging personality may be as much about your own perception as it is about the other person's style, because you may be the only person interpreting it negatively.

There are other situations, however, when most people in the group perceive one member's personality style as difficult or challenging. Some interesting terms developed by Gary and Ruth Namie (2000) to describe difficult personality types include the "bully", the "sniper", the "know-it-all", the "think-they-know-it-all", the "yes-person" and the "whiner".

Bullying, withdrawing, joking and whining have all been described in the section on non-functional behaviour in Chapter 4 or in the section that overviews coping with destructive uses of power in Chapter 5. These behaviours take the focus away from decision making and make the process of reaching a shared understanding that much more laborious. All of the creativity necessary to reach decisions through consensus gets diverted to dealing with confrontation and self-protection.

The know-it-alls, the think-they-know-it-alls and the yes-persons have not yet been discussed. These personality types take on positions of authority in decision making and appear to have a very high opinion of themselves. These people may actually have expert or informational power, yet yield that power without consideration of anyone else's opinion. Group members may compete with this person or disengage and leave the decision to the authority. This is particularly dangerous if the person is not really an expert, does not know it all and just thinks he or she knows it all. The group may defer to someone who is actually off track and makes decisions based on an inflated sense of self. Assertiveness of all group members is vital here, with each member taking responsibility for having input into decisions. With both personality types, clarifying the information is important, because it may be difficult to figure out if the voice of authority is perhaps a think-they-know-it-all. Blindly following suggestions from this kind of authority without critical analysis of the information is risky.

Yes-persons bring yet another interesting dynamic to decision making. In their need to be liked and avoid conflict at any cost, yes-persons may agree to just about anything. Later in this chapter we discuss how conflict can be a creative problem-solving process. Having a yes-person in the group may limit a full and meaningful interchange of ideas by all group members. In order to engage the yes-person in a more honest dialogue, a process must be structured that encourages all group members to share their ideas. This takes time and will be more evident in later stages of group development (that is, norming and performing) if the group has demonstrated that it is okay to express differences of opinion. Be aware that some yes-persons may never feel safe enough to disagree with others (see Exercise 6.4).

Did you see any of these difficult behaviours as familiar (either because you have engaged in them or have been on the receiving end)? If so, reflect on the impact of this exercise.

EXERCISE 6.4 DEALING WITH DIFFICULT PERSONALITY DYNAMICS

Objectives:

1. To experience the frustration of making decisions with difficult personality types
2. To experiment with ways of responding to certain personality types

Students choose a partner for this exercise. Partners label themselves A or B. As each partner engages in a group decision-making exercise, the other partner observes the exercise in order to offer feedback on communication effectiveness and level of participation in the exercise.

Observers look for the following:

1. The reactions from other members of the decision-making group to their partners' contributions
2. The communication skills used by their partners
3. The overall impact of their partners' role in the decision-making exercise

The following role behaviour descriptions should be written on slips of paper:

Bully: Forcefully advocate for your ideas; interrupt others; use passion when communicating (lean forward, shake your head when you do not agree and look very intense).

Yes-person: Agree with everyone; offer to do any work necessary; do not offer any of your own ideas.

Whiner: When an idea is shared, complain about why it will not work; use a whining tone of voice and appear to be completely at the mercy of forces beyond your control.

Think-they-know-it-all: Use confidence with your ideas; make others believe that you know about organizing special events and have contacts that will be useful to the planning; make up believable examples of times when your suggestions have worked in the past.

Withdrawer: Say nothing; look out the window; write notes to yourself; appear uninterested without drawing attention to yourself; if asked for input, just shrug your shoulders and give a non-committal response like, I don't know, or, No comment, or, It doesn't matter.

Joker: Take every opportunity you can to make sarcastic comments that might draw a laugh from the group; joke around with side comments that poke fun at the conversation.

There should also be seven or eight blank slips of paper without any role described.

The group of Partners A forms a circle. Partners B station themselves around this group.

The instructor then distributes the following slips of paper to random members of the A group: bully, whiner and yes-person, with blank slips going to remaining members. It is not known who has the three specifically described roles. Those without a specifically described role (a blank piece of paper) are asked to engage in a typical decision-making process, responding as necessary to the ways all group members engage in this process.

Group A is asked to decide the following:

Christmas holidays are coming up, and the class wants to put together a Christmas hamper. Your group must decide how much money each student will contribute and what will go into the hamper. All group members must feel comfortable about the way the decision is made before the task is deemed complete.

Once this decision is made, each Partner A meets with his or her Partner B and feedback is shared.

The instructor then distributes the following slips of paper to random members of the B group: think-they-know-it-all, withdrawer and joker, with blank slips going to the remaining members. It is not known who has the three specifically described roles. Those without a specifically described role (a blank piece of paper) are asked to engage in a typical decision-making process, responding as necessary to the ways all group members engage in this process.

Group B is asked to decide the following:

Students have decided to raise money for a local charity. Your group must decide how to raise the money. All group members must feel comfortable about the way the decision is made before the task is deemed complete.

Once the decision is made, each Partner B meets with his or her Partner A and feedback is shared.

The whole class then meets to discuss the experience of these decision-making exercises. Of particular importance is the observation of how the difficult behaviours affected the group and ways in which group members responded to these behaviours.

Conflict Defined

Exercise 6.4 above provides a perfect transition into a discussion of *conflict* and has probably reminded you of the feelings of frustration that arise when decisions are stalled by the kinds of difficult interactions evolving from unique group member personality types. The terms *conflict* and *controversy* are often used to describe the kinds of behaviours that result from those uncomfortable times when frustration grows and group progress grinds to a stop because there is a difference of opinion between two or more group members.

The term *controversy* seems somewhat less powerful than the term *conflict* because it implies that even if two or more individuals have differing views on a particular manner there is some kind of action in place that is seeking compromise. Topics, rather than people, seem to be defined as controversial. Controversial topics, for example, already allude to there being components that may not be acceptable to all of us, yet hold the promise of a shared understanding as these topics are defined, explained and better understood by all. There is the potential for creative problem solving when groups acknowledge controversy and work toward unraveling the rationale for each difference of opinion. As with the process of reflection, the process of unearthing the values, beliefs and assumptions behind a point of view helps in understanding the rationale behind those beliefs and eventually re-assessing their meaning. This may or may not change the belief or behaviour of an individual, but does enhance that person's awareness of why he or she holds certain beliefs. In a group situation, structures that ensure that all members can explain the rationales for their points of view help others better understand the reasons for a particular group member's beliefs.

It is the term *conflict* that more readily evokes anxiety in all of us, as we think about that uncomfortable feeling that arises when we oppose another group member's opinion and there seems to be little room for negotiation. Our view of conflict and the emotion that it evokes is a product of our perception of others and how our values, beliefs and past experiences have shaped that perception. It is also affected by how much we value relationships and how much we value getting our own needs met.

Not all uncomfortable interactions necessarily fit within a definition of conflict. You may spend a lot of time clarifying someone else's point of view in a decision-making situation and openly disagree with someone else's perspective. If there is high trust in your group, this checking out or open disagreement is a natural and healthy part of group process (similar to our discussion of controversy). It may result in accepting differences and moving on, agreeing to disagree or simply deciding that the disagreement is not worth resolving. In other words, resolution of such a "conflict" does not feel necessary or productive.

Helga Rhode (1993) carefully discriminates between **disagreement** and conflict, suggesting that not all disagreements have to be resolved. We can debate for the fun of it, refuse to argue, agree to disagree or keep the disagreement to ourselves for the sake of saving a relationship (Rhode, 1993). Again, arguments and disagreements are not deemed conflicts unless your values, beliefs and interests are somehow at odds with those values, beliefs and interests of other group members. These divergent perspectives are so persistent that the goals of your decision-making task are not meeting your needs or other group members' needs.

Jay Hall (1996) offers a clear, all-encompassing definition of **conflict:**

> Holding different values — being motivated by different objectives — desiring the same goal when there is not enough to go around — all of these may create the potential for conflict. Differing ideological, philosophical, or strategic orientations may also set the conflict dynamics in motion. Thus, we define conflict as circumstances — both emotional and substantive — which are brought about by differences between parties who are, for whatever reason, in contact with one another . . . . Conflict is a natural part of the human condition, but the manner in which you respond to and manage its dynamics will help determine the success of your enterprise. (p. ii)

This definition differentiates among some of the sources of conflict we all experience in group situations. *Ideological issues* include those thoughts, ideas and assumptions that influence our individual perspectives. They provide the foundation for our world view and are a product of our learning and experience. As a student in the helping professions, you will find that ideologies are being established in your training that speak to the importance of caring and wellness, of advocating for vulnerable populations as a political stance and of the world view that improving social systems can make a difference in the lives of your clients. This view provides the foundation of your practice, yet can come in conflict with people who do not value the importance of these doctrines as a priority.

Our *philosophical orientation* affects our ideology, yet is the product of our beliefs, values and attitudes and includes our principles. These principles may include the professional, spiritual or professional "truths" that guide the way we live our lives. Statements of philosophy identify the values we place on all aspects of our lives and the way these values affect the way we behave. In the professional sphere, our philosophy guides our practice and tells the rest of the world what we believe and how we will provide service in ways that represent those beliefs. If others seek to provide the same service, yet have a different philosophical stance, there is the potential for a conflict of interest.

Strategic orientations include the structures, goals, styles of interaction and all other components we believe are helpful to accomplishing our objectives. Again, our ideology and philosophical stance affect our strategic orientation. In our discussion of leadership styles, we addressed how different groups are affected by those leadership roles that seek to structure tasks and maintain group stability. As well, we indicated how there might be times when these roles are in conflict with each other throughout the development of any group. Communication styles, relationship issues and the degree of structure individuals require when they work in a group all have the potential for conflict when decisions are being made.

All three potential sources of conflict are clearly areas of vital importance to our personal belief systems. However, when conflict occurs, we experience the product of that belief system, not necessarily the belief system itself. In other words, belief systems actualize themselves with behaviours that often mask differing interests. Conflict is a good thing when we work at understanding each other's point of view and work toward a healthy resolution of issues. Conflict can help bring about creative idea sharing and motivate change for the better. At the same time, conflict can enhance group trust and cohesion, as group members share ideologies, philosophies and strategies.

Unfortunately conflict can also be destructive to group process, as those behaviours that mask differing interests become detrimental to group process. If not given the opportunity for mutual understanding, conflict behaviours can lead to accusations and negative emotions. Issues become more complex because emotion and misinterpretation complicate them. When conflict is not recognized, issues fester and affect groups, leading to unnecessary stress, divisiveness and low levels of personal effectiveness.

Conflict Behaviour

Exercise 6.5 helps to identify possible strategies you use in conflict situations. The works of Blake and Mouton (1970), Hall (1996), Filley (1975), and Thomas-Kilmann (1974) are most often cited when discussing **conflict styles**. The quick test you completed in Exercise 6.5 offers some insight into your natural (or dominant) approach to conflict situations. Conflict styles are a product of our culture, values, beliefs and attitudes in decision-making contexts. Our first response in any confrontational situation will usually be a reflection of our dominant conflict style. Remember that your habitual responses to conflict may not always be consistent. That is, they may change, depending on the nature of the conflict and the people with whom you are in conflict.

Two factors affect your natural style of handling conflict: the degree to which you place importance upon meeting your own needs, and the value you place upon the relationship with the other person or people involved. The five conflict styles described in this section are defined by the combination of these two factors. Each conflict style brings different opportunities and risks to group decision-making situations.

The following scenario will help clarify the five conflict styles and suggests the risks and opportunities implicit in their approaches.

> Brenda works in an outreach program at the regional child development centre in a northern Alberta community. She works with another

family support worker (Makayla) under the supervision of a registered clinical counselor and has happily worked with this organization for about four years. Makayla has worked at the centre for about three months. Brenda has some autonomy regarding when she visits families off site and often creates her own schedule to accommodate some of her personal appointments. She feels very conscientious about fulfilling her work obligations and has never had any complaints about her work.

Her supervisor has recently questioned her about her whereabouts on the last three Friday afternoons. Brenda realizes that Makayla is the only person who could have commented to the supervisor about her Friday schedule. Even though Brenda knows that she has fulfilled her work responsibilities, she is upset that Makayla has passed on information to the supervisor before checking with her.

The Avoiding Conflict Style

People who avoid conflict have usually had very negative experiences in confrontational situations. They choose to withdraw totally from conflict, either by leaving it up to others in the group to settle any disagreements or by letting the situation simply play itself out. Those who avoid conflict are not committed to their own needs or the needs of others. Hall (1996) calls this the "lose-leave style" of conflict management because those who avoid conflict have low commitment to their own needs and little regard for building relationships with others.

If Brenda were to avoid conflict, she would simply talk to her supervisor and explain her ways of scheduling clients, without confronting Makayla about her suspicions. She would feel safe with this approach and would not have to face the discomfort of a confrontation. Avoiding has, however, the potential for pent-up frustration and further distrust, with the risk of a poor working relationship with both Makayla and the supervisor. People who avoid conflict might rationalize their behaviour by thinking that it is not important enough to talk about or that it may never happen again. Either way, this kind of avoidance lowers the commitment in any work situation and decreases trust.

If you are someone who tends to avoid conflict at all costs, it is important to recognize the risks involved in not expressing your point of view. How you manage to tell others what is bothering you will be a blend of respectful listening, paraphrasing and the ability to communicate your feelings in conflict situations. If avoiding conflict has become a pattern for you, this will not be an easy process.

The Competing Conflict Style

Those who approach conflicts with a competing style see their own needs as the focus of any argument or confrontation. People with this conflict style do not like to lose, believe that they are always right and have little regard for relationship building in groups. Competing can take many forms, from outright bullying to passive-aggressive, coercive manipulation. This stance is not open or flexible and is focused on pushing until the individual gets his or her own way. This style is termed an *I-win-and-you-lose* way of thinking, with little regard for the human relationships that deteriorate during the process.

If Brenda approached her situation with a competing conflict style, her primary objective would be to make Makayla understand that her behaviour was unacceptable. She would take the opportunity to meet with her, if possible, and with the supervisor, and tell both of them that her family visitation schedule is her business and that Makayla should mind her own business in the future. It would be important to Brenda that both Makayla and the supervisor know she is right. She might even try hard to catch Makayla not using her time well with clients, because being right is of utmost importance to her. Obviously Brenda risks any relationship with Makayla and may alienate her supervisor with her response to this situation. She will feel quite powerful in all of this and may gain some temporary satisfaction from showing them that she is not slacking off on the job.

You may be someone with a competing conflict style or work with someone who has a high need to be right, with little regard for your feelings. Sometimes this assertive way of approaching conflict can be useful. Advocacy for a worthwhile cause (e.g., standing up for the rights and needs of your clients) may require an assertive style that clearly represents what you believe to be to the betterment of those clients. However, in most group decision-making situations, fighting for goals with little respect for others could jeopardize your working relationships.

If you see some competitive characteristics in yourself, take the time to reflect on the outcome of recent conflict situations for you. Did you experience any loss of relationships, friendships or comfort as a result of your need to meet your goals at any cost? If so, re-think this approach: the risks to group cohesion are high.

Have you ever used a competing style of conflict resolution? If so, did that style of conflict resolution have any repercussions for you?

The Accommodating Conflict Style

People who use an accommodating conflict style value relationships at the risk of not meeting their own needs and goals. They do not trust that relationships will stand the test of confrontation and back off from their point of view as soon as they see that it may not be in agreement with the rest of the group. It is another kind of avoidance technique, in which the individual comes to the conflict believing that his or her thoughts, ideas and goals are not nearly as important as those of other group members. Often this conflict style is more about the need to be liked than it is about putting the needs of others above one's own. The process of yielding to others may take the form of re-directing the conversation in some way or using humour to mask any discomfort.

If Brenda were using an accommodating conflict style she might ask Makayla if they could meet over coffee (Brenda would buy). Without any mention of her meeting with their supervisor, she would talk about how sometimes people wonder about how she schedules her visits with families. By doing this, she would be sidestepping her real concern about Makayla's focus on her work commitments. Her motivation would be to make Makayla understand her better and perhaps approve of her creative scheduling, but she would be avoiding the real concern she has about someone else questioning her ethics. She may succeed in building her relationship with Makayla, yet would be still avoiding the real issue.

You may find that using an accommodating style is helpful with less important issues that you are not particularly concerned about. At times we all use this style of conflict in those kinds of situations, when our backing off will help the group move forward. However, if you are always the one giving in for the sake of group cohesion, you risk a certain loss of power in the group that may erode the effectiveness of your role in the eyes of other group members.

The Compromising Conflict Style

The compromising style of approaching conflict has as its goal that everyone can win a little bit if they simply all give a little. People who use this style avoid working through the discomfort of a conflict by suggesting to group members that splitting the difference and having each member sacrifice something will move the group forward. As positive as it might sound, compromising does not work through the conflict in ways that incorporate everyone's needs and can leave group members feeling somewhat dissatisfied. Often, people who use a compromising conflict style end up manipulating people and issues in order to find common ground. The atmosphere becomes somewhat tense and competitive as group members are asked to assess what they might give up for the common good. Creativity gets lost in this process of meeting people halfway, and decision making moves out of healthy consensus and into a less interactive approach.

If Brenda were to use a compromising style of conflict resolution, she would have to begin by meeting with Makayla and her supervisor and openly discussing how everyone in the centre validates his or her use of time. More than likely she will ask the supervisor to call this meeting, with the primary objective of finding some way for everyone to post her client schedules so that there is little or no question about the hours that are devoted to the families. Brenda's situation is not as much about compromise as it is about confronting Makayla and finding out why she questioned her (Brenda's) ethics. By suggesting some kind of open scheduling process, she is still not unearthing the real issue, yet is contributing to team cohesion by suggesting ways everyone might work differently. Her loss (and possibly Makayla's) is the freedom and trust implicit in a more autonomous way of scheduling visits.

If compromise is your preferred conflict style, think carefully about whether you are actually getting at the issues that may be stalemating the decision-making process. Is the process of asking group members to "give a little" actually masking the opportunity to work through conflicts? Compromise does come with a cost, as group members pull back on achieving their goals in the zest for everyone to meet halfway.

The Collaborating Conflict Style

When using the collaborating conflict style, everyone's goals are considered important. As well, the relationships amongst all group members are equally important in achieving those goals. The two are not mutually exclusive, as those who seek to collaborate see value in working through conflict. When they face a conflict stalemate, they see it as a chance for creative problem solving and team building. If all group members value this process, then cohesion, trust and creativity flourish through the active exchange of ideas. When exploring differences of opinion openly, conflict has the potential of moving a group into creative solutions that meet everyone's needs. Everyone's rationales for thinking the way he or she does must be on the table, or the chance for this kind of win-win problem solving diminishes.

In Brenda's situation, collaboration would begin in a meeting with Makayla, with the objective of finding out from her what concerns she may have about how she (Brenda) schedules her family visitations. There would be open and respectful questioning about these concerns, with the objective of engaging in a dialogue about scheduling issues, flexibility and ways of preserving autonomy while also trusting each other's work ethic. Even though both Makayla and Brenda have the families they work with to support, the ultimate goal of this conversation would be to ensure that both felt they had an equitable workload. This would build trust, cohesion and a team-work atmosphere.

A collaborative conflict-resolution style contributes to the environment of consensus building discussed earlier. If you can overcome your fear of confrontation and see it as an opportunity for group growth, then it will be that much easier for you to start from a collaborative place when conflict builds. As with our discussion of consensus building, approaching conflict with a collaborative style requires enough time to fully listen to each other's points of view and to explore all of the rationales on both sides of issues. It is not always possible to take this kind of time when quick decisions have to be made.

EXERCISE 6.5 HOW YOU ACT IN CONFLICTS

Objectives:

1. To identify typical responses in conflict
2. To provide the foundation for further learning about conflict styles

The following proverbs can be thought of as descriptions of some of the different strategies for resolving conflicts. Proverbs state traditional wisdom; the proverbs below articulate traditional wisdom for resolving conflicts. Read each proverb carefully, and, using the following scale, indicate how typical each proverb is of your actions in a conflict.

5 = very typical of the way I act in a conflict
4 = frequently typical of the way I act in a conflict
3 = sometimes typical of the way I act in a conflict
2 = seldom typical of the way I act in a conflict
1 = never typical of the way I act in a conflict

Try to make a clear choice rather than rely on number 3.

______ 1. It is easier to refrain than to retreat from a quarrel.
______ 2. If you cannot make a person think as you do, make him or her do as you think.
______ 3. Soft words win hard hearts.
______ 4. You scratch my back, I'll scratch yours.
______ 5. Come now and let us reason together.
______ 6. When two quarrel, the person who keeps silent first is the most praiseworthy.
______ 7. Might overcomes right.

_____ 8. Smooth words make smooth ways.
_____ 9. Better half a loaf than no bread at all.
_____ 10. Truth lies in knowledge, not in majority opinion.
_____ 11. He who fights and runs away lives to fight another day.
_____ 12. He hath conquered well that hath made his enemies flee.
_____ 13. Kill your enemies with kindness.
_____ 14. A fair exchange brings no quarrel.
_____ 15. No person has the final answer, but every person has a piece to contribute.
_____ 16. Stay away from people who disagree with you.
_____ 17. Fields are won by those who believe in winning.
_____ 18. Kind words are worth much and cost little.
_____ 19. Tit for tat is fair play.
_____ 20. Only the person who is willing to give up his or her monopoly on truth can ever profit from the truths that others hold.
_____ 21. Avoid quarrelsome people, as they will only make your life miserable.
_____ 22. A person who will not flee will make others flee.
_____ 23. Soft words ensure harmony.
_____ 24. One gift for another makes good friends.
_____ 25. Bring your conflicts into the open and face them directly; only then will the best solution be discovered.
_____ 26. The best way of handling conflicts is to avoid them.
_____ 27. Put your foot down where you mean to stand.
_____ 28. Gentleness will triumph over anger.
_____ 29. Getting part of what you want is better than not getting anything at all.
_____ 30. Frankness, honesty and trust will move mountains.
_____ 31. There is nothing so important you have to fight for it.
_____ 32. There are two kinds of people in the world, the winners and the losers.
_____ 33. When one hits you with a stone, hit him or her with a piece of cotton.
_____ 34. When both give in halfway, a fair settlement is achieved.
_____ 35. By digging and digging, the truth is discovered.

SCORING

Each number in the columns below corresponds to the questions you have just answered. Transfer the number that you assigned to each question to its proper column placement, and total each column.

Avoiding	Competing	Accommodating	Compromising	Collaborating
_____ 1	_____ 2	_____ 3	_____ 4	_____ 5
_____ 6	_____ 7	_____ 8	_____ 9	_____ 10
_____ 11	_____ 12	_____ 13	_____ 14	_____ 15
_____ 16	_____ 17	_____ 18	_____ 19	_____ 20
_____ 21	_____ 22	_____ 23	_____ 24	_____ 25
_____ 26	_____ 27	_____ 28	_____ 29	_____ 30
_____ 31	_____ 32	_____ 33	_____ 34	_____ 35
_____ Total	_____ Total	_____ Total	_____ Total	_____ Total

The higher the total score for each conflict management strategy, the more frequently you tend to use that strategy. The lower the total score for each conflict management strategy, the less frequently you tend to use that strategy.

A Model for Resolving Conflict

The following **model of conflict resolution**, based on the work of Thomas Gordon (1975), outlines a clear process that will help guide you through any conflict situation. The process involves defining the problem, brainstorming ideas to solve the problem, choosing an idea that every group member is comfortable with, implementing it and then evaluating whether it meets everyone's needs after it has been implemented. If only this process was as easy to follow in conflict situations as it is to explain on paper! However, by following a step-by-step model of conflict resolution, those stalemates you might face during the process of decision making will have some hope of resolution.

Step 1: Defining the Problem Affecting Group Members

This step is usually ignored because it is assumed to be obvious in conflict situations. This step is not just about defining the problem; it is about defining the problem as it affects each group member. We usually assume that everyone knows what is causing a conflict. In reality, unless each group member has the opportunity to describe the problem from his or her perspective and come to a shared understanding of it, a lot of energy may go into solving a problem that does not address what everyone is really concerned about. Often when groups get stuck trying to solve a problem, it is because they have not adequately defined it in the first place. Interestingly, this can be the most difficult step to work through (see Exercise 6.6).

EXERCISE 6.6 DEFINING THE PROBLEM

Objectives:

1. To practise stating your personal perspective in conflict situations
2. To practise discriminating the definition of a problem from the description of solutions
3. To envision a problem from another person's perspective

Think about a conflict you have faced in the recent past that you are comfortable revisiting and then discussing with others.

Ask yourself (you may want to record this information) the following:

1. Who was involved in the conflict?
2. What was the issue?
3. What is your definition of the problem?
4. Would others involved define the problem in the same way?

Move into your Base Group and share the answers to your questions. When you are sharing your conflict and you are answering Question 3, have other group members assess whether or not you have truly defined the problem. Then, when you answer Question 4, have other group members assist you in defining the problem from the perspectives of others in your example.

Group members have to agree to clearly state their perspectives about how they view the problem. Sometimes people jump to offer solutions when they think they are describing the problem. A statement like, "When you two are side talking, I cannot concentrate on the project" states the problem someone might have when a group of students are attempting to work on an assignment together, and the work is blocked. It states someone's perception of the reason that her or she cannot work and the group seems stalled on the project. In contrast, a statement that does not focus on the problem but jumps to a solution might be "This work would go a lot faster if we would all be quiet and listen to each other." This statement may evoke defensive arguments from other group members. In the first statement, the person is taking responsibility for his or her point of view and is explaining what is bothering him or her. In the second statement, the person is trying to solve the problem, but the group might not understand this.

After hearing everyone's perspective, the next step a group must take is to attempt to define the overall problem for everyone involved. Essentially what the group is saying is, "You have a problem. I have a problem. What is the problem we have together?" For example, you and your partner may have conflicts about the way you spend money. One day your partner decides to look at a new boat, and you are not very happy about it because you have both agreed to curb your spending. You define this problem as, We have made an agreement, and he is not living up to our deal; I am worried about owing money. Your partner's definition of the problem might be, We have enough money coming in to justify looking at new investments; I feel pressured by the reaction I get when I want to spend money and have some fun. Each of you has defined the problem for himself or herself. The next step is to move away from your personal perspective and focus on the problem you have together. In this case it might be, We have a different outlook on the importance of budgeting, and we cannot seem to agree on how to spend our money.

In defining the problem, the questions you ask yourself might be:

- How am I affected by this situation?
- What is really going on here?
- What is blocking the group, and how does that affect all of us?

When defining the problem for the whole group, all members clarify their perspectives and assist each other in supporting that process in order to reach a shared understanding of the issue that is stalling progress. Again, defining the problem is the most difficult part of conflict resolution. However, once this work is done, the other steps will follow more smoothly. You will find that in some decision making you may move back to defining the problem when other steps in the conflict resolution process seem to get held up.

Challenges to this step in the resolution of any conflict include:

- Figuring out how you are affected by the situation.
- Risking talking about difficult issues.
- Taking personal responsibility for your perception of the problem.
- Being able to all state your perceptions of the problem during more emotional conflict situations.
- Being able to manage your emotions while stating the effect the problem is having on you.

- Taking the time you need to define the problem to everyone's satisfaction.
- Stepping back and looking at the problem objectively.

How might what you have learned about defining the problem help you in other conflicts you experience in your life?

Step 2: Brainstorming Solutions

Once the problem is defined for all group members the task is then to generate as many ideas as possible to reach a solution. This process should be organized, with time for each person in the conflict situation to generate ideas. You may choose to openly brainstorm everyone's ideas, recording them for all to see (using a flipchart, board or other kind of observable medium). Another alternative, after everyone has agreed on the definition of the problem, is to have each member privately list his or her own ideas and then share them later as a group. There are many ways of brainstorming (some are described in Kaner, Fisk and Toldi, 1996). Ultimately the goal is to accumulate as many ideas as possible from all members of the group. It is important to include all ideas, even if some seem unrealistic. Often there is something valuable in every idea that might serve as a foundation for a workable solution.

All of these solutions should be recorded, even if only two people are in conflict. This helps everyone actually see what they have to work with for Step 3.

Challenges in this step of conflict resolution include:

- Evaluating solutions prematurely and rejecting them before writing them down.
- Not respecting everyone's ideas.
- Stopping after all obvious solutions are generated and not taking the time to come up with new, unique and creative ideas.

Step 3: Evaluating All Solutions and Choosing One

In this step of conflict resolution, well-developed communication skills are vital. Each member of the group is now expected to evaluate all the ideas that have been collected during the brainstorming exercise. We refer you now to the process of consensus building described from pages 156 to 159. Essentially this process investigates the pros and cons of each idea, exploring its possibilities and its short- and long-term consequences.

We cannot emphasize enough the importance of respectful speaking and listening behaviour at this stage of conflict resolution. This means remembering some basic communication rules. When taking the opportunity to respond to someone's suggestion, remember to use language that makes explicit that this is your interpretation. This means using "I" statements and taking responsibility for your opinion. When listening to others, respectful acknowledgment (waiting for others to finish their thoughts before clarifying them) is vital. You should be focusing consistently on factors that appear to have the potential for agreement by making connections between ideas brainstormed, while at the same time building on others' ideas. The last important communication rule is being mindful of your body language and the message it sends. Do you look judgmental, uncomfortable or bored, or do you convey interest and hopefulness? Building an evaluation climate that is mutually respectful takes great patience and refined communication ability.

The question remains, How do you decide which brainstormed solution is the one that will work for everyone? Obviously, with each situation, the criteria for evaluation will differ in some way. As suggested by Kaner, Fisk and Toldi (1996), group members should decide what these criteria should be before evaluating any solutions. For example, the criteria might be that the solution is simple to implement, that it falls within a certain budget allocation and that it can be achieved by all employees. Other criteria might include identifying the challenges and opportunities implicit in each suggestion, as well as the ability of the group to realistically accomplish the chosen solution.

As each solution is considered, group members should have some way of identifying their level of acceptance of that solution. You must determine ahead of time whether decisions are to be made by consensus or some other method of decision making (e.g., taking a vote). There are innovative methods some groups use to give group members a sense of the degree to which they support ideas being discussed. For example, one can use hand gestures to quickly gauge group-member support for an idea. A closed fist indicates no support and an open hand with outstretched fingers indicates full support. The openness of the hand defines the level of support. This can be used in two ways. It can be a way of getting a quick idea of how much support the group has for each given solution, with those having no support being eliminated immediately. Or, the group can decide what level of support is needed to move any solution forward to implementation. For example, only those choices that receive a half-open fist from all group members will be considered as a viable option.

Challenges in this step of conflict resolution include:

- Jumping too quickly to a solution.
- Not being able to step out of your own frame of reference to consider other alternatives.
- Not creating evaluation criteria that are workable.
- Getting off topic to the point where group members become frustrated with the process, and it falls apart.

Step 4: Implementing the Solution

This is the time to try out the solution that is chosen. It is helpful to agree on a time frame in order to move to the next step, assessing the solution's effectiveness. If all group members have agreed to the solution and the first steps in conflict resolution have been followed, the challenges in this step should be minimal.

Step 5: Evaluating the Solution

This is the time to re-convene and assess whether the agreed-upon solution is meeting everyone's needs. Knowing ahead of time that this step is built into the implementation process helps alleviate any fears that group members will somehow be trapped into a solution that does not work. When the solution is working, this step is very expedient, as group members check back and acknowledge that the problem seems to be solved and the process can continue. If there are problems with the chosen solution, group members must start over. Chances are they may have neglected to fully explore the issues and did not adequately define the problem or moved to a solution prematurely. Challenges arise if people are unwilling to start the process over.

Final Comment

Conflict resolution takes time, effort and a willingness to carefully work through the issues that stall progress. Sometimes issues are resolved quickly, and sometimes they require the time and effort necessary to move the group back on task. It is hard to risk exploring the real issues and sharing your perspective when you anticipate the discomfort this brings to any group. Decision making and conflict resolution skills are the tools that support you in taking this risk. As you work in groups, the process will become more comfortable for you over time. Successful conflict resolution will likely produce higher group creativity, some innovative solutions, heightened group productivity and enhanced cohesion.

Summary

When groups reach a shared understanding about the way members will work together, the processes of decision making, problem solving and conflict resolution become opportunities for creative exchange. This process is in direct contrast to the traditional expectation that conflict is uncomfortable and should be avoided at all cost.

Commonly understood decision-making models include decision making by an authority figure with or without discussion, decision by an expert assigned by either the group or assigned leader, decision through the averaging of group member opinion, decision by a minority group assigned to make the decision on its own, decision by a majority vote and decision through consensus. All of these methods have advantages and disadvantages, depending on the authority structures and other elements of the group situation.

The decisions made in a group are affected by the procedures it creates to complete its tasks. As well, the group's stage of development at the time of making the decision will affect the decision's quality and its level of acceptance by all group members. Certain personality types also affect the process and product of group decision making. Challenging, difficult personality types include bullies, snipers, know-it-alls, yes-persons, whiners and jokers. Dealing with these behaviours detracts from the group and impairs decision making.

Conflicts arise when individuals in the group have differing ideologies, philosophical orientations or strategies for the way the group should be structured or for how people should interact with each other. All individuals have certain natural conflict styles. Some avoid conflict, and some compete assertively for their needs. Others see great importance in preserving relationships with other group members and focus less on getting their own needs met, while others choose to work toward some kind of compromise on everyone's part. Finally, there are those who seek to collaborate and work through conflict in ways that meet everyone's goals.

A model of conflict resolution built from a collaborative approach is one where group members note the conflict, define the problem from everyone's perspective, brainstorm solutions, evaluate the solutions offered by everyone and then choose one. Finally, in this model of conflict resolution, group members implement the decision made with a promise to evaluate its effectiveness later, to see if it meets all group members' needs. Conflict resolution that seeks to meet everyone's goals takes time and energy, yet builds group cohesion and trust.

Key Terms

Conflict *(p. 165)*
Conflict styles *(p. 168)*
Consensus *(p. 156)*
Decision making *(p. 151)*
Disagreement *(p. 165)*
Majority *(p. 156)*
Minority *(p. 155)*
Model of conflict resolution *(p. 172)*
Personality problems *(p. 161)*
Procedural problems *(p. 160)*
Process problems *(p. 160)*
Shared understanding *(p. 151)*
Synergy *(p. 157)*

Case Studies

The following case studies, taken from classroom, human service team and community contexts will help clarify the topics covered in this chapter, using real-world examples. These case studies focus on ways of responding to conflict styles and conflict resolution strategies that enhance the decision-making process.

Case Study 6.1 The Disrespectful Student

CATEGORY: STUDENT

A group of 24 human service students have been together for about two months (in a four-month semester). It is becoming increasingly evident to most class members that one of the student's attitudes in this class (and all of the other classes in the program) is highly negative, sarcastic and generally erodes the classroom environment. Not only is this student disruptive with other students, he also side talks and is generally disrespectful of the instructors in all of the classes. A small group of students has now approached the chairperson of the human service program to discuss this student and complain about his behaviour. The chairperson, after listening to their concerns, rightfully explains that she cannot discuss this particular student with them and that, because they are students learning how to work in groups, they should handle this situation themselves.

QUESTIONS:

1. Based on the information in this chapter, identify all of the evident issues in this scenario.
2. What would be the goals of any kind of conflict resolution strategy?
3. Describe some kind of strategy that might help in addressing this problem.
4. What would be the short- and long-term consequences of this strategy?

Case Study 6.2 **Project at Risk**

CATEGORY: STUDENT

It is near the end of the second semester of a two-year early childhood education diploma program. Students have been assigned to work in groups of four on a program-planning project that is worth 40 percent of their programming course final grade. The project is a group assignment, and all students will be given the same grade for the work they do together. Andrea, Tasha, Sabrina and Jasleen have been assigned to a group.

At this point in the diploma program, most of the students have learned that Sabrina has learning-support needs when doing assignments. Unfortunately, she has not always taken the opportunity to get the support she needs from the learning assistance department at the college when doing assignments and has gained a reputation for not participating fully in group work. Andrea has stated that she is not willing to risk her grade by working with Sabrina and has gone to the instructor to complain. The instructor has said that the group must remain as is.

Andrea meets with Tasha and Jasleen and states again that her grade is the most important thing to her and she does not want anything to interfere with a high-quality product. She expresses frustration and anger about the fact that the instructor did not make some kind of change to the group structure and is unsure about how to resolve the situation. Tasha and Jasleen begin to worry that the whole project is at stake. Sabrina is unaware that other members of the group are discussing issues about working with her.

QUESTIONS:

1. What kind of conflict style is evident in Andrea's behaviour?
2. What might be the consequences of Andrea's behaviour to others?
3. Define the problem from each group member's perspective.
4. Define the problem for the whole group.
5. How might this group work through this difficulty?

Case Study 6.3 **Quick Decision Making**

CATEGORY: TEAM

Lydia is the team leader at a mental health facility for school-age children with severe behaviour disorders. This is a group facility for children ages 10 to 18 who require expert support from human service and community mental health workers who specialize in behaviour disorders. Lydia has worked here for about 12 years and, as team leader, works at the centre and oversees the day-to-day management of the staff and support workers on every shift.

Each child in the facility has a transdisciplinary team of professionals made up of the team leader, a psychiatrist, a social worker, a behaviour management consultant and a primary support worker at the group home. A 10-year-old child in this facility has become quite violent over the past two weeks, physically acting out with behaviours so unpredictable and severe that other staff and children are being put at risk. Staff members have reported on the escalating behaviour, but a transdisciplinary meeting is not due for three days. Lydia has been considering the status of the situation and makes a preliminary call to the local psychiatric facility at a nearby hospital in order to research possible courses of action to take with this child. She finds out quite unexpectedly that a space has become available in the psychiatric unit, and she must decide by the end of the day whether to move this child to the hospital. Time is of the essence and she needs to make this important decision quickly.

QUESTIONS:

1. What information does Lydia need?
2. How should she get this information?
3. What kind of decision-making style best suits this scenario?

Case Study 6.4 **Personality Dynamics**

CATEGORY: TEAM

A group of three early childhood educators (Tom, Mariah and Chiara) each work in different daycares in a large seven-centre childcare facility. They have been given time away from their centre responsibilities to plan a float for the local winter carnival. It is November, and the carnival is in mid-January. They have a small budget and not much time. Tom feels really excited about this project and knows all kinds of community people involved in the carnival. It is important to him that the float be classy and impressive. Mariah is a strong environmentalist and believes that simple is best and that preventing any overuse of materials is important. Chiara is just happy to be off from work to do this project.

Tom comes to the first meeting laden down with fabric samples, decoration models and all kinds of shiny, slinky materials to show the others. After a quick discussion of the timeline and the nature of the task, Tom proudly pulls out his items to show the others. As Mariah begins to comment about her concerns about the materials, Tom just keeps talking about how wonderful the float will look with them. He then tells the others he has already told people he knows about how the float is going to look. Mariah then begins to argue about the inappropriateness of the materials and begins to explain how each of the items Tom brought along contributes to global warming and overwhelming landfill use. Chiara just sits there and listens, hoping that the two will work this out.

QUESTIONS:

1. What kinds of personality dynamics do you see happening here? How might you describe the dynamics of the interaction between all three people?
2. Define the problem from the perspective of each person in this scenario.
3. Step back and define the problem they have together as a group.

Case Study 6.5 **Transdisciplinary Meeting**

CATEGORY: COMMUNITY

Joel is a behaviour consultant recently assigned to work with four-year-old Emile, a child with autism. As part of his responsibilities, Joel takes part in transdisciplinary meetings with a physiotherapist, a speech therapist and a preschool teacher. He sees himself as an advocate for Emile and the one person in Emile's life who will get to see him on a consistent basis, in all contexts. Joel's past experiences with other professionals linked to children with special needs have not been particularly positive. He has come to the conclusion that speech therapists and physiotherapists think they are experts on everything and that their objectives, specific to their discipline, should take priority. As well, he sees the preschool teacher as yet another authority trying to tell him what to do with Emile.

As he heads into this meeting with the rest of the transdisciplinary team, he thinks to himself that this first meeting together should set the stage for further interactions. Therefore, he has decided to tell the other members of the group that he will take their ideas and think about them, but he alone will decide how they will be implemented. That way he will show them that he is the expert on this child and that they can't push him around.

QUESTIONS:

1. How might you label Joel's style of interaction? What conflict style do you see him using at this first meeting?
2. What do you predict the implications of his behaviour might be for other team members and for Emile?
3. If you were one of the other members of the transdisciplinary team, how would you feel in response to Joel's anticipated approach to this group?
4. How would you respond to Joel, based on your conflict style and what implications would this have for the group?

Reflection Tool

What?

What stood out for you in this chapter? Describe a reading, exercise, incident, person's behaviour, etc.

So What?

1. Emotional impact?

2. Why do you think you had this emotional response?

3. What assumptions might you be making in this situation? What beliefs and values were touched off by this situation?

Assumptions:

Beliefs, values:

4. Write about the meaning this has for you. Some helpful questions might be: Do you think your values might be clouding your interpretation of the situation? If so, how?

Have you been affected by similar situations in the same way? How have you responded?

5. Is it important for you to change your behaviour? Why?

Now What?

6. Based on the learning from this chapter, what other behaviours might you consider?

7. What might stop you from engaging in these new behaviours?

Objectives

What Questions Remain?

Chapter 7

You and Others

Objectives

In this chapter, students will acquire the knowledge, skills and attitudes to:

1. Integrate their learning about group skill development.
2. Appreciate the importance of a lifelong learning approach to working in groups.
3. Understand the unique group participation needs in a variety of professional contexts.
4. Use a self-assessment framework that evaluates group participation.
5. Set personal objectives for more effective group participation.
6. Understand their role in contributing to the possibility of transformational change in groups.

Integrating the Learning

With the help of your reflection tools and Base Group feedback, you should now have come to the conclusion that the skills or competencies that contribute to effective participation in groups do not develop in isolation from each other. As you move in and out of the many kinds of groups in your professional career, this **personal skill set** that you develop will have to adapt to the many different contexts and group dynamics you experience. Your learning about groups, their development and their unique dynamics is but the first step in what will become a process of self-awareness and lifelong learning about yourself and others.

In Chapter 1 we asked you to consider questions about your history in groups, the kind of group member you believe yourself to be, any feedback from others about the quality of your interaction in groups and any natural abilities you would like to pay attention to in group situations. By now you should have a better understanding of your leadership skills, your communication style and perceptions others have of your influence (or power) in groups. You should also have a number of objectives listed that spell out areas that you will pay attention to in your ongoing participation in groups. These objectives will help to direct changes in your behaviour and your level of self-awareness during an ongoing analysis of group effectiveness.

Learning will become more integrated as you pull together all of the elements of group development, leadership, power and problem solving into an organized framework for reference as you move into practice. Integrating learning is vital to successfully turning theoretical understandings into principles of practice. This process does not end when you say goodbye to the classroom. *Self-assessment* and a **lifelong-learning** approach allows you to make use of each group experience to consistently fine-tune your group skills and enhance your personal skill set in order to adapt more effectively to the many unique group contexts you will face in the helping professions. This is not an easy process and requires the support of some kind of guided *self-assessment framework*. Only then can the process of reflective practice truly support the many daily professional judgments you will make in your work in the field.

Concluding the Base Group Experience

Your Base Group has provided you with a consistent opportunity to share feedback, observe specific areas of group skill development and support each other's learning throughout the various exercises explored in this text. Bearing witness to each other's learning has been an invaluable process that has focused attention on developmental change in each Base Group member.

The healthy development of any group experience involves the process of putting closure to, or adjourning, that particular group's work. As we explained in Chapter 3, closure involves sharing the learning, celebrating the overall experience and acknowledging that the Base Group has completed its time together (see Exercise 7.1, 7.2 and 7.3).

EXERCISE 7.1 SUMMARIZING REFLECTION TOOLS WITH BASE GROUP MEMBERS

Objectives:

1. To take the opportunity to review learning from completed reflection tools
2. To review outstanding questions from the reflection process
3. To hear feedback from others regarding issues explored during ongoing reflection
4. To support your own and others' learning as evidenced in the sharing of reflections

This exercise gives Base Group members the opportunity to pull together completed reflection tools and share with others the issues, concerns and celebrations explored during the process of reflection.

In preparation for this exercise, students should take the time to collect all completed reflection tools. These questions may take some time to collate. Make sure all Base Group members are prepared when you come together to share answers and offer feedback.

Consider the following questions:

1. Are there issues explored in your reflection tools that seem to repeat themselves? In other words, are there certain issues that you have grappled with more than once? If so, what are they?

2. As you review the objectives set for yourself at the end of each reflection, which have proven to be more significant to you than others?
3. What outstanding questions about yourself would you like to share with your Base Group for feedback?
4. What are three conclusions you can make about your behaviour in groups as you review the completed reflection tools?

Once all members are prepared, Base Groups should meet to share the answers to these questions with each other. As the information is debriefed, members should offer input and support to each person's review.

EXERCISE 7.2 REFLECTION COLLAGE

Objectives:

1. To give individual Base Group members a chance to recall significant learning from the ongoing process of reflection
2. To create a representation of the Base Group composed of symbolic learning identified by individual members
3. To celebrate closure of a long-standing, significant group

MATERIALS NEEDED:

- Coloured newsprint or construction paper
- A selection of coloured markers or crayons
- Tape or glue
- Scissors
- Other collage materials, as desired

Each person in the class takes a piece of paper and his or her favourite selection of coloured pens (and collage materials, if desired). Individuals create a drawing or design that symbolizes the learning gleaned from Exercise 7.1. Take lots of time to think about and produce this design.

After creating this design, class members move into their Base Groups and discuss the meaning behind their design with the rest of the group.

As a group, create a new collage from all members' designs that characterizes the Base Group and represents and celebrates each member's learning. This requires cutting out each person's design and incorporating it into the whole group design.

Each Base Group then places its collage on the wall of the classroom for all to see.

EXERCISE 7.3 MESSAGES OF APPRECIATION

Objectives:

1. To put closure to the Base Group experience
2. To express appreciation for each other
3. To share each Base Group member's expression of his or her experience of all other members of his or her Base Group

MATERIALS NEEDED:

- Envelopes
- Writing paper
- Writing utensils

Each class member is given an envelope and pieces of paper to write a message to each member of his or her Base Group. Class members write their names on the front of their envelopes and leave them for others in their Base Group to see.

On each piece of paper, write a note of appreciation to a member of your Base Group. This can be simply one word, or it can be a small paragraph. It is most important that you think carefully about this message because it is a message of appreciation about your experience of that person.

Once your message is written, fold it, and place it inside the recipient's envelope. Each class member then reads the enclosed messages at a time that feels the best for him or her.

Once this process is complete, it marks closure of the group because it involves doing something special for each group member on an individual basis.

Reflective Practice and Ongoing Assessment

As discussed briefly in Chapter 1, reflective practice examines everyday experiences in terms of their meaning to you. Reflection involves consideration of the learning in this text in terms of your experiences, assumptions, values and beliefs. Upon reflection, the choices you make in terms of changing (or not changing) your behaviour will help to reinforce your skill development in specific areas of group practice.

The process of reflection does, however, have a somewhat limited scope when you move into an overall assessment of group skills and abilities in the many contexts of practice in the helping professions. What begins with the process of self-reflection now moves into a place of overall self-assessment. A guided process of **self-assessment** helps you look closely at each group situation and then step back and analyze, over time, ways that you can improve your practice on an ongoing basis.

Analysis over time is an invaluable process for a number of reasons:

1. It allows you to analyze the effects your behaviour has had on the group's function as you take the time to step back and actually think about the group's process.
2. It focuses attention on how you may or may not act differently in the many different group situations you are a part of. This allows you to investigate possible reasons why your behaviour may change and helps you to make decisions about how much you are willing to adapt to the different elements that have affected your level of interaction.
3. It clarifies your style of interaction and helps you make choices about how you are going to participate in groups in general, based on past positive and negative experiences.
4. It takes reflection to a whole new level and enhances your ability to make professional judgments based on careful consideration of your behaviour with others.

5. It checks your understanding of new learning in all of the components of successful group participation by assessing these components on one integrated tool.

Group Contexts in the Helping Profession

A guided self-assessment should be seen as helpful to an ongoing observation of your group experiences while yielding enough information that you can track your behaviour. Only then can you come to significant conclusions about your skills as a participant and make choices as to what you might or might not change for your next group experience. We have created a framework that will help focus your attention on skills that are important to ongoing development as a group member in most contexts relevant to students and practitioners.

Student contexts range from whole-class participation to small project groups. Even short-term classroom discussion groups charged with the task of working for 20 minutes on a classroom exercise provide an opportunity for self-assessment of your participation. The membership of these in-class discussion groups may change daily, affecting how you use your group skills. Tracking this kind of change offers valuable information about how the people you work with on a short-term basis affect factors like your leadership ability, use of power and overall commitment. This short-term group situation may also differ from the longer-term student project groups where a task must be completed, and there is a mark at stake. How might you use your group skills differently in these two situations where the potential risks to you are very different?

Other student group situations include representation on college or university committees. Again, taking your newly learned group skills to these venues and assessing your effectiveness in a role that represents others offers a rich opportunity for learning about how this kind of situation affects your level of participation.

As a practitioner, self-assessment helps you continue to hone your group skills as you move into the many possible group contexts in the helping professions. We refer to these professional contexts as the **field of practice** in an attempt to capture the essence and variety of workplace, facility and community spheres where those in the helping professions find themselves.

When in your field of practice, the actual department, sector, division, unit or team that houses the other employees you work with will comprise, for most of you, one of your most changeable, active and significant groups. Tracking your skills in this group situation would be a rich source of information, yet realistically extremely time-consuming. You might choose meeting times (structured in some way where all personnel can come together on a regular basis) to focus on your group skills. This will allow you to more easily pay attention to your behaviour and the behaviour of others in a predictable setting. However, if there are certain times you work in a team and feel the need to focus on elements of your work environment, the self-assessment framework can easily be altered to capture patterns of behaviour you would like to examine more closely. For example, if shift changes in a group home are posing difficulties as staff check with each other about client needs, then this is the time to take a close look at your behaviour and the behaviour of others through guided assessment. Only then can the elements of effective group process be differentiated and necessary changes made.

Other common group contexts in the field may include **transdisciplinary** committee work (representing your relationship with people in your care in a forum with a number of other professionals), group meetings with families of the people in your care and groups where you will be an advocate for your client(s). You will know well your professional obligations with respect to your representation on any of these committees by the time you graduate from your program of studies.

Other group contexts in your field of practice will include various kinds of committee work. This may be a part of your actual job description or a professional choice you make in an effort to represent your work in the community. Invitations for committee membership abound in most communities in Canada for those of us in the helping professions, as we are seen as extraordinary resources in the social service sector. As well, shared values of supporting people of all ages and abilities inspire most graduates in our professions to contribute what they can to their communities. Ultimately, most of you will have the experience of community committee work and will find that paying close attention to your role in these group situations offers rich self-assessment information.

Self-Assessment Framework

There would be little value in using a guided self-assessment if the framework felt cumbersome and time-consuming. The **self-assessment framework** suggested here is meant to be a guide that quickly summarizes the important areas of your participation as well as your perception of the general group dynamics. We have provided a documentation format that includes rating scales, multiple-choice questions and direct questions. You may want to note comments in some of the sections that include simple ratings, or you may want to place additional thoughts on the back of the form. Whatever way you use this form, see it as a way to focus your observations, not as an onerous and lengthy obligation.

It would be useful to use this framework in a variety of settings over a designated period of time. This will offer you feedback in a number of contexts and allow you to monitor your behaviour, as well as look at the way all of the elements we discussed in this text affect your performance.

We are re-visiting the "What?", "So What?" and "Now What?" stages of reflective process by organizing this framework into those three general headings. The "What" section sets the stage for assessing overall group participation. It helps you to describe the context of the group and your perception of your own participation as well as that of others. In the "So What?" section you are taking your observations and impressions and digging deeper into their link to your behaviour in the group situation. There are questions that relate to your leadership, your use of power and your feelings of personal effectiveness during the group interaction. There is also a question that asks you to compare your participation in this group situation to others you are tracking over time. Finally, the "Now What?" component of the framework is a place for you to identify either the behaviours you would like to enhance or areas of growth you would like to pay more attention to.

Most of the framework is self-explanatory. However, some sections require further explanation. What follows is an explanation of the sections that may merit some clarification, using a descriptive example and a copy of the completed form as a reference.

Using the Self-Assessment Framework in Practice

Lyric has been working in childcare for about four years, having graduated with a diploma in early childhood education. She is in a university childcare complex that houses 10 separate childcare programs (among the following types of childcare: infant toddler, childminding, preschool and daycare [for preschool-aged and school-aged children]). Originally Lyric was hired as an early childhood educator in two of the centres in the complex and has just taken a position as a full-time supervisor in the Busy Bee Daycare. This position means a wage increase, working full-time as a leader of a team of four caregivers, extra responsibility for programming decisions and overall centre operation, and the opportunity to represent the centre on various committees. Lyric not only works in a team on site with three others, she also represents Busy Bee Daycare in monthly meetings of all the centres in the university childcare complex.

Lyric has already joined some community committees, so this responsibility is not totally new to her. The external committee work includes a citywide childcare committee, a small group of people who take on a children's festival each summer (on behalf of the city) and monthly meetings with others who are local members of the provincial professional association.

As the years have gone by, after graduation from the diploma program, Lyric has found that working in any group committee has been energizing and stimulating and has contributed to her values about the healthy development of young children. Lyric is becoming more conscious of her overall effectiveness in group situations, particularly now that she is holding a new position in her daycare. She wants to be sure that the time she spends in all of the positions she holds in committees and work groups is well-spent and that the way she participates contributes to productivity. As well, Lyric values the relationships she is building in each of her committee contexts and sees that paying closer attention to her group behaviour might help her make positive changes and build on her professional presence in the community.

She decides to use the self-assessment framework to track her next two months of meetings in all of her groups. It will be time-consuming work to do this, but it will help her answer the following questions:

1. In what ways does her behaviour change when some of the elements of the group differ (e.g., size, length of meeting, whether there is an assigned leader, and where and when the meetings are scheduled)?
2. How might her level of power and influence change in her committee or group situations?
3. What leadership role does she take when the group has an assigned leader in comparison to when all group members share leadership?
4. In which groups does she feel a high level of trust, cohesion and accepting climate, and is there some pattern that evolves regarding her part in that?

5. Does her conflict style shift in varying group contexts? If so, how does it shift, and is it helpful and appropriate to the group, or does it detract from effective problem solving?

By tracking her behaviour and focusing on these areas of interest to her, Lyric hopes to make the changes necessary to meet these goals:

- That she contribute to overall task accomplishment and overall group satisfaction in all groups she is a part of
- That she take on a leadership role that is comfortable and effective during all group interactions, regardless of the context
- That others in all of the groups she is a part of see her as someone who shares power, contributes to the goals of the group and cares about others

The meetings Lyric will track include:

- Team meetings with the staff of Busy Bee Daycare (once every two weeks).
- Meetings with the other programs in the childcare complex (once a month).
- Childcare committee meetings away from the centre (once every two months).
- Children's festival meetings (once every two weeks at City Hall).
- Professional association meetings (once a month, held in different daycares around the city).

Lyric has already attended one team meeting and two children's festival meetings. The one team meeting she attended was fairly productive, and Lyric feels comfortable in her assigned leadership role. She is also feeling at home in the children's festival meetings because she has worked with this group for a couple of years.

Now that she is heading into the centre complex meeting, she is interested in knowing how her behaviour might change as a result of the different context and dynamics. At the end of this meeting she fills out the self-assessment framework (see the sample Self-Assessment Framework on p. 191). Lyric's example will be used in explaining the components of the self-assessment framework.

What? Meeting Observations and Impressions

Context of the group: Any workable assessment framework for self-analysis in groups begins by identifying the most obvious elements that affect the context, climate and developmental stage of each group.

Group situations usually involve meetings of some kind. These may occur regularly or be a one-time event. The regularity or number of meetings may have an impact on your participation, so it is noteworthy information and is identified in the framework as a choice between "Once" and "Regular."

Self-Assessment Framework

What? Meeting Observations and Impressions

Context of the Group:

Where Staff Room When 5:30 to 7:30 P.M. Time Together overall in centre: 10 years; Membership changes

Purpose of Meeting Childcare-Complex Monthly Meeting Once/(Regular)

Structures or Norms Each centre in complex is represented; complex director is assigned leader; rotating recorder for minutes; snacks provided; *other norms unknown to me at this time*

Size/Composition 10 people plus director

You in This Meeting:

What are the expectations of your behaviour and role in this group meeting?
I am expected to actively participate as a representative of my centre. We discuss issues common to all centres in the complex.

How do you feel going into this meeting (physically and emotionally)?
Nervous — This is a new position and a big responsibility. Worried — I might look like I don't know what I am talking about. Physically okay — hungry & tired.

Observations of Yourself and Others:

	You	Others
Level of Interaction		
What was the level of verbal contribution?	1 2 (3) 4 5 6 7 8 9 10 Low … High	Director 1 2 (3) 4 (5) 6 (7) 8 (9) (10) 2 5 1 1 1 Low … High
What was the level of involvement in the group?	1 2 3 4 5 6 7 8 9 (10) Uninterested … Committed	Director (1) 2 (3) 4 (5) 6 (7) (8) (9) 10 1 2 1 3 1 2 Uninterested … Committed (of interest to me)
Leadership Skills Used		
What was the level of task focus?	1 2 3 4 5 6 7 (8) 9 10 Low … High Asked lots of questions to get information	Director (1) 2 3 4 (5) 6 (7) 8 (9) (10) 2 3 3 1 1 Low … High
What was the level of maintenance focus?	1 2 3 (4) 5 6 7 8 9 10 Low … High Told a couple of jokes	Director (1) 2 3 4 (5) 6 7 (8) 9 10 2 7 1 Low … High Hard to say?
Use of Power		
How was power demonstrated? (Circle terms that apply.)	Verbally Non-verbally (Attentiveness) Reward Coercion Legitimate Expert Nuisance Habitual Sanction	(Verbally) Non-verbally Attentiveness Reward Coercion (Legitimate) Expert (Nusiance) (Habitual) Sanction Legitimate, Habitual: Director Nusiance: Side talk from 2 members

Process of Decison Making

What methods of decision making were used?

Authority without Group Discussion | Decision by Expert | Averaging Opinions | (Authority after Group Discussion) circled
Minority | Majority Vote | Consensus

Seems like we offer input and the director makes the decisions.

What was the level of comfort you experienced in decision making?

I'm new — so felt okay without having to make decisions.

1 2 3 4 (5) 6 7 8 9 10
Low — High

If there was conflict, what conflict style did you use?

(Avoiding) Competing Accommodating Compromising Collaborating

What conflict styles were used by others?

Avoiding (Competing) Accommodating Compromising Collaborating

Tavis and Petra seemed to compete for use of outdoor play equipment.

What was your level of satisfaction with the conflict experience?

I was only observing; a bit uncomfortable, but not my problem.

1 2 3 4 (5) 6 7 8 9 10
Low — High

Perception of the Group:

Group Development

What stage do you think the group is in?

Hard to tell because I am new — a bit of everything

Forming (Storming) (Norming) Performing OR (Inclusion) Control Openness

Storming: Some competing
Norming: Productive discussion
Inclusion: of me

Perceived Level of Trust and Cohesion

To what degree did you experience a climate of openness, mutual respect and a sense of safety?

Even with minor conflict observed, felt welcome here.

1 2 3 4 5 6 7 (8) 9 10
Low — High

What was the level of commitment to goals and a teamwork atmosphere?

Some high, some low. Group seems split on their level of commitment.

1 2 3 4 (5) 6 7 8 9 10
Low — High

Perceived Level of Productivity

How much was accomplished with respect to the goals of the meeting?

A task-driven agenda. We managed to cover all but two items on the agenda.

1 2 3 4 5 6 7 (8) 9 10
Very little — A lot

So What? How Does This Information Have Meaning for You?

Your Role in Developing Trust, Cohesion and Productivity:

How helpful do you think your contributions were to overall group productivity?

I am not confident enough yet. I asked questions rather than contributing information.

1 (2) 3 4 5 6 7 8 9 10
Not helpful — Very helpful

How satisfied were you with your participation (your openness, your respect for others, your level of acceptance of others)?

Even in my nervousness, I think I came across as respectful. I am trying hard to fit in.

1 2 3 4 5 6 7 8 (9) 10

Not very satisfied — Very satisfied

How personally effective did you feel?

Considering my being new, I think I represented the centre well.

1 2 3 4 (5) 6 7 8 9 10

Not very effective — Very effective

How committed do you feel to the work of this group?

This is an important place for me to be.

1 2 3 4 5 6 7 8 9 (10)

Not very committed — Very committed

Linking Group Context and Your Behaviour:

Look back on the group description and comment on the impact one or all of these elements may have had on your behaviour.

- Late meetings are hard for me—I can't seem to think clearly and stay alert.
- I tuned out when it seemed the conversation went on and on in this large group.
- The fact that minutes are recorded made it a bit easier for me to focus.

You and Others during the Group Situation:

Describe the impact your task and maintenance leadership roles had on the group.

Task: My questions may have slowed down the progress of decision making, yet seemed to clarify things for others as well.
Maintenance: My jokes seemed to lighten the mood a bit.

How did your level of power and influence affect the group?

I may have appeared a bit helpless and uninformed. Other group members may have taken care of me a bit in this meeting.

Was there anything about the influence of others that you would like to emulate?

Not really. My sense is that I will align with those in this group committed to working toward high standards for their centres.

Patterns of Group Behaviour over Time:

What differences and similarities are there in your behaviour here compared to other group experiences?

In my team meeting I am the assigned leader, so the experience here seemed different. I was much quieter and my verbal input was focused on questions. In my team meetings I gave information and accessed opinions.
With the children's festival meetings I use more humour and seem less task-focused.

As you analyze group situations over time, what group elements might be directly affecting your leadership roles or use of power?

Time spent together obviously affects my behaviour. The children's festival group is in openness, and I feel comfortable and valued. I think because of the new situation at work and the large number of people in this centre-complex group, I am more inhibited than I usually am. I am not yet sure how to use my power effectively and I appear to be more task-driven.

What patterns are emerging as you consider your recent group experiences?

I seem to be more focused on the task when I am new to a group.
Late meetings affect my participation and I cannot think clearly.

Now What? Goals for Change:

1. Continue to monitor the value of my task leadership role and consider the other leadership behaviours I might use to enhance group commitment and effectiveness.
2. Carefully consider how I might use my power to best represent the needs of my centre in the midst of others using a competing conflict style.
3. Find a way to be more energized for late afternoon or evening meetings.

Structures or norms are elements described in Chapter 2. There will be more notes in this section if you are assessing meetings that occur regularly. Structures include whether there is an agenda, a designated leader, scheduled breaks, formal seating arrangements or other pre-planned ways of organizing the meeting.

In Lyric's example, the structures are common to regularly scheduled meetings with a designated leader. This is a fairly large group, which may affect Lyric's participation.

You in this meeting: The questions here look at not only what others expect of you in a particular meeting, but also your own physical and emotional state of being. For example, if you have just fallen in love, this is an element that affects your participation in the group, which in turn affects the overall group process. On the contrary, if you are hungry, sick or tired, your input will be affected in a different way.

In Lyric's case, she is feeling nervous and worried about her new responsibility and has noted that she is the representative for her centre.

Observations of yourself and others: This section links to earlier discussions of levels of interaction, use of leadership skills and power, and the process of decision making. We have separated your perception of your own performance from your perception of the performance of others. If there are a number of people in your group situation, there will be several numbers circled in the "Others" section. Under each circle place the number of people you believe are exhibiting the noted behaviour. For example, in the assessment filled out by Lyric, she has noted two people participating at a level 3, five at a level 5 and one at levels 7, 9 and 10 in the question asking for levels of verbal contribution.

Lyric has also noted that she has asked lots of questions to get information, as well as attempted some humour during the meeting. When looking at the behaviour of others, she has discriminated between the director and the rest of the group. This may or may not have much significance later, but is important to her because this is her first meeting in her new capacity in the centre complex.

When filling out the multiple-choice questions, you might want to add comments to help you remember more clearly whom you are referring to in the group situation. As you can see on Lyric's form, she has made a couple of comments in these sections. For the decision-making and conflict questions, Lyric has added notes to help her remember specific information. That way, when she returns to it in the future she can more easily identify patterns in her own behaviour. For example, if Lyric analyzes later meetings with this same group and finds that she still avoids conflict, she will want to examine why this is happening and what, if anything, she wants to do about it. Specifying the people who engaged in competitive behaviour will help in this analysis. When she looks at meetings in the future, she will be able to note whether the same people are still involved in this behaviour and make some decisions about whether her role needs to change.

Perception of the group: In this section you are noting a more subjective experience of the current group, having stepped back and reviewed the process. Here you must make reference to earlier text discussions of group development and levels of trust and cohesion experienced, as well as your sense of how productive this group appeared to be during the time you were together. Again, there is room to make notes on details you believe are important to clarifying your perceptions.

Because Lyric is new to this group, she acknowledges that she is in the inclusion stage and that the rest of the group seems to be in transition from the storming to the norming stage. Even though she is new, she feels welcomed by the group, though she is still bit unsure of their level of commitment. Productivity seems high, which, according to Lyric, is the consequence of a ready-made agenda and task-driven assigned leadership.

So What? How Does This Information Have Meaning for You?

At this critical point in the self-assessment framework, the observations are complete and you begin to take a closer look at your part in the overall group experience.

Your role in developing trust, cohesion and productivity: This is your **subjective evaluation** of yourself in the group. You are focusing more deeply on the role you play in co-creating the group experience. The questions ask you to rate your performance, satisfaction and overall level of commitment to this particular group.

Again, Lyric realizes that being new to the group may have contributed to her low rating of helpfulness, yet she is satisfied with her level of participation and commitment to the group. She also considers her earlier identified nervousness in this representative position.

Linking group context and your behaviour: This section helps you connect the first section of the self-assessment framework to your performance in the current group situation. For example, if this is a regular meeting, how has that affected your behaviour? How does the size of this group affect your behaviour?

This was a critical question for Lyric. The meeting time did not work for her, and even though she was excited and nervous about her position in the group, she tuned out because she felt tired. Because she is new to the group, she may have to find ways to deal with this group element because it is the norm for this group to meet after work.

You and others during the group situation: Again, you are asked to make specific connections between what happened in the current group situation and your leadership and level of power and influence. For example, if you took a strong task role as initiator during this group experience, how did it affect the overall function of the group? Did you keep the group on task or did your attempts fall flat? Did the group appreciate your role, or did the group members seem irritated with your need to structure discussion?

Regarding your power and influence, and with reference to the content of Chapter 5, you will want to consider the factors of dependency and perception when you assess the rating you give yourself when you observe your use of power. Do you appear to be less assertive when, for example, you are in meetings with an assigned leader? Or are you in a position where you have expert power and feel extremely influential during the group experience? Ultimately, the answers to these kinds of questions help you clarify how your use of power affects the group.

Lyric acknowledges that at times she felt helpless and uninformed, which may be perceived as dependency on others in the group. Because she has earlier identified that, unlike the other group members, she is at the stage of inclusion in this group, Lyric understands that a certain level of dependency is expected and understood and, therefore, does not seem too upset by this.

Patterns of group behaviour over time: All three questions in this section ask you to step back and consider your behaviour and the way in which it is similar or different in comparison to your behaviour in the other group situations you are tracking. The first question is a general look at similarities and differences, while the second question asks you to consider how group elements seem to be affecting your leadership and power in different contexts. This question is different from the earlier question that asks about group elements and your behaviour, as it focuses on the current group situation in comparison to others you have experienced in the past. The third question integrates the answers to the first two questions, as you identify noticeable patterns from your experiences over time.

Here Lyric has clearly identified some differences in her behaviour. She recognizes that her behaviour changes when she is an assigned leader of a small group in contrast to being a group member when somebody else is the assigned leader. She also sees some leadership differences linked to her feelings of comfort in the different contexts. She notes the effect of the stage of group development and the size of the group on her comfort level, use of power and the shared leadership roles she assumes.

Now What? Goals for Change

Here is where you identify goals for yourself now that you have taken the time to analyze all other components of your group behaviour. These goals also mark your progress and may build upon earlier directions noted from other self-assessments. We suggest that you also use this section to note areas of observation you might want to take a closer look at in further self-assessments.

In Lyric's example, she has already begun to make the connections between the many factors that affect the group's function and her role in its development. The goals she articulates are specific to this meeting. Because she is seeing behaviours not evident in her other analyses of group contexts, she wants to continue to pay close attention to her behaviour in this group in order to take on a leadership role that is effective, productive and natural to her. This is a goal that holds great importance to her new position in the centre complex and ultimately to her professional career.

Professional Considerations

When you are using this guided self-assessment framework, there are some **professional considerations** that merit discussion. You will be functioning as a group member on two levels as you note your observations while being an active participant in the group. It is difficult to participate to the same degree when you are also engaging in the process of observation. For this reason it is important to tell other group members that you are engaging in an additional task that you hope will serve to enhance your future participation in all group situations. This includes informing others that you are noting their behaviour as well as yours.

It has been our experience that this kind of disclosure is seldom a problem for groups we have been a part of. Most of the time other group members are curious about the information you are noting and quite often ask for feedback on what you may have noticed about their group interactions. Obviously, all information recorded in any process of observation is discreet, confidential and only used for your personal growth.

The length of time you devote to tracking your group participation depends on the number of groups you are involved in and the frequency of their meetings. We suggest that you look at six to eight different meetings over a period of time. The more diverse the contexts, the more information you will glean from your different assessments.

The process of self-assessment takes time, energy and commitment, but will serve to enhance your self-awareness in groups. As well, this process goes hand in hand with the reflective practice we advocate throughout the text. In the helping professions, your goal is to reach a level of personal and professional competence that enhances your work with others. You do this best when you have a strong sense of who you are and understand your ability to adapt in ways that promote healthier interactions. Only then can you best support transformational change in others.

Summary

All components of group skill development discussed in this text can be seen as learned competencies that you will take into your field of practice in the form of a personal skill set that enhances your work with others in groups. The use of reflection tools helps you to carefully consider values, beliefs and attitudes when you are engaged in new learning about yourself in group situations. However, you also need to broaden the scope of this self-assessment and utilize your new learning about group work to engage in an ongoing observation of your behaviour in a variety of group contexts. These contexts include college or university environments, practice sites, community work or any kind of group situation where you work in collaboration with others.

The self-assessment framework has been designed for the purpose of tracking your group behaviour over time. This way you will be able to monitor your behaviour with the use of a guided framework of questions focused on all of the components of skill development discussed in this text. Used over time, it will help you take note of how you are affected by those factors, perceptions and contexts inevitable in group situations. You can then examine the role you take in contributing to the development of trust, cohesion or productivity in all of the groups you will be a part of. Any links or patterns you examine as you work with others can be used to set goals for change and, ultimately, lead to more fulfilling and productive group participation in the future.

Key Terms

Field of practice *(p. 187)*
Lifelong learning *(p. 184)*
Personal skill set *(p. 183)*
Professional considerations *(p. 196)*
Self-assessment *(p. 186)*
Self-assessment framework *(p. 188)*
Subjective evaluation *(p. 195)*
Transdisciplinary *(p. 188)*

Self-Assessment Framework

What? Meeting Observations and Impressions

Context of the Group:

Where ___________ When ____________ Time Together ______________________________

Purpose of Meeting __________________ Once/Regular ______________________________

Structures or Norms ____

____

Size/Composition ____

You in This Meeting:

What are the expectations of your behaviour and role in this group meeting?

How do you feel going into this meeting (physically and emotionally)?

Observations of Yourself and Others:

	You	**Others**
Level of Interaction		
What was the level of verbal contribution?	1 2 3 4 5 6 7 8 9 10 Low High	1 2 3 4 5 6 7 8 9 10 Low High
What was the level of involvement in the group?	1 2 3 4 5 6 7 8 9 10 Uninterested Committed	1 2 3 4 5 6 7 8 9 10 Uninterested Committed
Leadership Skills Used		
What was the level of task focus?	1 2 3 4 5 6 7 8 9 10 Low High	1 2 3 4 5 6 7 8 9 10 Low High
What was the level of maintenance focus?	1 2 3 4 5 6 7 8 9 10 Low High	1 2 3 4 5 6 7 8 9 10 Low High
Use of Power		
How was power demonstrated? (Circle terms that apply.)	Verbally Non-verbally Attentiveness Reward Coercion Legitimate Expert Nuisance Habitual Sanction	Verbally Non-verbally Attentiveness Reward Coercion Legitimate Expert Nusiance Habitual Sanction

Process of Decison Making

What methods of decision making were used?

Authority without Group Discussion   Decision by Expert   Averaging Opinions   Authority after Group Discussion
Minority   Majority Vote   Consensus

What was the level of comfort you experienced in decision making?

1 2 3 4 5 6 7 8 9 10
Low High

If there was conflict, what conflict style did you use?

Avoiding   Competing   Accommodating   Compromising   Collaborating

What conflict styles were used by others?

Avoiding   Competing   Accommodating   Compromising   Collaborating

What was your level of satisfaction with the conflict experience?

1 2 3 4 5 6 7 8 9 10
Low High

Perception of the Group:

Group Development

What stage do you think the group is in?

Forming   Storming   Norming   Performing   OR   Inclusion   Control   Openness

Perceived Level of Trust and Cohesion

To what degree did you experience a climate of openness, mutual respect and a sense of safety?

1 2 3 4 5 6 7 8 9 10
Low High

What was the level of commitment to goals and a teamwork atmosphere?

1 2 3 4 5 6 7 8 9 10
Low High

Perceived Level of Productivity

How much was accomplished with respect to the goals of the meeting?

1 2 3 4 5 6 7 8 9 10
Very little A lot

So What? How Does This Information Have Meaning for You?

Your Role in Developing Trust, Cohesion and Productivity:

How helpful do you think your contributions were to overall group productivity?

1 2 3 4 5 6 7 8 9 10
Not helpful Very helpful

How satisfied were you with your participation (your openness, your respect for others, your level of acceptance of others)?

1 2 3 4 5 6 7 8 9 10
Not very satisfied Very satisfied

How personally effective did you feel?

1 2 3 4 5 6 7 8 9 10
Not very effective Very effective

How committed do you feel to the work of this group?

1 2 3 4 5 6 7 8 9 10
Not very committed Very committed

Linking Group Context and Your Behaviour:

Look back on the group description and comment on the impact one or all of these elements may have had on your behaviour.

You and Others during the Group Situation:

Describe the impact your task and maintenance leadership roles had on the group.

How did your level of power and influence affect the group?

Was there anything about the influence of others that you would like to emulate?

Patterns of Group Behaviour over Time:

What differences and similarities are there in your behaviour here compared to other group experiences?

As you analyze group situations over time, what group elements might be directly affecting your leadership roles or use of power?

What patterns are emerging as you consider your recent group experiences?

Now What? Goals for Change:

Glossary

Adjourning the last stage in Tuckman's model of group development. Adjourning refers to the completion stage of group development when group members recognize their time together is coming to an end.

Assumptions the immediate thoughts and ideas that initially enter our minds when we first react to a person, a situation or a concept that we have never considered before.

Attachment the emotional tie that forms between infants or children and the adults in their lives.

Authoritarian a parenting style that demands obedience from children and uses punitive, forceful methods to ensure children do as they are told.

Authoritative a parenting style that provides rules for children while still allowing for their negotiation and input.

Base Group a small group of people that meets regularly to discuss issues and ideas in order to support each other's learning process through giving and receiving feedback.

Beliefs what we think is true.

Coercive power the ability to influence others by using punishment to get them to do things against their will.

Cohesion the degree to which group members feel an overall sense of comfort, mutual respect and productivity together.

Communication Patterns the frequency and quality of the way group members interact with each other.

Competency the work-related knowledge, skills, and behaviour needed to effectively perform in a specific occupation.

Conflict when two or more people have differing values, beliefs or interests that interfere with their ability to make decisions that reflect the goals of the group.

Conflict styles a framework to describe the way we typically respond to conflict. The styles include competing, avoiding, accommodating, compromising and collaborating.

Consensus a style of decision making that involves discussion and exploration of options and leads to a decision that all group members can support.

Constructive process assessing new information in terms of our existing thoughts, beliefs, values and attitudes. This may mean reframing or adjusting our existing thought patterns and eliminating what no longer makes sense to us.

Control the second stage of group development in Schutz's model. The control stage occurs when group members begin to challenge each other. It is characterized by an increase in tension as arguments over discussion points and decisions that need to be made become more frequent. Successful resolution of this stage leads to increased cohesion and productivity.

Cooperative group development the increasing level of trust and respect experienced by group members who are open and accepting and risk both giving and receiving feedback.

Decision making the process of coming to a conclusion as a group. There are several different methods for reaching a conclusion.

Defensiveness excessive sensitivity to criticism, or the protective response when feeling threatened by another person. May be demonstrated through silence or angry comments.

Dependency the degree to which we rely on others to meet our needs.

Destructive power a style of interaction that influences a group by preventing it from working cohesively and productively.

Disagreement a difference of opinion that does not impair group decision making.

Disclosure the sharing of thoughts, feelings and experiences that are relevant to the situation at hand. Mutual disclosure usually serves to increase feelings of group cohesion and trust. Unreciprocated disclosure usually erodes mutual trust.

Egalitarian having to do with a social and/or political structure that allows for equality among its members.

Empowerment helping others gain personal power through such supports as teaching or advocacy or providing opportunites for them to have valid input into decisions that concern them.

Expert power the ability to influence others as a result of possessing special knowledge or skills that others do not have.

Field of practice the variety of workplace, facility and community contexts associated with your area of specialization.

Formalized leadership roles the assigned responsibility for leading a group in the completion of a task.

Formalized leadership structure the organizational structure that defines the levels of authority that exist within a work environment. The levels of authority are the formalized leadership roles.

Forming the first stage in Tuckman's model of group development. Forming is characterized by questions geared to getting to know each other and clarifying the reason for the group's existence. This is a time of "niceness" and a desire to make a good impression.

Goals — the clear, attainable objectives that a group agrees upon and works toward.

Groups — two or more people who work toward common goals, influence each other and interact on a regular basis within a framework of mutual expectations.

Groupthink — a term coined by Irving Janis to describe the pitfalls of a group that becomes too cohesive. Groupthink occurs when members desire group agreement so much that they disregard important information or do not look closely at the decisions they are making. Decisions become driven by a desire for consensus rather than a desire for the most successful outcome.

Habits of mind — the habitual, routine ways we think, feel and act, based on our early experiences and cultural heritage. Habits of mind are influenced by our assumptions and, if left unexamined, are responsible for our disregard of new information, new learning and potential personal growth.

Habitual power — influence that results from history. A person has power because he or she has been in a particular position for a long time and others are reluctant to question or challenge that individual.

Hidden agendas — personal goals that are not openly expressed to the group and are usually in conflict with or not "in sync" with the identified goals of the group.

Human element — the impact that the individuals present in a group have on each other.

Inclusion — the first stage in Schutz's model of group development. Inclusion is characterized by the degree to which we feel a sense of belonging.

Informational power — influence that comes with the ability to articulate clearly and appear knowledgeable.

Interdependence — the ability of group members to work together toward a common goal. The coordination amongst group members is affected by the level of trust in the group, the interpersonal style of its members and the stage the group is at in its development.

Leadership roles — the task and maintenance functions performed by group members that help the group operate effectively. These roles are not assigned or formalized and shift amongst group members.

Legitimate power — influence as a result of a particular position; for example, president, chief executive officer or chairperson.

Lifelong learning — refers to the notion that learning continues past graduation from an educational institution. It is the ongoing acquisition of knowledge and skills through formal and informal educational opportunities.

Maintenance leadership functions the leadership functions that contribute to effective group process. These functions contribute to group cohesion and group member satisfaction. These functions include gatekeeper, encourager, harmonizer, describer of emotional climate, consensus tester, process observer and tension reliever.

Majority more than 50 percent of the group.

Mediated discussion any discussion between two or more people that is facilitated by a neutral party in order to increase successful communication. The goal is to resolve issues that are blocking the ability to relate openly or work together satisfactorily.

Minority less than 50 percent of the group.

Model of conflict resolution a guide that outlines specific steps to follow when attempting to resolve a conflict.

Mutuality working cooperatively and interdependently toward a common goal.

Mutually decided norms norms that the group has discussed or agreed to openly.

Natural roles the task and maintenance leadership roles that feel natural to each individual. Natural roles are distinguished from those roles an individual takes on when he or she recognizes a need for more balanced leadership. Taking on a needed role may feel awkward rather than natural.

Non-functional behaviours behaviours that impede the progress of the group. These behaviours include blocking, joking, competing, sympathy seeking, special-interest pleading and withdrawing.

Norms the rules and expectations that guide the behaviour of group members.

Norming the third stage of Tuckman's model of group development. Norming refers to the time in the group's development when members have moved through the discomfort of the storming stage and have an increased acceptance and understanding of each other. Roles, responsibilities and work structures are clear to everyone and the group functions well together.

Nuisance power influence that results from annoying or irritating behaviour that others would rather not deal with. If not confronted, the individual using nuisance power gets away with behaviour that would otherwise be unacceptable.

Openness the third stage in Schutz's model of group development. Openness is characterized by group members who risk sharing their ideas and opinions, accept each others strengths and weaknesses and share the workload in an equitable manner.

Perception the interpretations or meanings we give to what we observe or experience.

Performing the fourth stage in Tuckman's model of group development. Performing is an evolution of norming because it builds upon the acceptance of each other's individual contributions and style of interaction, resulting in high productivity and appreciation of the overall group experience.

Permissive a parenting style that makes few demands on children and allows them to define rules and limits.

Personal effectiveness the degree to which individuals feel useful and able to influence others in the group.

Personal power the influence we have over others, based on our personal characteristics, talents and skills.

Personal skill set the abilities, attributes and personal characteristics that reflect both your educational training and your personal style.

Personality problems personality styles of interacting that affect the decision-making process. These personality styles include the bully, the sniper, the know-it-all, the think-they-know-it-all, the yes-person and the whiner.

Power the ability to influence others.

Power-from-within an inner feeling of competence and self-confidence.

Power-over the attempt to influence or control others through the use of coercive, controlling and manipulative techniques.

Power struggles the impasse that occurs when two or more people attempt to influence each other in unwanted ways. A power struggle is often experienced as controlling.

Power-with collaborative influence, where all individuals in an interaction support and influence each other.

Preconceived norms expectations about the way the group will operate or the way individuals within the group will conduct themselves. Preconceived norms are not openly discussed, are specific to the individual and result from our background, socialization and general life experience.

Preconceived notions the thoughts, feelings and expectations we bring to the group that we have not formally confirmed. These notions could be about other members in the group, the task the group will engage in, or the way the group will work together.

Procedural problems a lack of clarity about how the group will function that impedes the decision-making process.

Process problems factors such as stage of development, group size and clarity of goals, which affect the ability of the group to make decisions.

Productivity the amount of meaningful work that gets accomplished and meets the overall goals of the group.

Professional considerations the factors to consider when using the self-assessment framework in group situations. These factors include ethical considerations that are necessary when engaging in self-assessment in groups. Examples include letting others know that you may be making note of their behaviours and that you are engaged in a self-reflective process to help further enhance your skills as a group member.

Professional judgment the constant review and self-analysis of potential outcomes of one's behaviour that results in decisions that reflect the expectations and standards of the profession.

Referent power the ability to influence others by virtue of the individual's personal characteristics or charisma that others wish to emulate.

Reflection critical analysis of our experiences, beliefs, values and assumptions that results in new learning, increased self-awareness and personal growth.

Reflection tool the form provided in this text to help guide your reflective process.

Reward power the ability to influence others by delivering positive consequences or removing negative consequences.

Sanction power the ability to prevent or interfere with someone's course of action through the use of standards, rules or policies, or coercive power.

Self-assessment the process of analyzing and reflecting on your skills and abilities with the goal of improving your performance.

Self-assessment framework the observation template provided in the text that helps guide your self-analysis and reflection.

Self-efficacy the belief that we are competent, capable human beings who are able to achieve what we set out to achieve.

Self-esteem the way people feel about the strengths and weaknesses that comprise who they are.

Shared understanding the foundation for effective group decision making that comes from the open sharing of ideas and opinions and the willingness to listen to and accept differing points of view.

Storming the second stage of Tuckman's model of group development. Storming describes the time in a group's progress when members challenge perceived leadership and assert themselves in an effort to gain some power and control. This stage is characterized by tension, conflict and arguing.

Subjective evaluation the perception you have of the quality of your participation in groups.

Synergy an energized feeling of cohesion and productivity that results from group members sharing power.

Task leadership functions the leadership functions that contribute to the accomplishment of the group's goals. These functions include initiator, information giver, opinion giver, information seeker, opinion seeker, elaborator/clarifier and summarizer.

Transdisciplinary groups of people that represent a variety of organizations and professions.

Transformational change the personal change that occurs through enhanced self-awareness after a significant life event (in this case, participation in a group experience).

Transformative learning occurs when we expand our worldview or frame of reference as a result of a reflection process that leads to new understanding and a shift in the way we operate in our daily lives.

Trust the degree to which group members believe others in the group will respond respectfully to their openness and will follow through with their commitments. Honesty, faith and mutual disclosure are components of trust.

Values what we hold to be important.

References

Ainsworth, M. D. S. (1978). *Patterns of attachment: A psychological study of the strange situation.* Mahwah, NJ: Lawrence Erlbaum Associates.

Avis, W., Drysdale, P., Gregg, R., Neufeldt, V., & Scargill, M. (1983). *Gage Canadian dictionary.* Toronto: Gage Educational Publishing.

Bales, R. F. (1950). *Interaction process analysis.* Cambridge, MA: Addison-Wesley.

Baumrind, D. (1978). Parental disciplinary patterns and social competence in children. *Youth and Society, 9*, 239–276.

Blake, R. R., & Mouton, J. S. (1970). The fifth achievement. *Journal of Applied Behavioral Science, 6*, 413–426.

Bowlby, J. (1958). The nature of the child's tie to his mother. *International Journal of Psycho-Analysis*, *39,* 350–373.

Brilhart, J. K., & Galanes, G. J. (1992). *Effective group discussion* (7th ed.). Dubuque, IA: Brown.

Cragan, D. W., & Wright, C. R. (1991). *Communication in small group discussions: An integrated approach* (3rd ed.). Minneapolis: West Publishing.

Cragan, D. W., & Wright, C. R. (1995). *Communication in small groups: Theory, process, skills* (4th ed.). Minneapolis: West Publishing.

Cranton, P. (2002). Teaching for transformation. *New Directions for Adult and Continuing Education,93*(spring), 63–71.

Dimock, H. D. (1993). *How to observe your group* (3rd ed.). North York, ON: Captus Press.

Filley, A. C. (1975). *Interpersonal conflict resolution.* Glenview, IL: Scott Foresman.

French, J. R. P., Jr., & Raven, B. (1959). The bases of social power. In D. Cartwright (Ed.), *Studies in social power* (pp. 259–268). Ann Arbor, MI: University of Michigan.

Gordon, T. (1975). *Parent effectiveness training.* New York: New American Library.

Guralnick, M. (1993). *Assessment of peer relations.* Vancouver, BC: Making Friends Project, Health and Welfare Canada.

Hall, J. (1996). *Conflict management survey.* The Woodlands, TX: Teleometrics International.

Janis, I. L. (1972). *Victims of groupthink: A psychological study of foreign-policy decisions and fiascoes.* Boston: Houghton, Mifflin.

Johnson, D. W., & Johnson, F. P. (2006). *Joining together: Group theory and group skills* (9th ed.). Boston: Allyn & Bacon.

Kaner, S., Fisk, S., & Toldi, C. (1996). *Facilitator's guide to participatory decision-making.* Gabriola Island, BC: New Society.

Landy, S. (2002). *Pathways to competence: Encouraging healthy social and emotional development in young children.* Baltimore: Paul H. Brookes.

Mayer, B. (2000). *The dynamics of conflict resolution.* San Francisco: Jossey-Bass.

Mezirow, J. (1997). Transformative learning: Theory to practice. *New Directions for Adult and Continuing Education, 74*(summer), 5–12.

Namie, G., & Namie, R. (2000). *The bully at work.* Naperville, IL: Sourcebooks.

Patton, B. R., Giffin, K., & Patton, E. N. (1989). *Decision-making: Group interaction* (3rd ed.). New York: Harper & Row.

Raven, B. H. (1965). Social influence and power. In I.D. Steiner & M. Fishbein (Eds.). *Current studies in social psychology* (pp. 399–444). New York: Wiley.

Rhode, H. (1993). *Dealing with conflict and confrontation: How to keep your cool, stand your ground and reach a positive resolution* [supplementary guide to video series]. Boulder, CO: CareerTrack Publications.

Schon, D. (1983). *The reflective practitioner: How professionals think in action.* New York: Basic Books.

Slater, P. E. (1958). Contrasting correlates of group size. *Sociometry, 21,* 129–139.

Steiner, I. D. (1972). *Group process and productivity.* New York: Academic Press.

Thomas, K. W., Kilmann, R. H. (1974). *Thomas-Kilmann Conflict Mode Instrument.* Tuxedo, New York: Xicom Inc.

Tuckman, B. (1965). Developmental sequence in small groups. *Psychological Bulletin, 63*, 384–399.

Tuckman, B. W., & Jensen, M. A. (1977). Stages of small-group development revisited. *Group & Organizational Studies, 2*, 419–427.

Index

A

Affection stage of group development. *See* Group development, openness (affection) stage of
Ainsworth, Mary, 127, 129
Assumptions, 9, 10, 11, 12, 13–14, 15, 17
Attachment, 128–129

B

Baumrind, D., 127, 128
Behaviours, non-functional, 102
Beliefs, 9, 10, 12, 13–14, 15
Blake, Robert R., 166
Bowlby, John, 127
Brainstorming, 174
Brilhart, John K., 27, 28, 55

C

Cohesion. *See* Group(s), cohesion of effective
Communication patterns. *See* Group(s), communication patterns
Communication skills, 50–52
  power and, 130, 132, 134
Community, 91
Competency, 3, 10
Conflict, 164–166
  accommodating style, 168–169
  avoidance style, 167
  behaviour, 166–172
  collaborating style, 169–170
  competing style, 167–168
  compromising style, 169
  resolution model, 172, 174, 175, 176
  sources of, 165
  styles, 166
Constructive process. *See* Reflection (constructive process), process of
Controversy, 164
Cooperative group development, 53
Cragan, John F., 31, 35, 58
Cranton, Patricia, 9, 55

D

Decision making, 150, 151
  methods of, 152, 153, 159
    authority after group discussion, 153, 155
    authority without group discussion, 152, 153–154
    average everyone's opinion, 152, 154–155
    consensus, 153, 156–159
    expert, 152, 154
    majority vote, 152, 156
    minority, 153, 155–156
  personality problems, 159, 161–162, 163–164
  procedural problems, 159, 160
  process problems, 159, 160–161
Defensiveness, 131
Dimock, Hedley, 59
Disagreement, 165
Disclosure, 51

E

Effectiveness, personal, 50–51, 64–65, 67, 68–69
Egalitarian, 140
Empowerment, 125–126
Evaluation, subjective, 195

F

Field of practice, 187–188
Filley, Alan C., 166
FIRO. *See* Fundamental Interpersonal Relationship Orientation (FIRO) model of group development
Fisk, Sarah, 174

Formalized leadership,
roles, 106–107
structure, 84
Frame of reference. *See* Values (frame of reference)
French, John R. P., 121, 122, 123, 131–132, 137
Fundamental Interpersonal Relationship Orientation (FIRO) model of group development, 58

G

Galanes, Gloria, J., 27, 28, 55
Giffin, Kim, 35, 159
Goals. *See* Group(s), goals
Gordon, Thomas, 172
Group development,
adjourning stage of, 57–69, 70
closure stage of, 68–69, 70, 71
control stage of, 58–59, 64–65
effective group function and, 61, 63
forming stage of, 56–57, 61, 63
historical theories of, 56, 58–59
inclusion stage of, 58, 61, 63
norming stage of, 57, 67–68, 161
openness (affection) stage of, 59, 67–68, 161
performing stage of, 57, 67–68
storming stage of, 57, 64–65
Group tasks,
additive, 36–37
conjunctive, 37
discretionary, 37
disjunctive, 37
Group(s), 1, 2, 3, 7, 9–15
assumptions about membership and roles in, 34–35
base, 5, 6, 39, 63, 83, 118, 121, 129, 184, 185, 186
behaviour(s), 2
characteristics of effective, 48, 49
cohesion of effective, 54–55, 62, 65–66, 67–68, 69
common behaviours of, 47
communication patterns, 35, 36
context(s) (environment), 2, 28–29, 187–188, 190–195, 196
definitions of, 24–25
development of, 2, 47–48
dysfunction in, 106
effectiveness of, 3, 17
elements of, 27–28, 29
goals, 33, 34, 55
historical theories of development of, 56, 58–59
interdependence of, 37–38
leadership issues in, 100–101, 102, 104, 105
norms, 30–31
participating in effective, 50
participation, 2, 3
personality factors of, 35
perspective, 15
power in, 117–119, 135
preconceived notions about purpose of, 32–33
process, 4
productivity of effective, 55
roles, 81–82
size, 27–28
student, 1
task accomplishment by, 36–38
time together of, 28
transformational change in effective, 55–56, 63, 66
trust in effective, 51–53
Groupness, 57, 68
Groupthink, 54–55, 161
Guralnick, Dr. Michael, 151

H

Habits of mind, 10
Hall, Jay, 165, 166, 167
Helping professions. *See* Human service (helping) professions
Hidden agenda, 10
Human factor, 29
Human service (helping) professions, 1, 2, 4, 5, 10, 11, 20, 24–25, 187–188
considerations, 196–197

I

Interdependence. *See* Group(s), interdependence of

J
Jarvis, Irving, 54
Johnson, D. W., 27, 28, 31, 50, 53, 54–55, 153
Johnson, F., 27, 28, 31, 50, 53, 54–55, 153
Judgment, professional, 3–4

K
Kaner, Sam, 174

L
Landy, S., 128, 129
Leadership,
  assigned (formal), 84
  definitions of maintenance functions, 91–93, 94, 95
  formal roles, 106–107
  informal (expectations), 84
  roles and power, 135, 136
  roles, 84–85, 98
  shared, 85
  task functions, 85–86, 87, 88, 89
Learning,
  integrating, 183–184
  lifelong, 184
  transformative, 11
  transformative theory, 9

M
Maintenance leadership functions, 90, 91, 96, 97, 99
Mayer, B., 123–124, 137, 138
Mediated discussion, 51
Mezirow, Jack, 10
Mouton, Jane S., 166
Mutuality, 53

N
Norms,
  context-specific, 31
  mutually decided, 30–31
  preconceived, 30
  see also Group(s), norms
Notions, preconceived, 32–33
  see also Group(s), preconceived notions about purpose of

O
Orientation,
  philosophical, 165
  strategic, 166

P
Parenting,
  authoritarian, 127–128
  authoritative, 128
  permissive, 128
Patton, Bobby R., 35, 159
Patton, Eleanor Nyquist, 35, 159
Perspective sharing, 158–159
Power, 119, 141
  coercive, 121–122
  communication skills and, 130, 132, 134
  dependency, 120, 121
  destructive, 138–140
  developing through lifespan, 127–129
  expert, 123
  formal leadership and, 140
  forms of, 121–123, 124
  French and Raven's bases of, 121–123
  habitual, 124
  informational, 123
  leadership roles and, 135, 136
  legitimate, 122
  maintenance leadership and, 137, 138
  Mayer's categories of, 123–124
  nuisance, 124
  perceived, 124
  perceptions of, 66, 117–118, 119–120
  personal, 124
  referent, 123
  reward, 121
  sanction, 124
  struggles, 119
  task leadership and, 136–137
Problem defining, 172
Productivity, 62–63, 66, 68, 69, 70

R
Raven, Bertram H., 121, 122, 123, 137, 138
Reflection (constructive process), 3–4, 7, 10
  group process and, 10–11
  importance of, 11

Reflection (constructive process) (*Continued*)
process of, 7–8
theories of, 8–9
Reflection tool, 11–12, 15, 39, 55, 183, 184–185, 186
sections of, 12, 13
use of, 15, 17
Reflection-in-action, 8, 9, 102
Reflection-on-action, 8
Reflective practice, 3, 186
Rhode, Helga, 165
Roles,
blockers, 102–103
competitors, 104
consensus testers, 94
elaborators (clarifiers), 88–89
emotional climate describers, 93
encouragers, 92
formal leadership, 106–107
gatekeepers, 91–92
harmonizers, 92–93
information givers, 86–87
information seekers, 87
initiators, 86
jokers, 103
leadership, 84–85
natural, 82, 83
opinion givers, 87
opinion seekers, 88
process observers, 94–95
special interest pleaders, 104–105
summarizers, 89
sympathy seekers, 104
tension relievers, 95
withdrawers, 105

S
Schon, Donald, 8, 9
Schutz, William C., 56, 58, 59, 61, 67
Self-assessment, 8, 184, 186–187
framework, 188–190
Self-awareness, 10, 61
Self-efficacy, 127, 129
Self-esteem, 127, 129
Self-reflection, 2, 8, 10, 19
template, 4
Shared understanding, 150–151
Skill set, personal, 183
Slater, P. E., 28
Steiner, I., 37
Synergy, 157

T
Tasks. *See* Group tasks; Group(s), task accomplishment by
Toldi, Catherine, 174
Transdisciplinary group context, 188
Transformational change, 55–56, 68
Transformative learning. *See* Learning, transformative
Trust, 51, 62, 65, 67, 69
personal, 54
see also Group(s), trust in effective
Tuckman, Bruce, 56, 57, 59, 61

V
Values (frame of reference), 8, 9, 10, 11, 12, 13–14, 15, 17, 19

W
Wright, David W., 31, 34–35, 58